S0-BRI-373

Art and Society

Essays in Marxist Aesthetics
by Adolfo Sánchez Vásquez

Translated by Maro Riofrancos

Monthly Review Press
New York and London

Copyright © 1973 by Monthly Review Press
All Rights Reserved

Originally published as *Las ideas estéticas de
Marx: ensayos de estética marxista,* copyright
© 1965 by Ediciones Era, S.A., Mexico

Library of Congress Cataloging in Publication Data
Sánchez Vázquez, Adolfo.
   Art and society; essays in Marxist aesthetics.
   Translation of Las ideas estéticas de Marx.
   Includes bibliographical references.
   1. Communism and art.   2. Communist aesthetics.
I. Title.
HX521.S313   111.8'5   72-92025
ISBN 0-85345-269-5

Monthly Review Press
116 West 14th Street, New York, N. Y. 10011
33/37 Moreland Street, London, E. C. 1

First Printing

Manufactured in the United States of America

Contents

✳ *Foreword*

This volume will attempt to analyze the aesthetic ideas of Karl Marx, little known and studied, and examine several questions vital to a Marxist aesthetic. Aesthetic problems are of increasing interest to Marxist thinkers. There is a general need to go beyond, in this field as well as others, the dogmatic and sectarian conceptions which were prevalent during the years of the Stalinist deformations—theoretical and practical—of Marxism. We must not forget that those deformations were particularly grave in the realm of artistic theory and practice. Furthermore, as aesthetic problems have become increasingly important, the content of Marxism has been enriched, and its humanist character—which includes the essential aesthetic relationship—has increasingly been emphasized. There is also the need to overcome old, one-sided views of the artistic phenomena of our time. Modern art, apart from the place we assign it socio-historically—as part of an ideological superstructure—and regardless of the value we attribute to it on an aesthetic plane, is a rich, complex, and contradictory phenomenon which cannot be approached with the schematic and simplistic criteria that dominated Marxist art criticism until recently.

All this obliges us to bring to the fore the true nature of Marx's aesthetic ideas, not in order to limit ourselves to an exegesis and reiteration of them, but to develop them creatively, in a living and constant relationship with life itself, with artistic experience, and thus to lay the foundations for a true Marxist aesthetic. We can find in Marx the roots for a conception of aesthetics in general, and of art in particular, which in my view allows us to deal successfully with the most complex artistic problems. The essays in this book are devoted both to discovering and examining those roots and to taking into account artistic experience in its entirety, with special attention to contemporary artistic experience. These essays therefore share a common concern, without being a systematic whole. They are approaches, using different themes, to one cardinal question: What is the nature of man's aesthetic relationship to reality, and of art in particular? It has been impossible, because of the nature of this book, to avoid some repetition with regard to this question.

Throughout this study we have kept in mind other Marxist interpretations which enjoy or have enjoyed a certain authority, since the debate is wide open and the old dogmatism will no longer be able to end it. The important thing is to deal with the various views on this subject critically and creatively. To the great debate among Marxist aestheticians about views which differ from or are opposed to Marxism, our book contributes a voice, however modest, in the Spanish language.

Furthermore, we should add that the author has had the opportunity to propose and expound some of the fundamental theses of this book in his classes on aesthetics and in his seminar on aesthetics at the Universidad Nacional Autónoma de México, as well as in lectures and at conferences at the universities of Guadalajara and Michoacán. They were presented to, and debated by, a brilliant group of university professors and researchers in the "Círculo de Discusiones Filosóficos." Finally, they were presented in socialist Cuba, fertile crucible of Marxist theory and practice, where aesthetic problems arouse vital interest. These presentations and discussions have been a vigorous stimulus for the author, who recognizes and acknowledges this assistance.

The author's ideas now emerge, in printed form, into a public forum. Before beginning any further work in this field, we pause and await the helpful words of readers and critics.

Adolfo Sánchez Vázquez

Mexico City, February 1965

I. In Returning to the Aesthetic Ideas of Marx and the Problem of a Marxist Aesthetic

"Man therefore also forms things
in accordance with the laws of beauty."
Karl Marx,
The Economic and Philosophic Manuscripts of 1844

"An *objet d'art* creates a public that has
artistic taste and is able to enjoy beauty—
and the same can be said of any other product."
Karl Marx,
A Contribution to the Critique of Political Economy

1. The Vicissitudes of the Aesthetic Ideas of Marx

Marx never wrote a treatise on aesthetics; nor did he deal extensively with any specific aesthetic problems. Nevertheless, as the various anthologies of his comments on art and literature show, he always took a keen interest in questions of aesthetics in general, and of art and literature in particular.[1] In his philosophical and economic works, such as *The Economic and Philosophic Manuscripts of 1844, Critique of Political Economy, Capital, Theories of Surplus Value,* etc., we find ideas which have a direct bearing on such fundamental aesthetic and artistic problems as: art and work, the nature of aesthetics, the social and creative aspects of art, the social nature of the aesthetic experience, art as part of the ideological superstructure, the class origin and relative autonomy of a work of art, the uneven development of art and society, the relationship between art and reality, ideology and cognition, artistic creation and material production under capitalism, the durability of a work of art, etc. We also find in Marx's writings numerous critical evaluations of various writers. These comments, because of their theoretical content, are of great value in deepening our understanding of Marx's aesthetic and artistic views. Marx's ideas on aesthetics can be found scattered throughout his work, and some—perhaps the most important—appear in his earlier works; those in his later works are found in the context of an examination of fundamental Marxist questions. The aesthetic thought of Marx does not constitute, therefore, an organic doctrine, a fully developed aesthetic, but this does not diminish in any way its importance as an essential aspect of his views on man and society.

Marxism, humanism, and art

Marx could not ignore aesthetic and artistic issues—his world outlook constantly brought him face to face with them. In the light of these issues we can perceive Marx's conception of the *total* man, his alienation conquered and his essential powers fully at his disposal. Certainly, artistic creation and aesthetic gratification presupposed, in Marx's eyes, the specifically human appropriation of things and of human nature that is to prevail in a communist society, a society that will mark humanity's leap from the realm of necessity into that of freedom.

A true appreciation of Marx's aesthetic ideas cannot be separated from the human and artistic praxis which corroborate them. But at the same time, if they are to stand out in all their intensity they cannot be made marginal to the vicissitudes of Marxist thought. It is no coincidence that those interpreters of Marx's thought who have proven least capable of sensing his vitality have also been blind to his aesthetic ideas. The question of the value and range of these ideas, as well as of the possibility of constructing an aesthetic using them as *starting* points (rather than as a fully developed system), requires an understanding of Marxism as a philosophy of praxis; more precisely of a praxis which aims to transform human reality radically (on a concrete historical level, to transform capitalist society) so as to establish a society in which humanity can give free rein to its essential powers, frustrated, denied, postponed, and emasculated for so long. This understanding of Marxism as the true humanism, as the radical transformation of humanity on all planes, fulfills Marx's aspiration, already formulated in his youthful works, that "man's Supreme Being should be man himself." Aesthetics cannot be alien to this humanist Marxism, since, as we shall see in the course of this book, it is an essential dimension of human existence. Because of this, Marx necessarily had to deal with aesthetic problems, perhaps too briefly and not well enough articulated, but with a depth informed by his conception of humanity and by his thesis of the revolutionary transformation of society.

Kautsky's Marxism "without aesthetics"

The problem of extracting the germinal value of Marx's compact and suggestive aesthetic formulations thus can be approached only in the context of his world outlook, and on the basis of an understanding of Marxism as the true humanism of our times. It is not possible to appreciate the full value of Marx's aesthetic ideas, and grasp the potential for a Marxist aesthetic, when his entire doctrine is reduced to mere economics and politics, interpreted from a reformist point of view that ignores its philosophical essence. But such was the theoretical position of German Social Democrats at the end of the nineteenth and the beginning of the twentieth centuries. Karl Kautsky, for example, saw in Marxism only a specific conception of society, not a philosophy. Having been emaciated until nothing remained but the bones of a simplistic economic and philosophical theory, Marxism had to be fleshed out with a borrowed philosophy, called in to explain the existence of the realm of human values, to which art belongs. In this way, aesthetic problems were left out in the cold, exiled from the Marxist discourse, their analysis put in the hands of an idealist philosophy—usually of Kantian derivation—used to fill the gaps left by historical materialism. The official theoreticians of Social Democracy—Kautsky and Eduard Bernstein among others—thought that the only contribution Marxism could make to the field of aesthetics was in an explanation of the influence of economic factors on art. But with this quirk: the central thesis of historical materialism on the determining role of economic relations was, in the final analysis, interpreted by these theoreticians in such a schematic and one-dimensional way that its real significance was entirely lost.

Marx's aesthetic ideas, and consequently a Marxist aesthetic, could gain no inspiration from this tendency to emasculate the humanist and revolutionary content of Marxism and to vulgarize the fundamental thesis of historical materialism regarding the relationship between the base and the superstructure, which includes artistic activity. Thus we can see why the aesthetic ideas of Marx were ignored and his literary criticism was taken to be purely personal taste without any general theoretical significance.

Contributions and limitations of the first Marxist art theoreticians

The situation changed in the last decades of the nineteenth and the beginning of the twentieth centuries, when several Marxist art theoreticians attempted, for the first time, to recover the vitality of Marxism, although their endeavors were not free of error and one-sidedness. In the process of reestablishing Marx's legacy, they began to get a glimpse of the importance and fruitfulness of his aesthetic ideas. Among those who dealt most brilliantly and innovatively with aesthetic questions were Paul Lafargue in France, Franz Mehring in Germany, and G. V. Plekhanov in Russia.

Lafargue was interested in highlighting the relationship between art and social and class interests; but in underlining the ideological character of a work of art he lost sight of its specific mode of reflecting reality. Nevertheless, although he showed a certain class subjectivism, Lafargue, like Marx, recognized art as a social phenomenon.

Mehring likewise stressed the class character of art and denounced the pretensions of pure art, aloof from social concerns; yet he sustained a fondness for certain Kantian theses which he considered essential complements to Marxism. On the one hand, he conceived of art as a social phenomenon and a part of the superstructure; in that sense he saw that it is conditioned by class interests and incapable of reaching a totally universal plane. On the other hand, he attempted to free art from that conditioning with the help of Kantian formalist aesthetics. His study of a work of art thus placed him at the fork of two roads, an analysis of content and an analysis of form, causing him to waver between a sociological schematism and a Kantian formalism.

Plekhanov attempted to overcome this contradiction between social determinism and the autonomy of art. In a series of concrete studies he underscored the intimate relationship between art and class struggle; at the same time, he showed the relativism of the concept of beauty and pointed out the unity of content and form as well as the determining role of ideological content. However, he did not always clearly establish the social nature of art and of the aesthetic sense: he acknowledged the existence of psychological laws in the historical development of society and art, and fell into a kind of biological determinism in speaking of the sense of beauty. There is no doubt that Plekhanov made substantial contributions to the Marxist theory of the social conditioning of art and to the exegesis of the historical succession of aesthetic ideals and artistic tastes; but he failed to resolve the problem of the relative autonomy of the creative work. Although he recognized the necessity for analyzing the artistic merits of a work of art, as well as of situating it in the social dimension, he did not succeed in linking one with the other. Consequently, his work took him on a search for what he termed the sociological equivalent of a given literary phenomenon.

It is no accident that Plekhanov's work gave rise to a tendency that reduced Marxist aesthetics to a sociology of art and overlooked the question of relative autonomy which Engels had already begun to emphasize, especially in his letters during the 1890s. Marx himself laid the foundations for the concept of autonomy when he evolved his law of the uneven development of art and society, and when he called attention to the durability of Greek art despite, or as a result of, its social and ideological conditioning.

Lenin and art

Lenin claims a prominent place in the movement to re-cover and enrich the philosophical heritage of Marx and Engels, the heritage that the Second International either corrupted or ignored.

In "Party Organization and Party Literature," an article written in 1905, Lenin touched on questions of great importance to a Marxist aesthetic: the relations among art, ideology, and society; the party spirit of a work of art; etc. Starting with Engels' thesis that a tendentious spirit is intrinsic to the nature of art, Lenin put particular emphasis on the class character and social and ideological roles of art and literature. When, with the emergence of Marxism, the social and ideological perspective of the process of transforming society becomes clear, the artist who desires to link his creative work to the revolutionary cause consciously adopts that perspective and fuses his creative work with the revolutionary struggle. In this sense, literature has a party character. Behind the absolute freedom of creative work constantly paraded by bourgeois thinkers is hidden the most wretched dependency; only in the solidarity between his creative efforts and those social forces which are struggling for an authentic human and social liberation can the artist hope to assure his own liberty. This is the core of Lenin's "Party Organization and Party Literature."

Nowhere is there the slightest indication that Lenin felt the need to regiment artistic work or outline the permissible range of themes, styles, forms, etc. On the contrary, he understood that "literature is least of all subject to mechanical adjustment or levelling, to the rule of the majority over the minority. There is no question, either, that in this field greater scope must undoubtedly be allowed for personal initiative, individual inclination, thought and fantasy, form and content."[2] Indeed, as is shown by the cultural and artistic policies of the Soviet Union and the Communist Party during its first years in power, Lenin always held firmly to these principles, not only in theory but in practice. But if these principles are interpreted in a sectarian and mechanical way, with prescriptive intentions—as was done during the Stalinist period—the result runs counter to Lenin's aims: namely, to bring the artist closer to life, to develop a clearer and more deeply rooted view of reality, and to guarantee a true freedom of artistic creation.

In *Materialism and Empirio-Criticism,*[3] published in 1909 and written after the temporary defeat of the Russian Revolution—a time rife with attempts to revise Marxism with new varieties of old subjective idealism—Lenin developed and enriched Marxist epistemology with his theory of reflection. In this work, Lenin does not deal with the relationship between art and science, nor does he at any length investigate art as a specific cognitive process. Nevertheless, we can infer from his analysis that art, like other agencies of ideology, is historically conditioned, although this does not preclude artistic truths from having an objective and extra-artistic validity.

Lenin thus cleared the way for discrediting the class subjectivism into which Marxist art theoreticians had fallen, and accordingly he made it possible to understand art as a particular reflection of reality. In no way did it follow that the Leninist theory of reflection could be transplanted automatically from the field of scientific knowledge, for which it was developed, to the realm of art; for the purposes of developing an aesthetic, there was no justification for assigning to this theory a central role, one that Lenin himself did not give it. But, beginning in the 1930s, most Soviet aestheticians attributed to Lenin's theory precisely such a role, to such an extent that it became the philosophical base of Marxist-Leninist aesthetics.

Actually, the concept of art as reflection is relevant only when discussing the cognitive function of art, or, more precisely, when this reflection possesses certain unmistakable characteristic features: the specificity of the reflected reality; the particular activity of the artist in the aesthetic field; the particular functions of the imagination, the senses, or the emotions; the process of thinking about these functions; etc. In sum, even in a work of art that reflects reality, artistic reflection differs radically from scientific reflection. That is why we cannot share the categorical views of such theoreticians as the Soviet author Boris Meilakh: "From Lenin's views on aesthetic problems in *Materialism and Empirio-Criticism* we can deduce, with ample evidence, that the general laws of the Marxist theory of reflection are also applicable, without alterations, to the field of art."[4]

Once we identify the characteristic features of artistic reflection and the reality it reflects, we can begin to speak of the cognitive value of art. At the same time, we should not forget that in reflecting reality the artist reflects himself, and in the process his time and class as well, so that we cannot reduce art to its cognitive function, as indeed its history shows.

Lenin was well aware of this, and in his articles on Tolstoy he succeeded in resolving the subject-object relation in artistic creation, overcoming the sociological and subjectivist distortions of such theorists as Lafargue, Mehring, and Plekhanov. Without underestimating the subjective element in creative work, which is for the most part determined by the artist's world view, Lenin did not limit himself to a conception of art as a merely ideological expression; he emphasized instead that every great artist exceeds his ideological limitations to reveal a truth about reality.

To sum up, the Leninist theory of reflection is not the philosophical key to a Marxist aesthetic. Nevertheless, when it is used to analyze specific elements of artistic reflection and is not applied mechanically to aesthetics in general, it can contribute to an understanding of the relationship between the artist's world view and whatever truths about reality his work contains.

Artistic, theoretical, and practical problems
after the October Revolution

After the victory of the Revolution of October 1917, there was a growing demand for an art that responded to the needs of the men and women who were building a new society. As a result, the vital and pressing problems of artistic practice came to the fore. The need was felt for a new, revolutionary art, for new forms in which to express the vitality of a victorious ideology and the birth of a new society. The road was not easy: during the years immediately following the revolution there was an open struggle among diverse artistic trends, each with a different understanding of what this new art should be.

Lenin did not attempt to hide his personal taste in artistic matters but he was careful not to let his taste become a norm; he opposed any tendency of any group of artists toward a monopoly of artistic activity and refused to commit the revolutionary government to any official position on art, leaving the road open for artistic experimentation. Although he acknowledged that art has an ideological content and that it therefore plays a social and educational role, he was the first to recognize that art and politics operate on essentially different levels. It was in this spirit that shortly after Lenin's death the Bolshevik Party, in its 1925 resolution on the relationship between the party and literature, stated that "the class character of art in general and literature in particular is expressed in forms infinitely more varied than, for example, in politics."

In this way the party remained faithful to the Marxist thesis that art as an ideological form expresses class interests, without ignoring that—in view of the complex network of intermediary connections—art is not simply a direct and immediate expression of those interests. A. V. Lunacharsky, commissar of education from 1917 to 1929, was primarily responsible for carrying out the cultural and artistic policies of the new regime, and his approach to the momentous problems of creating a new art was greatly influenced by Marx's aesthetic ideas. A hotly debated question during those years concerned the value of the classical legacy in literature and art, and Lunacharsky—in the face of a quite prevalent nihilist desire to obliterate the past—frequently turned to Marx's reflections on the enduring appeal of the Greek classics and even more to his comments on the peculiarities of artistic development. In this openminded and dynamic attitude to the values of the past, Lunacharsky was supported by Lenin; both were opposed to the "hothouse culture" of the Proletcult movement.

And yet it was Plekhanov, not Marx, who during the 1920s was considered the foremost authority on the theory of art. Marx's aesthetic ideas were seen primarily through a Plekhanovian prism. This resulted, as noted above, in "ideologizing," and in a sociological concept of art which dominated Marxist art and literary criticism in those years. The narrowness of this view made it impossible either to grasp the rich implications of Marx's aesthetic thought or to understand its organic relationship with his philosophical outlook.

In 1923 Lunacharsky proposed a revision of Marxism to accommodate aesthetic questions,[5] in a polemic with Denike, author of an article entitled "Marx and Art." Mikhail Lifshitz—who in 1933 compiled the first anthology of texts by Marx and Engels on art and literature—noted that as late as 1929 the well-known Soviet historian Pokrovsky had said: "For quite some time we have had at our disposal a theory of historical process, but we have yet to develop a Marxist theory of artistic creation." Referring to Marxist contributions to that field, he added: "Except for certain works by Plekhanov and Mehring, we have nothing."[6]

The period between 1931 and 1933 was very important for the study and propagation of Marx's aesthetic ideas. Those years saw the publication of several key texts by Marx and Engels on the problem of literature: two of their early works, *The Economic and Philosophic Manuscripts of 1844* and *The German Ideology*—both, but especially the former, touching on basic aesthetic questions—appeared for the first time (the full texts were published in German, and selections in Russian); and Lifshitz and Schiller edited, with the active collaboration of Lunacharsky, the first anthology of writings by Marx and Engels, *On Literature and Art.* As a result, there was a renewed interest in Marx's aesthetic ideas; their integral role within Marxism as well as their relationship to previous aesthetic thought again began to be asserted. An indication of the renewed Marxist research in this field was Lifshitz's excellent *On the Problem of Marx's Ideas,* published in Russian at about the same time as his anthology.

However, the favorable conditions created in the Soviet Union in the early 1930s, in which a thorough and creative study of Marx's aesthetic ideas might have provided the foundation for a scientific, openminded, non-normative Marxist aesthetic, were seriously undermined when the Stalinist regime began to give rise to increasingly dogmatic, sectarian, and class subjectivist methods in aesthetic theory and artistic practice.

On socialist realism

Socialist realism was conceived, in different ways and from diverse artistic perspectives, during the mid-1930s. At its inception—and above all during its gestation period—it represented attempts to generalize and synthesize the artistic experiences accumulated after the October Revolution, and to respond definitively to the need for a new art, an art serving the new society and nourished by a socialist ideology. Its underlying assumption, clearly justified, was that the Marxist-Leninist world view placed the artist in a new relationship to things and people; and that consequently an art that was to reflect this new human and social reality needed new eyes. This led to a demand for a new realism that could reflect reality and its dynamism, development, and internal contradictions; it would of necessity have to be socialist. Even Lunacharsky, opposed as he was to a dogmatic and normative approach to art, joined this new movement, while making it very clear that he did not envision a realism with predetermined and rigid formal boundaries. On the contrary, he conceived of a socialist realism in which "fantasy, stylization, and every possible freedom of expression play a very important role in the depiction of reality." He stressed that this new realism would employ "many different methods."[7]

Two years before, in 1931, when opposing a trend toward stylistic uniformity, he had defended vigorously the right of artists to develop a realism without stylistic limitations. He felt that this was necessary to assure a great diversity "not only of genres but also of basic methods." It was in this spirit that Lunacharsky became an advocate of the new realism, which in his view would accommodate the most varied forms of expressing and reflecting reality.

However, when socialist realism became institutionalized on both the theoretical and practical levels, it began to close itself off behind increasingly rigid lines, causing such a deep schism between its content and its form that in many cases it became nothing more than a new content pumped into an old form. This contradiction, which never existed for Mayakovsky or Eisenstein, just as it never existed for Prokofiev, Eluard, Brecht, Alberti, or Siqueiros, tore into the very guts of an artistic theory and practice which had the potential to develop a radically new approach to both form and content.

This rigid conception of realism, allowing only one approach and closing the door on formal experimentation, ended any benefits that a new socialist art might draw not only from other artistic trends, whether alien or opposed to it, but also and above all from the formal breakthroughs that the new ideological content demanded. Moreover, the administrative and authoritarian interpretation of the Leninist thesis on the party spirit of a work of art in many cases put a damper on artistic freedom, transforming the vital inner urge to create into an external necessity, in a different context, with the kind of negative results that Marx had pointed out.

All of this led to a socialist realist aesthetic which ceased to postulate infinitely diverse ways of dealing with reality and began to establish norms and fix models, thus turning into a normative aesthetic, incompatible with the Marxist principles on which it pretended to base itself.

However, the dogmatism and sectarianism that imposed themselves on the relationship between art and reality in the name of socialist realism could in no way invalidate the legitimacy of an open, profound, and rich realism—a realism as broad and diverse as reality itself; a realism, moreover, which, far from finding Marxism-Leninism to be a restraint on its attempt to capture reality, found it instead to be the ideological perspective best suited to grasping the complexities and dynamics of reality. It was just this kind of realism that was engendered by the first films of Sergei Eisenstein and even, in the difficult years of the Stalinist period, by the novels of Mikhail Sholokhov.

Toward a Marxist theory of art

After the Twentieth Congress of the Communist Party of the Soviet Union in 1956, the criticism of Stalin's dogmatic and sectarian methods led to the restoration of the forgotten or denatured Marxist-Leninist principles: efforts were made to enrich and revitalize them by reestablishing their bonds with social practice, with people's lives. This process of liberation from Stalinist dogmatism—the vital and creative assimilation and application of the fundamental theses of Marxism—has already yielded results, as much in the Soviet Union as elsewhere, in the study of the aesthetic ideas of Marx and Engels, and more generally in the analysis of the fundamental questions of a Marxist aesthetic which, using Marx's and Engels' ideas as a starting point, attempts to base itself firmly in artistic and social reality.

The return to the source—to Marx's ideas on the nature of aesthetics and art, to Engels' precise formulations on the relationship between ideological and socioeconomic phenomena—as well as the careful study of historico-artistic experience and of the complex artistic experience of our times: all this is contributing to the depth, diversity, and breadth of Marxist research in the field of aesthetics. It is necessary to point out that Marxist aestheticians from both socialist and capitalist countries have made important and relevant contributions and by their collective work have thus rejected the exclusively national manifestations that are proof of dogmatism in the universal field of aesthetics. As a matter of principle, Marxist aestheticians of all countries can and should contribute to the clarification and propagation of Marx's aesthetic ideas, and on the basis of these ideas lay the foundations for a true Marxist aesthetic, one constantly nourished by artistic experience, as diverse, complex, and contradictory as it may be.

Notes

1. The best anthologies are those prepared by Mikhail Lifshitz, published in Russian in 1933, 1947, and 1948 (the latter also appeared in German in 1948). A two-volume edition was published in Russian by Iskusstvo in 1957 under the title *Karl Marx and Frederick Engels: On Art*. Less expensive is an anthology prepared by Jean Freville in French, *Karl Marx–Frederick Engels: Sur la littérature et l'art* (Paris: Editions Sociales, 1954). The first edition of Freville's volume has been translated into Spanish under the title *Sobre la literatura y el arte* (Mexico: Editorial Masas, 1938).

2. V. I. Lenin, "Party Organisation and Party Literature," *Collected Works*, vol. 10 (Moscow: Foreign Languages Publishing House, 1962), p. 46.

3. V. I. Lenin, "Materialism and Empirio-Criticism," in *Collected Works*, vol. 13 (New York: International Publishers, 1927).

4. Boris Meilakh, *Lenin and the Problems of Russian Literature* (Moscow, 1954); French edition (Paris, 1956), p. 203.

5. A. V. Lunacharsky, *In the World of Music* (Moscow, 1958), pp. 224-25.

6. Mikhail Lifshitz, introduction to Karl Marx and Frederick Engels, *On Art,* vol. 1, p. xi.

7. A. V. Lunacharsky, *Articles on Soviet Literature* (Moscow, 1958), pp. 238-39.

* 2. Contemporary Marxism and Art

Several basic tendencies can be seen in the panorama of current Marxist research, all reflecting a return to the source of Marxism, but their principles differing in response to the enriching and invigorating contact with artistic practice. Art is a phenomenon that constantly defies vacuous and hasty generalizations that result from a one-dimensional point of view. Within the Marxist camp today we can see profound differences in the emphasis given a particular aspect or function of artistic creation. These emphases derive from a shared conception of humanity and society and should not be considered exclusive as long as no one of them walls itself in and closes its doors to a different basic approach to art. It is only when a relative truth elevates itself to the level of the absolute that what was valid invalidates by this transgression whatever contribution it might have made to our knowledge, and in this way ceases to be an open aesthetic conception and becomes rigid and closed. It is precisely this kind of open conception, which does not mutilate the richness, diversity, and dynamism of art in its historical development or in its current manifestations, that Marxist aestheticians are seeking through a variety of interpretations. Very well then, what are these different interpretations?

Art as ideology

Let us look first at the concept of art that reduces it to a form of ideology. Of course, this view of art carries good credentials as Marxist thought; in fact, Marxism has all along emphatically insisted on the ideological nature of artistic creation. According to its cardinal thesis of the relationship between the economic base and the superstructure, art belongs to the superstructure and, in a society divided into classes, is linked to definite interests of particular social classes. But the expression of these interests takes on form: the artist's political, moral, or religious ideas are integrated in an artistic structure or totality that has its own set of laws. As a result of this process of integration or formation, the artistic work appears to be endowed with a certain internal coherence and relative autonomy which thwarts its reduction to a mere ideological phenomenon. The writings of Marx and Engels on the complex web in which artistic phenomena exist, on the endurability of Greek art across changing historical conditions, on the autonomy and dependence of spiritual creations, including art, and on the uneven development of art and society, proscribe the placement of an equal sign between art and ideology in the name of the ideological character of an artistic work. Nevertheless, until only a few years ago one of the most frequent temptations for Marxist aestheticians—and, above all, for literary and artistic critics confronted with specific works of art—has been to overestimate the role of the ideological factor and consequently to minimize the form, the internal coherence, and the specific laws of the work of art.

The Marxist thesis that the artist is socially and historically conditioned, and that his ideological positions play a particular role, in some cases bearing on the artistic fate of his work, does not in any way imply a need to reduce a work of art to its ideological components. And there is even less justification for equating the aesthetic value of a work with the value of its ideas. Even when a particular work clearly shows its class roots, it will continue to live, although those roots—already dry—may not bear new fruits. The work of art thus outgrows the socio-historical ground which gave it birth. Because of its class origin, its ideological character, art is an expression of the social division or gash in humanity; but because of its ability to extend a bridge between people across time and social divisions, art manifests a vocation for universality, and in a certain way prefigures that universal human destiny which will only be effectively realized in a new society, with the abolition of the material and ideological particularisms of social classes. Just as Greek art survived the ideology of slavery, the art of our times will outlive its ideology.

To characterize art according to its ideological content ignores a key historical fact: class ideologies come and go, but true art persists. If the specific nature of art lies in its transcendence, because of its durability, of the ideological limits which made it possible; if it lives or survives by its vocation for universality, thanks to which people living in actual socialist societies can coexist with Greek, medieval, or Renaissance art, then its reduction to *ideology*—and to its particular elements, its *here* and *now*—is a betrayal of its very essence. But at the same time we should not forget that art is made by men who are historically conditioned, and that the universality that art achieves is not the abstract and timeless universality that idealist aestheticians speak of after creating an abyss between art and ideology, or between art and society, but the human universality that is manifested *in* and *through* the particular.

Thus we see that the relationship between art and ideology is extremely complex and contradictory, and in dealing with this relationship we must avoid—as two equally noxious extremes—either an identification or a radical opposition between art and ideology. The first is characteristic of ideologizing, subjectivist, or crudely sociological positions; and the second is found at times among those who carry their distinction between art and ideology to the point of denying the ideological character of art, thus placing themselves outside Marxism.

Artistic decadence and social decadence

In the last few years Marxist aestheticians have taken important steps to overcome these false positions, particularly the crudely sociological position, which as we have seen is the most prevalent and has the oldest roots. However, this process has encountered grave difficulties when it has attempted to go beyond a formulation of general theoretical theses to an analysis of concrete artistic phenomena. This is what happens, for example, in dealing with the phenomenon of modern painting, or contemporary novels with roots in Proust, Joyce, and Kafka. As we know, these artistic manifestations formerly were rejected *en bloc,* in the name of Marxist-Leninist aesthetics, because they were considered decadent. This attitude does not find the support it did a few years ago among Marxist aestheticians.

The essence of this position—which inspired the famous Lukácsian dilemma, "Franz Kafka or Thomas Mann," decadent vanguardism or realism—is substantially the following: art is decadent when it expresses or portrays a decadent society, when its view of such a society leaves its socio-economic pillars intact, or when its ideological content is decadent or contains elements of decadence. Now then, even given this debatable characterization of artistic decadence, the concept is inapplicable to Kafka's novel *The Trial,* for example, since the author here gives us a key to an understanding of the abstract, alienated, and absurd nature of human relationships in capitalist society.[1] With regard to the requirement that the artist consciously shake the foundations of society by offering not only a critique but also a set of solutions, Engels has already given a full and convincing retort.[2] And in any case, after we have read Kafka, the pillars on which bureaucratized human relationships rest can no longer appear to us as firm as before.

What concerns us here is not whether the concept of decadence is applicable to Kafka—who clearly will not let himself be confined within the narrow framework of Lukács' dilemma—but whether the very concept of decadence is valid in its application to art. From our point of view, this application shows the same simplistic conception of the relation between art and ideology we criticized above. This simplification results from a hasty move from the social and ideological to the artistic, thus in a way burning bridges, ignoring the intermediate links and peculiarities that must be taken into account.

The concept of decadence is not immutable, to be applied indiscriminately to all ideological forms or to specific artistic phenomena or social periods. Decadent art is not the same as the art of a decadent society; decadence in artistic terms is not the same as decadence in social terms. An artistic movement can be called decadent when, after reaching its apogee, it begins to descend for lack of further creative possibilities. It can also be said that a decadent ideology, or elements of it, may inspire the artistic creations of a society in which the dominant social class, at one time progressive, has entered its period of decline. But none of this leads to the conclusion that a society in decadence necessarily engenders a *decadent art* in the sense we give to that term—art in decline due to a weakening or exhaustion of its power to innovate or create. That is as false as the contention—made by A. A. Zhdanov in 1948—that socialism engenders a vanguard art, superior by the mere fact of its being an expression of a superior stage of social development. Likewise, we cannot apply the category of progress—and indeed, Marx never did—to two related but distinct fields. In short, what is false with regard to the ascendant phase of a social movement or dominant class is also false in dealing with its decadent phase.

In our opinion, no true art can be decadent. Artistic decadence appears only with the falsifications, constriction, or exhaustion of the creative forces which are objectified in the work of art. The elements of decadence a work may contain—pessimism, loss of energy, attraction for the abnormal and morbid, etc.—express a decadent attitude toward life. But from an artistic point of view those elements can take only one of two roads: either they are so powerful that they wear out the creative impulse, or they are integrated and transcended in the work of art, thus contributing, through the curious dialectic of the negation of the negation, to an affirmation of man's creative power, which is precisely the negation of a decadent outlook on life.

The application of the concept of decadence to art—either in the simplistic manner of Zhdanov or using the more subtle approach of Lukács—shows that we need to proceed with great care in examining the relationship between art and ideology. The discussions recently elicited by the application of this concept demonstrate that within Marxist aesthetics there is already an attempt to overcome the old sociological error of identifying artistic decadence with social decadence.[3] But at the same time there is a renewed urgency to discover the nature of art at a level deeper than that of ideology; so that, far from disappearing, it will flourish in the future, when the class ideologies which have so far nourished art will be, like other particularist ideologies, a thing of the past.

Art as a form of cognition

In response to the excesses of the ideologizing and vulgar sociological positions, a Marxist aesthetics emphasizes the conception of art as a form of cognition. The cognitive function of art, and of literature in particular, was pointed out by Marx and Engels in their opinions of various works by the great realist writers of the nineteenth century, and by Lenin in his articles on Tolstoy. All three called attention to the cognitive character of art without ignoring its ideological nature: they recognized that the relationship between these two functions of art is extremely complex and at times contradictory, as evidenced by their analyses of Goethe, Balzac, and Tolstoy. Marx's reflections in *The Holy Family* on Eugène Sue's novel *Mystères de Paris* and the critical observations of Marx and Engels on Lasalle's tragedy *Franz von Sickingen*[4] demonstrated that a false ideological perspective can adversely affect the artistic truth and the aesthetic merits of a work. On the other hand, the analysis by Marx and

Engels of Balzac's *Human Comedy* and Lenin's writings on Tolstoy—"Mirror of the Russian Revolution"—revealed, in Engels' words, "one of the greatest triumphs of realism,"[5] that is, the victory of artistic truth over a false ideological outlook. Balzac's monarchic legitimism is artistically transcended in his work: what stands out is his realistic portrayal of a decrepit aristocracy in a bourgeois world. Tolstoy's mysticism could not, as Lenin noted, keep Tolstoy's work from reflecting certain essential features of the Russian Revolution, just as it could not prevent the working class of Tzarist Russia from *learning more* about its enemies.[6]

Art thus appears in the classics of Marxism-Leninism as a form of knowledge; and that is why the cognitive value of art is currently given an emphasis opposed to merely ideological interpretations, and instead informed by the writings of Marx, Engels, and Lenin on the great realist writers of their time. While according to the ideological conception the artist addresses himself to reality in order to express his vision of the world, as well as of his time and class, the conception of art as cognition emphasizes that the artist is approaching reality. The artist approaches reality to capture its essential features, to reflect it, but without dissociating his artistic reflection from his attitude to reality, that is, from the ideological content of the work. In that sense, art is a means of cognition.

The concept of reflection as applied to art does not infer, or at least should not infer, as we previously pointed out, a mechanical transformation of an epistemological category into an aesthetic one. Artistic truth is not determined by a full correspondence between art and ideology, but neither is it determined—and this differentiates it from scientific knowledge—by a complete congruence with an objective reality existing apart from and independently of man. In a painting or a poem about a tree, for example, what we have is not a tree in itself, or a tree as seen by a botanist, but rather a humanized tree, a tree that attests to a human presence. Consequently, when we speak of artistic truth or the reflection of reality in art we must go beyond a general philosophical level to aesthetics itself. Only in this way, by giving it a specific significance, can we speak of art as a form of knowledge. What does that humanized tree refer to? Purely and simply, the real tree that grows alone, untouched by human hand? Or man himself, humanizing the tree? These questions are enough to make us realize the need to proceed cautiously when speaking of art as a form or means of knowledge, until we can establish *what* it is that we know, definitively, in art, and *how* this knowledge comes to us.

For a long time the theory of the cognitive function of art was limited to one fundamental question: What is the specific form in which art reflects reality? Art, the answer went, reflects reality in images; science and philosophy in concepts. The roots of this conception go back to Hegel, to whom art did not have an intrinsic content and object: its object was the same as the object of religion and philosophy. These forms in the development and self-knowledge of the Absolute Spirit were differentiated by the manner in which they gained this knowledge. In art, which is the "sensory manifestation of the Idea," the spiritual was still attached to the sensory; only in philosophy—after the changes made necessary by religion—did the Idea appear in its pure state: the concept. Therefore, the difference between art and philosophy—as specific forms of knowing the same object— was necessarily determined by the development of the Spirit, which achieved its full truth and reality only in its total conceptual self-knowledge.

Marxist aestheticians have spoken, and still speak—very much à la Hegel—of art and science as two distinct ways of knowing reality (different in form, identical in object and content). But it is not enough to characterize art as a specific form of knowledge, even if it uses new cognitive means which preclude reducing it to a "thinking in images"; Ernst Fischer emphasizes that a reality which is itself deformed or grotesque can best be reflected by recourse to fantasy, parable, or symbolism, as it is by Kafka. As A. I. Burov has correctly pointed out, the form in which art reflects reality does not justify a distinction between art and other manifestations of social consciousness. If we characterize art exclusively according to its form and not according to its object or content, we will fail to understand the peculiarities of art as knowledge.[7]

The formal differences between art and science do not lead us beyond the concept of art—Hegelian in its origin—as specific knowledge without an object of its own. But if art and science are different forms of knowledge, what sense is there in this duplication of the cognitive function? What is the point of this new knowledge, which in truth does not enrich the knowledge we already have about the object but simply provides us with a new form of knowing? Or could it be that art pretends to compete with science in its domain? "Artistic creation, just like science," according to A. Yegorov, "leads us to a knowledge of the essence of phenomena, and enriches humanity with new knowledge."[8] If art as a form of knowledge fulfills a certain need, and if it is not merely a duplication (using images, metaphors, or symbols) of what science or philosophy already gives us (using concepts), it can be justified only if it has its own specific object, as Burov pointed out, which in turn conditions its specific manner of reflecting reality. This specific object is man, or human life.

Man is the specific object of art even if he is not always the object of artistic representation. Nonhuman objects that are represented artistically are not simply represented objects, but are objects in a certain relationship to humankind; that is, they show us not what they are in themselves, but what they are for man—they are humanized. The represented object embodies a social significance, a human world. Therefore, in reflecting objective reality the artist involves us in human reality. In this way, art as knowledge of reality can show us a portion of reality—not in its objective essence, which is the specific task of science, but in its relationship to human nature. There is a science which deals with trees, classifying them, studying their morphological and functional characteristics; but where is the science that deals with *humanized* trees? These are precisely the objects art is concerned with.

But what happens when the object of artistic representation is man, not man revealed by things in relation to him, but man in a direct and immediate way? Here again, art does not duplicate the work of what are called the human or social sciences. Dostoevsky does not limit himself to repeating psychiatric truths, nor is Balzac's *Human Comedy* an explanation of the ideas about capitalist economic relations in Marx's *Capital.* Art does not look at human relationships in general, but rather in their individual manifestations. It presents concrete live human beings in the unity and richness of their determinations, where the general and the particular merge in a particular way. But the knowledge art can give us about people is gained by particular means which do not include the imitation or reproduction of concrete reality; art goes from what we will call an objective concreteness to an artistic concreteness. The artist sees before him the immediate, given, concrete reality, but he cannot remain on that level, limiting himself to reproducing it. Human reality reveals its secrets to the artist only to the extent that, starting from the immediate and individual, he rises to a universal level, to return again to the concrete. But this new individual or artistic concreteness is precisely the fruit of a process of creation, not of imitation.

Art can only be knowledge—specific knowledge of a specific reality: man as a unique, concrete, and living totality—which transforms external reality, departing from it to bring forth a new reality, a work of art. Artistic knowledge is the fruit of an activity: the artist makes art into a means of knowledge not by copying a reality, but by creating a new one. Art is knowledge only to the extent that it is creation. Only thus can it serve truth and discover the essential aspects of human reality.

Definitions of realism

Art which thus serves truth as a specific means of knowledge both in its form and object is realism. We call realist art all art that, starting with the existence of an objective reality, constructs a new reality which gives us truths about concrete men who live in a given society, in historically and socially conditioned human relationships, within which they work, struggle, suffer, rejoice, or dream.

In the definition of realism we just formulated, we find the category of reality on three different levels: external reality, marginal to man; the new or humanized reality man engenders, transcending or humanizing external reality; and human reality, radiating through humanized external reality and enriching our knowledge of man. This definition enables us to distinguish between realism, which represents a reality that reflects the essence of human phenomena, and art, which cannot or does not want to have a cognitive function. The latter category includes primarily the false realism which, by trying to deal exclusively with either an external reality or an internal human reality, fails to enrich our knowledge of man, either because man ceases to be the specific object of artistic knowledge, or because the artistic methods it uses preclude a penetration into the essential aspects of human reality.

It is a false realism which, in the name of knowing reality—an expression used vaguely by some Marxists—makes the representation of things an end rather than a means at the service of truth. This type of realism is not a way of knowing reality, but simply a way of representing it; that is, it is an attempt to present it anew in the way a copy or an imitation presents the original. The boundaries of this supposed realism are rigid: they extend no further than the boundaries of the object. Sometimes the artist pretends to reproduce every detail, thus falling into naturalism, or a documentary, anecdotal, photographic realism; at other times the artist presents the object on a higher level, pretending to capture the essence of things, their secret rhythms or intimate structures, in a doomed attempt to compete with science or philosophy. It is a hopeless enterprise: things and their essential reality go on waiting for the scientist, while the artist—absorbed by things, by their objective essence—loses his grip on the human content they may bear.

Another type of false realism is that which has human

reality as its object, but seeks in it not what it is but what it should be, and transforms things so that they reflect a pretti-fied human reality, with the edges smoothed. This type of realism falls into the trap of artistic unrealism or idealism. For the most part, what was made to pass for socialist realism during the Stalinist period was nothing but its transformation into "socialist" idealism. Of course, not all the artistic and literary works of that time presented the new socialist reality through rose-colored glasses, and the novels of Sholokhov are but one example; those that did deserve to be called neither socialist nor realist. True socialist realism has no reason to mystify reality. Lies kill it; the truth it can reveal justifies and legitimizes its existence. Therefore, if art is a form of knowledge that captures human reality in its essential aspects and tears off the veil of its mystification, if art in the service of truth can serve humanity in its construction of a new human reality, then there is nothing—short of some new form of dogmatism—that can prevent a socialist realist conception of art that is neither sectarian nor exclusive.

The task of presenting a profoundly realistic vision of new social realities from the ideological perspective—Marxism-Leninism—that facilitates such a vision, far from being an enterprise without a future, still has a long way to go. A truly realist and socialist art has yet to say its last word on the new social reality that is in the process of emerging—a reality with light and shadow, conflict, and a vital, constant, and at times dramatic struggle between the old and the new.

Identifying art and realism

Once we discard the conception of realism as a copy or imitation of reality and admit that realism cannot be en-closed in the aesthetic canons of previous historical periods, there arises the question of defining the relation between art and realism. If by using diverse forms of expression, realism is a way of knowing man by means of creating a new reality, then we have to answer the following questions: Does realism exhaust the sphere of art? Is all realism art, or is all art realist? Is there anything that precedes or goes beyond realism?

Let us analyze one response to these questions.

> The trends that manifest a rigorous adherence to all the formalistic principles, such as abstract art or surrealism, are not artistic methods in the strict sense of the word. When reality is deformed to the point of making it unrecognizable, and when the principle that art must penetrate the aesthetic essence of life is denied, it is impossible to create an artistic image. The works that are nourished by these formalist methods remain, in fact, at the margin of the sphere of art.[9]

Everything in our times that does not fit into a narrow definition of realism—futurism, cubism, expressionism, surrealism, etc.—is here lumped under the rubric of formalism. This sectarian and dogmatic position is indefensible, for it narrows the sphere of art, ignoring its specific nature in order to apply exclusively ideological criteria to it. From the point of view of the specific nature of art, the works of art produced by those artistic movements the above writer banishes from the world of art might have the following points cited in their favor: (1) they are particular ways of presenting or objectifying human reality; (2) they represent a new reality or product created by man in which he freely expresses his creative capacity, although in this case they may not strictly speaking fulfill a cognitive function; and (3) they contribute to the development of art insofar as they satisfy the need—always vital for art—to discover new forms and means of expression.

Applying exclusively ideological or political criteria to works of art and denying their artistic character on that basis can only serve those criteria as such, demonstrating, as Antonio Gramsci very accurately put it, "that somebody as an artist does not belong to a specific political world and that, since his personality is essentially artistic, in his intimate life, in the life he actually lives, the political world under discussion plays no role, does not exist."[10] And even then, the efficacy of those criteria is doubtful, as shown by these two facts: (1) modern art has developed, for the most part, in opposition to the tastes, ideals, and values of the bourgeoisie; and (2) after the October Revolution, important figures of the new or vanguard art movements were linked ideologically and politically to the revolutionary vanguard, the Marxist-Leninist parties.

Reiterating what we discussed above with regard to the mechanical application of the concept of decadence to art and the attendant oversimplification of the relationship between art and ideology, we believe that it is impossible to equate nonrealist trends in art with the reactionary and decadent ideology of the imperialist bourgeoisie; nor is it possible to equate realism with the ideology of progressive and revolutionary classes. On the other hand, there cannot be, nor is there, a total lack of communication between realism and what is called the vanguard of art. The formal techniques of the modern novel, such as the interior monologue and the discontinuity or reversibility of time, are integrated increasingly into the realistic novel, which up to a few years ago was constructed according to classical norms. It is not merely a question of formal innovations, but rather one of changes in the formal structure made necessary by changes in content, which in turn were the result of transformations in human reality itself. The Italian Marxist theoretician Carlo Salinari comes to the same conclusions, observing that "the form also becomes irregular, faster, less melodious, unable to ignore the technical discoveries made by the European vanguard in the field of prose."[11]

The same need to experiment is felt by the young Soviet novelist Daniel Granin: "I must recognize that frequently one becomes aware of one's own impotence in trying to find more profound creative possibilities using the methods of the traditional novel. It is necessary to discover new methods, and I believe that this is nothing but a natural process."[12] Without this fruitful assimilation of new methods of expression, the artistic personalities of the great figures of socialist art would have been stunted in their development. Mayakovsky would not have existed without futurism, nor Siqueiros without modern painting, Brecht without expressionism, Neruda, Aragon, or Eluard without surrealism, etc. Thus realism does not exhaust the sphere of art, and the artistic phenomena that lie outside realist art cannot be excluded from it.

The aesthetics of Georg Lukács

Throughout the aesthetic writings of Georg Lukács we find a less restrictive formulation of the thesis that equates art and realism. Art is for Lukács one of the forms through which man can reflect or grasp reality. He insists on the need to distinguish between artistic and scientific reflection. He finds the special character of artistic reflection in the category of particularity, the midpoint in the process of reflecting reality at which both the particular and the universal are transcended. The special character of art is also manifested in the relationship between phenomenon and essence: while in scientific knowledge the essence can be conceptually separated from the phenomenon, in art it cannot maintain its autonomy apart from the phenomenon. Thus art is one of the forms through which man discovers the world and reality.

Reality, of course, is in a constant process of change, and therefore requires varied means of expression. The historicity of objective reality in turn imposes a historicity on the means of expression, and thus determines the actual development of art. However, what enables us to distinguish great art and at the same time explains its durability is its capacity for reflecting reality, the strength and depth with which it grasps the essence of the real. From this Lukács concludes unequivocally that true art is realist art, and that realism is the yardstick by which to evaluate any artistic work, whatever its period and whatever conception of the world it may express. Thus, in an interview with the Czech journalist Antonin Liehm in 1964, Lukács said: "All great art is realist art; this has been the case since Homer's time because it reflects reality, and this is the irrefutable criterion for all great periods of art, even if the means of expression varies infinitely."[13] In this way, Lukács defined once and for all the limits of great art.

Using this definition, Lukács opposes the denaturalized realism of the Stalinist era, above all vanguard (decadent) art, which is for him particularly exemplified by Kafka's *angst*, "the experience *par excellence* of modernism." Lukács is not so myopic or dogmatic as to deny the existence of phenomena that are within the realm of art but not contained within the limits of realism. He recognizes the formal accomplishments of the modern novel, and admits that Kafka penetrated his reality to a certain extent, although in Lukács' judgment it was a penetration "in one dimension only." In sum, although he acknowledges the existence of nonrealist (in his terms) art and literature, he maintains that true art—authentic art, art that endures—is realist art. His preference for critical realism, with its great exemplars, Balzac, Goethe, and Tolstoy, and for socialist realism—once it is liberated from its subjectivist and naturalist deformations—derives precisely from their superior grasp of reality.[14]

Lukács' aesthetics represent, in the Marxist camp, the most fruitful exposition of the conception of art as a form of knowledge. As an aesthetics of realism it captivates us with its penetrating analyses and suggestive findings, but by setting up those conditions that can only be satisfied by realism as criteria of value, it becomes a closed and normative aesthetic.

From a narrow realism to a realism without boundaries

Art refuses to be enclosed within the limits of realism, even less of a realism that does not go beyond the pictorial canons of the Renaissance, or the formal criteria which in literature are exemplified by Goethe, Balzac, or Tolstoy. Realism as an artistic category exceeds the boundaries of any particular school of realism,[15] and can therefore have no boundaries because, as Roger Garaudy points out, "the development of human reality has no limits."[16] And if it is to develop and extend itself, realism must go beyond the object, beyond objective reality and its actual configurations. Certainly we cannot equate, in creating pictures, realism and representational painting. Realistic painting involves more than the visible forms of external reality. True realism begins when these visible figures or forms are transformed into insights into the human world which the artist wants to reflect or express. We therefore insist that realism must break the representational barrier, in a dialectical transcendence that reabsorbs real figures and forms to elevate them to a higher synthesis. The real, external figure is an obstacle that must be overcome if realism is to be more than mere representation, that is, transfiguration. *To transfigure is to place the figure on a human plane.*

Realism must open itself so that it can reflect not only the appearance of reality—fed by fidelity to detail and to the external figure—but rather the profound and essential reality that can be reached only by placing real figures on a human plane. The fidelity of the strictly representational painter— the painter who remains with the object, without transcending it—is really an infidelity to reality because it is precisely the transfiguration of the object that allows true realism to approach reality.

In breaking the representational barrier by transforming rather than by abandoning the figure, realism, far from losing itself, affirms itself, and thus emerges as an infinitely developing realism that does not need to encompass the totality of artistic phenomena. In order to defend a true realism without boundaries, such as the one proposed by Garaudy,[17] it is not necessary to deliver to it all of art, including abstract art. What do we stand to gain by subsuming all artistic phenomena under the category of realism, or by establishing, from this new perspective, the oneness of art and realism? In order to recognize the undeniable existence of an art that, starting with Kandinsky's famous watercolor in 1910, neither makes use of the figure nor fulfills a cognitive function, an art that testifies to a distinct human presence—as do all artistic phenomena, including decorative art—it is not necessary to redescribe any of the characteristics of realism, which as we noted previously consist of a threefold mode of presenting reality: as represented *external reality* (real forms, figures) with which a *new reality* (work of art) is created, essentially reflecting and expressing *human reality*.

Both realism and nonrealism are artistic facts. Each fulfills different functions—including an ideological one—each satisfies different human needs, and each makes use of diverse means of expression. But each has its pitfalls: while the appeal to real forms can lead to the desert of cold and inexpressive representationalism, a total break with the forms and figures of the real world can result in the frigidity and monotony we suffered with geometric abstractionism. One recent painter, Jean Bazaine, whose works border on the abstract, has underlined the mortal dangers of a total break with the external world: "We cannot cast off the external world as if it were too heavy a mantle . . . A systematic denial of the external world amounts to a denial of oneself: a form of suicide."[18] But the dangers that beset both realism and abstract art do not invalidate the fact that they are both proof of the creative life of man, without implying that one art dissolves into the other.

Art as creation

So let realism extend its boundaries without excluding or absorbing other artistic phenomena, and let us look for a more profound and primary stratum of art, one that does not identify art with a particular tendency—realist, symbolist, abstract, etc.—or rigidly restrict its development, and one that enables us to understand art in its totality as an essential human activity. Only in this way can we avoid, from a Marxist point of view, the limitations of a merely ideological, sociological, or cognitive conception of art.

Certainly, art has an ideological content, but only in the proportion that ideology loses its substantiveness by being integrated into the new reality of the work of art. That is, the ideological problems that the artist chooses to deal with have to be solved *artistically*. Art can have a cognitive function also, that of reflecting the essence of the real; but this function can only be fulfilled by *creating a new reality,* not by copying or imitating existing reality. In other words, the cognitive problems that the artist chooses to deal with have to be solved *artistically.* To forget this—that is, to reduce art to ideology or to a mere form of knowledge—is to forget that the work of art is, above all, creation, a manifestation of the creative power of man. In the failure to recognize this lie the limitations of the concept of art we examined previously.[19]

From a truly aesthetic point of view, the work of art does not depend for its life on either the ideology that inspires it or its function of reflecting reality. It exists by itself with its own reality, into which that which it expresses or reflects is integrated. A work of art is primarily a human creation, and it exists through the creative power it incarnates. This point of view allows us to see the historical development of art as an infinite process that cannot be enclosed within the limits of a determinate movement. Ideological or sociological criteria ignore the law of the uneven development of art and society. They talk of superior and inferior art, or progressive and decadent art, ignoring the specific nature of artistic activity as a manifestation of the creative power of man. Realist criteria underline the cognitive function of art, making it the sole function, overlooking the other functions art can fulfill and has fulfilled historically; realist criteria ignore the fact that art, as a human product, not only represents or reflects man, but also makes him present, objectified. Certainly, human presence is not the exclusive property of works of art, and even less of a particular tendency in art. If, as Marx said, technology is an opening to the essential forces of man, then we have even more reason to say that so is art, whether it be ornamental, symbolist, realist, or abstract. Precisely because it is a superior form of creation, an exceptional testimony to creative existence, humanity is present in every work of art. In this sense, man is as present in the pre-Colombian *Coat-licue* as in the shoes of Van Gogh's peasant, or in a Christ by Rouault, or in an apple by Cézanne. The organization of colors and forms does not cease to be a manifestation of man's creative capacity whether it depicts a human face, a stone, or a tree, or even if its reference to external reality is minimal. Man is not lost in the transition from representational to nonrepresentational art; what happens is that the process of humanization, characteristic of art, follows a different road. That is why there is no point in speaking rigidly of the dehumanization of art where there is real creativity. The dehumanization of art—its alienation—would be its own negation, the exclusion of all objectification or presence of human reality. By emphasizing the human presence in art— whether realist or not—we point to its most profound and basic level: its quality of being a particular form of creative work.

The roots of this idea can be found in one of Marx's youthful works, *The Economic and Philosophic Manuscripts of 1844.* In order to arrive at this conclusion we must overcome, as Marx did, the idea that art and work are antagonistic activities, an idea which resulted either from a failure to see the creative character of human work (a forced, mercenary activity, according to Kant), therefore excluding it from the sphere of freedom, or from reducing work to a merely economic category, without understanding its relationship to man, to the human essence (work, according to Adam Smith and David Ricardo, was to produce material goods, and was the basis of all material wealth).

Hegel had perceived the commonality of art and work, although in an idealist manner (see *The Phenomenology of the Spirit* on the role of work in the development of man, or man as a product of his own work), but it was Marx who first saw clearly that the relationship between art and work lay in their common creative character. Consequently, Marx conceived of this creative character not only as an economic category (source of material wealth) but as an ambivalent philosophical category (source of *human* wealth and misery).

The idea that art is an activity that, by prolonging the positive aspect of work, manifests the creative capacity of man permits an infinite extension of the boundaries of art, without confining it to any particular *ism.* Although the work of art can fulfill the most diverse functions—ideological, educational, social, expressive, cognitive, decorative, etc.—as it has throughout the history of art, it can only fulfill these functions as an object *created* by man. Whatever internal or external reality it may refer to, a work of art is, above all, a creation of man, a *new* reality. The essential function of art is to broaden and enrich, with its creations, a reality already humanized by human work.

The idea of art as creation precludes the establishment of formal criteria that can be applied to any future artistic work. Rooting ourselves firmly on this basic level, we can avoid falling into a closed, dogmatic idea of art. If creation is the substance of all true art, then we cannot exclude any particular artistic tendency; realism, therefore, has no monopoly on creation. But we would be creating a new dogmatism if we saw the break with visible reality as the only creative impulse. The theory that the growing infidelity of painting to external reality, which began with impressionism, is an advance toward the conquest of the true creative nature of art forgets that a truly realistic painting is always creation. Realist art deserves its name not because it has recourse to external reality, but above all because it can order real forms and figures in such a way as to place them in a relationship to man. Real creation is just as opposed to direct, formless expression as to an imitation or copy; on the other hand, it does not exclude a formed or structured expression—of an ideological nature, for example—any more than it rules out the use of real figures. The representation does not in itself constitute creation, but neither is its abolition a necessary guarantee of, or condition for, creative activity. Those who think this way will find themselves in a situation similar to that of Kant's famous dove, who thought that if it were not for the resistance of air it would be able to fly in total freedom.

The idea of art as creation does not demand a unanimous attitude to reality (a fidelity to its shapes and figures, or a distancing from them); it underlines, above all, the relationship between art and the human essence. Man elevates and affirms himself in the process of transforming and humanizing reality, and art satisfies this need. That is why there is no such thing as "art for art's sake," nor can there be; there is only art by and for man. Since man is essentially a creative being, he creates works of art to feel his affirmation, his creativity, that is, his humanity.

This fertile idea, which is gaining ground in current Marxist aesthetics, has come about only by a reevaluation of Marx's idea that art and work are two essential spheres of human life. The idea of art as a particular form of creative work does not prevent us from recognizing its possible ideological or cognitive functions; but neither does it reduce art to its ideological content or its cognitive value. To reduce art to ideology is to lose sight of its essential dimension, the creative one; and to see art only as a form of reflecting reality is to fail to understand its fundamental character: the artistic product is a new reality that attests, above all else, to the presence of the human being as creator.

Notes

1. See chapter 7.
2. "But I believe the tendency must spring forth from the situation and the action itself, without explicit attention called to it; the writer is not obliged to offer to the reader the future historical solution of the social conflicts he depicts." Letter to Minna Kautsky, November 26, 1885.
3. The Prague conference on the concept of "decadence" included writers from various countries: Jean-Paul Sartre, Ernst Fischer, J. Hajek, and others; an account can be found in the Czech review, *Plamen,* no. 2, 1964. Contributions translated into French appeared in *La Nouvelle Critique,* nos. 156, 157 (June-July 1964), pp. 71-84. Marxist theoreticians and writers opposed the dogmatic and mechanical use of the concept of decadence. Ernst Fischer: "We must have the courage to say: if writers describe decadence in all its nakedness, and if they denounce it morally, this is not decadence. We must not abandon Proust, Joyce, or Beckett, and even less

Kafka, to the bourgeoisie." E. Goldstucker: "We must distinguish the elements of decadence in the 'philosophy of life,' critically examining and deeply appreciating the new techniques of artistic creation which this decadent and pessimistic vision of life and of the world has brought with it." Milan Kundera: "We have arrived at a truly dialectical position in regard to what is called decadent literature, and we have understood that ideological struggle does not consist in the rejection, but rather in the overcoming of obstacles."

4. See chapter 6.

5. "That Balzac was thus compelled to go against his own class sympathies and political prejudices, that he *saw* the necessity of the downfall of his favorite nobles, and described them as people deserving no better fate; and that he *saw* the real men of the future where, for the time being, they alone were to be found—that I consider one of the greatest triumphs of Realism, and one of the grandest features in old Balzac." Letter to Margaret Harkness, April 1888.

6. V. I. Lenin, "Party Organization and Party Literature," in *Selected Works* (New York: International Publishers, 1967).

7. A. I. Burov, *The Aesthetic Essence of Art* (Moscow, 1956), particularly chaps. 1 and 5.

8. A. I. Yegorov, *Arte y sociedad* (Montevideo, 1961).

9. *Ensayos de estética marxista-leninista,* trans. and ed. A. Vidal Roget (Montevideo), p. 199.

10. Antonio Gramsci, *Letteratura e vitla nazionale,* in *Opere,* vol. 6 (Turin: Einaudi, 1947-71).

11. Quoted by Jiri Hajek at the Leningrad Conference of European Writers, August 5–8, 1963. In *Esprit,* no. 329, p. 39.

12. Daniel Granin, ibid., p. 78.

13. *La Nouvelle Critique,* nos. 156–157 (June–July 1964).

14. Georg Lukács, *Realism in Our Time* (New York: Harper and Row, 1964). See also his "Prolegomena to a Marxist Aesthetic," *New Hungarian Quarterly,* no. 47.

15. Stefan Morawski, "Realism as an Artistic Category," *Recherches internationales* (Paris), no. 38 (July–August 1963), pp. 53, 62.

16. Roger Garaudy, "Philosophical Materialism and Artistic Realism," *Europe,* nos. 419-420, p. 335.

17. Roger Garaudy, *D'un réalisme sans rivages: Picasso, Saint-John Perse, Kafka* (Paris, 1963).

18. J. Bazaine, "Notes sur la peinture d'aujourd'hui" (Paris, 1953), in Walter Hess, ed., *Documentos para la comprensión de la pintura moderna* (Buenos Aires, 1959), p. 156.

19. These limitations also existed in my earlier writings on aesthetics: my doctoral thesis, *Conciencia y realidad en la obra de arte* (1955), and "Sobre el realismo socialista," in *Nuestras Ideas* (Brussels), no. 3, 1957. Starting with my study on "The Aesthetic Ideas of Marx's *Economic and Philosophic Manuscripts*" (1961), I have attempted to relate Marxist aesthetics to thepraxis of Marx's thoughts.

*

3. The Ideas of Marx
on the Source and Nature
of the Aesthetic

The aesthetic and the human

In his youthful works, particularly in *The Economic and Philosophic Manuscripts of 1844,* Marx was occupied with clarifying the source and nature of the aesthetic; and in the framework of man's aesthetic relationship to reality, he paid particular attention to art as "creation that conforms to the laws of beauty."

At that time Marx was interested in defining man as producer, not only of objects or material products but also of works of art. There was an aesthetic dimension to human existence that needed to be explained.

But why did Marx insist so vigorously in this early work on explaining the aesthetic, on searching out its sources and defining its nature? We believe that it was not the aesthetic as such that he was looking for; he was after something else, and on the way he found aesthetic creation "that conforms to the laws of beauty" to be an essential dimension of that something. He was looking for man, or more precisely social, concrete man, man who, in the historical and economic conditions of capitalist society, destroys, mutilates, or denies himself. This mutilation or loss of humanity takes place in work, in material production—that is, in the sphere which has made possible aesthetic creation and in which man should affirm his humanity. In his search for the human, for our lost humanity, Marx found in the aesthetic a stronghold, as well as an essential sphere, of human existence. If man is creative, he cannot keep from aestheticizing the world—that is, assimilating it artistically—without renouncing his human condition.

For Marx the aesthetic is integrated fully and necessarily in man. We can therefore understand why in his youthful works he peered so eagerly at the world of the aesthetic in his search for the roots of alienation and the real essence of man that is lost in work. Thus Marx began to look at the aesthetic in order to clarify just how much man had lost in his alienated society, and therefore how much he stood to gain in a new society—a communist society—governed by truly human relations.

Aesthetics and praxis

If the aesthetic appears as an essential dimension of man as a creative being, Marx's humanist vision demanded that aesthetics be placed in the foreground. But if the aesthetic shows man to be a productive, transforming being, then artistic activity must be rooted in a fundamental praxis from which it emerges as a superior expression. Praxis is a dimension of man as an active, creative being, and therefore the very foundation of artistic praxis must be sought in the basic and profound praxis that informs the consciousness and existence of man.

In linking aesthetics to praxis, Marx's concept of aesthetics, like all his philosophy, exists on a radically different level from that of idealist aesthetics. The first of the *Theses on Feuerbach* established, in opposition to idealism and pre-Marxist materialism, a type of relation between subject and object that permits the concept of the artistic object as product, as human sensory activity, as praxis, as objectified extension of the subject.[2] Praxis, as the basis of man as a socio-historical being, capable of transforming nature to create a world to a human measure, is also the basis of man's aesthetic relationship to reality.

When Marx referred to praxis as a primary relationship

between man and nature, he referred to man's real, effective action on nature, manifested above all by material production. This action, which is a transformation of the given world, is not demanded purely and simply by the need to exist, but by man's need to affirm his humanity, to keep or raise himself to a human level. Praxis is the creation or restoration of a new external or internal reality. The creative power of man unfolds in the creation of humanized objects and of his own nature. Man is already a creator since he produces objects that satisfy human needs: a new product emerges from his work, one that is human or humanized and that exists only because of and for him.

Marx's great contribution to aesthetics is his perception that the aesthetic, as a particular relationship between man and reality, has been forged historically and socially in the process of transforming nature and creating a world of human objects.

The relations between man and reality

While animals relate one-dimensionally to the world in a decisive, immediate, and individualistic way, man's relationship to it is multiple, mediated, and free. As a human being, his wealth is measured by the extent of his relations with the world, that is, by the extent to which he feels the need to appropriate reality in an infinite number of ways. Human wealth is the wealth of needs and of relations with the world. Under capitalism, man becomes a being who lacks needs, a being who reduces his life to the need for survival, or who renounces his truly human needs in exchange for one need: the need for money.

The wealth of human relations is therefore determined by the wealth of truly human needs. But the man who is truly rich in this sense "is simultaneously the human being *in need* of a totality of human manifestations of life,"[3] a man who overcomes the limitations on the universal development of his personality, developing in a many-sided manner and enriching his relations to the world. "Man appropriates his total essence in a total manner, that is to say, as a whole man."[4] While the animal exhausts its reality in a singular and exclusive relation with the world, which allows it to satisfy its immediate needs, human reality is affirmed only by enriching its relations with the world in order to satisfy a multiplicity of human needs.

Different types of relations between man and the world have been forged and reinforced in the course of his socio-historical development: practical-utilitarian relations with things; theoretical relations; aesthetic relations; etc. In each one of these relations the attitude of the subject to the world changes because the need that determines it changes, and the object that satisfies the need changes at the same time.

In practical-utilitarian relations, the subject tries to satisfy a specific human need; therefore, objects are judged by their usefulness or ability to satisfy that need. In theoretical relations, man continues to be present: knowledge satisfies the need for a real and effective affirmation of man before nature. In this sense, all sciences, including the natural sciences, have an anthropological character, as Marx said in *The Economic and Philosophic Manuscripts,* since they satisfy human needs and are therefore at the service of man. But the particular mode of human presence in theoretical assimilation demands, in turn, an absence of the human. In effect, what is sought in the theoretical assimilation of the world is "the objective measure of the object itself," that is, an insight into its essence; in order to achieve this, the subject must remove himself, place himself in parentheses, so that the object can reveal its essence. Science is thus a human product or creation designed to satisfy a human need; but the subject does not express itself directly in this product. Science tends to erase any traces of the subject—ideas, aspirations, or hopes—on the scientific object—truth, theory, law, or concept. The victory of objectivity implies the sacrifice of subjectivity.

The full potency of man's subjectivity unfolds in his aesthetic relations to reality, revealing the basic human forces of an individual who is essentially a social being. Art thus functions in the affirmation or expression of man, as science, especially the exact or natural sciences, cannot, without negating itself. In artistic creation, or the creative aesthetic relation of man with the world, the subjective becomes objective (object), and the object becomes subject, but a subject whose already objectified expression not only transcends subjectivity, outliving its creator, but which also can be shared by other subjects in its objectified state.

The work of art is an object in which the subject expresses, externalizes, and recognizes itself. To arrive at this concept of art it is necessary to see in the objectification of the human being a need that art, in contradistinction to alienated work, satisfies positively. In order to reach this conclusion, Marx had to establish the distinction between objectification and alienation—which Hegel did not grasp—and then to assign to the former a real and concrete content in the process of autoproduction or autocreation of man. Since man can only realize himself by getting out of himself, by projecting himself—that is, by objectifying himself—art plays a very important role in the process of humanizing man. But this in turn means that this objectification must be conveyed in all its positiveness, on a real, concrete, socio-historical basis. That is the gist of Marx's critique of Hegel in *The Economic and Philosophic Manuscripts of 1844,* where art is understood as the expression and objectification of the human being.

Marx's critique of Hegel's concept of objectification

Marx aimed his criticism primarily at the manner in which Hegel deals with objectification in his *Phenomenology of the Spirit.* The *Phenomenology* is a history of consciousness—the Spirit—seen through its relationships to its object. The types of relationships between subject and object range from the one in which the object appears to the consciousness as something external, alien, or opposed to it, to the stage of Absolute Knowledge, or knowledge of the object, by virtue of which the entire object is assimilated as subject in such a way that what appeared as alien or strange turns out to be the subject itself. Absolute Knowledge is the Spirit fully knowing itself as subject. But when it grasps itself as subject and understands the true nature of the object, then all objectification disappears, and with it all alienation.

Marx's critique pointed out the abstract and unreal character of the subject and the process through which it objectifies itself and cancels its objectification (or alienation). While Hegel admitted that man participates in this process, he clearly did not have in mind a real and concrete man, but one who is as abstract and unreal as the Spirit of which he is the mouthpiece. Nevertheless, Marx did not underestimate the merits of the *Phenomenology of the Spirit*. Man is present in that work, although in a mystified way, and thus Hegel put in our hands the key to an understanding of human history as a movement of objectification and transcendence of alienation. But with Marx, the concepts of objectification and alienation take on a practical and real dimension: man objectifies and alienates himself in the process of production. Hegel's contribution lies in having pointed out that in objectifying himself through his work, man has made himself. According to Marx:

> The outstanding achievement of Hegel's *Phenomenology* and of its final outcome, the dialectic of negativity as the moving and generating principle, is thus first that Hegel conceives the self-creation of man as a process, conceives objectification as loss of the object, as alienation and as transcendence of this alienation; that he thus grasps the essence of *labor* and comprehends objective man—true, because real man—as the outcome of man's *own* labor.[5]

Man is work, and through it he produces or creates himself. That is Hegel's central idea, which Marx underlined approvingly; but this idea manifests its full value only when work, understood as the production or creation of man, takes on a practical and real significance—such as in Marx's *Manuscripts*—and, moreover, when objectification is understood as necessary for man's self-creation or realization, an objectification which also contains the possibility—actualized historically and concretely in capitalist society—of man's denial of himself. Man exists only to the extent that he objectifies his essential powers, through work, but he can only objectify them as a social being, "through the joint action of men": from this emerges the possibility that one form of objectification (alienation) can become dominant, suppressing the positive role of work as creative, disalienated activity.

To sum up, Marx made two criticisms of Hegel's concept of work: (1) Hegel saw only the positive aspect of work: for him work not only gave form to things, it also formed and shaped man himself. In this sense it is positive: there is no humanity outside of work. But Hegel ignored the negative aspect of work: its concrete and historical form in a society based on private property, alienated labor; and (2) since Hegel referred to the objectification of the Spirit, the only kind of work he recognized was the work of the Spirit, or of man as a spiritual being.[6]

In order to recover the valuable content of Hegel's concept of objectification as the externalization of man's vital powers, we must make a distinction between objectification and alienation, between creative and alienated labor, and between Hegel's abstract objectification and the objectification of real, concrete men.

Revindication of objectivity

In Hegel's equating of objectification and alienation the object always appears as alien to the subject, as a limitation on its subjectivity; therefore, for the subject to reappropriate its true nature—its spiritual nature—objectivity must be negated. Because man—insofar as Hegel defined him by his spiritual subjectivity, his self-consciousness—overcomes his alienation and hence cancels objectification, in the absolute subjectivity of his thought. Objectivity lies outside the human essence, which for Hegel was purely and exclusively spiritual. Man, as self-consciousness, recovers his true essence when he overcomes objectivity. On this point Marx criticized Hegel:

> *Objectivity* as such is regarded as an *estranged* human relationship which does not correspond to the *essence of man,* to self-consciousness. The *reappropriation* of the objective essence of man, begotten in the form of estrangement as something alien, therefore not only is the annulment of *estrangement,* but of *objectivity* as well. Man, that is to say, is regarded as a *non-objective, spiritual* being.[7]

The Marxist revindication of objectivity is the revindication of the real, concrete man, for man gains his humanity only by externalizing his essential powers; it is also a revindication of art as an activity that belongs essentially to the field of objectification. To revindicate objectivity means to recognize that man's relationship to objects is a necessary one. Man becomes man only by objectifying himself, by creating objects through which he externalizes himself. We can thus say that man is subject and object at the same time, and that he becomes a human subject only to the extent that he objectifies himself. This objectification, far from depleting the subject, as Hegel believed, is precisely what humanizes man.

Thus, in the specifically human world, in the world of work and art, there is no such thing as an object in itself, because the object is a creation of the subject, a product in which the subject objectifies itself; nor does the subject exist by itself, but rather as a subject that objectifies itself. Marx pointed out that man objectifies himself because he is already an objective being, that is to say, he is himself an object and has an object: "A being which has no object outside itself is not an objective being. A being which is not itself an object for some third being has no being for its *object;* i.e., it is not objectively related. Its be-ing is not objective."[8] But a being with no relationships, one with no reality outside itself, which neither has an object nor is an object for another being—such a being is unreal: "A *non-objective* being is an unreal, nonsensical thing—a product of mere thought (hence of mere imagination)—a creature of abstraction."[9]

Therefore, not only does man objectify himself by creating a world of objects—in that sense his activity is objective—but by his very structure he is an objective being who exists only in the reciprocal subject-object relationship.

By revindicating objectivity, Marx turned away from Hegel, for whom the existence of the object always implied the existence of something external or alien to the subject; but at the same time he recognized an objectivity that turns against the subject, against man. He clearly distinguished between objectification and alienation, and applied this distinction on a concrete socio-historical plane, in the sphere of productive work. All work is objectification, but not all work implies the alienation of the human being. The objectification which is at the core of human labor is a necessary process for man, for only thus can he transcend his natural immediateness, that is, transform his own nature and *create* his human nature by producing a world of human objects. In other words, man is a natural human being, a fragment of nature that humanizes itself, without breaking with nature, transcending it in two directions: externally, by acting on the natural world to create a humanized reality, thus humanizing nature; and internally, by surmounting his instinctive, purely animal, biological existence, thus transforming his own nature. The activity that makes this double transformation possible is the objectification of the human being through work.

Objectification has enabled man to rise from the natural to the human; alienation inverts this process, and this is precisely what degrades the humanity of man. In the framework of the economic and social relationships of capitalist private property, man does not recognize himself in the products of his labor, in his activity, or in himself.

*Art as a practical activity and as a means
of the objectification and affirmation of man*

By equating objectification and alienation and reducing the former to the objectification of the Spirit, Hegel mystified the objectifications of man, his work, and his art. Thus, after acknowledging Hegel's concept of man as the product of his own work, Marx said that Hegel was dealing only with spiritual work and that, moreover, he only saw the "positive aspect of work," through which man has become conscious of his human reality and transcended his natural immediateness. But Hegel also understood, which Marx did not point out, that artistic creation enables man to manifest himself in external objects, thus raising to a new level the self-expression already evident in practical activity. Hegel noted that consequently artistic creation is a human activity through which man becomes conscious of himself. To the question of why works of art exist, Hegel answered in his lectures on aesthetics that they exist as a response to a need that

> has its source in the fact that man is a *thinking* consciousness . . . The things of nature are only *immediate and single,* but man as mind *reduplicates* himself, inasmuch as prima facie he *is* like the things of nature, but in the second place just as really is *for* himself, perceives himself, has ideas of himself, thinks himself, and only thus is active self-realizedness. This consciousness of himself man obtains in a twofold way: *in the first place theoretically,* insofar as he has inwardly to bring himself into his own consciousness, with all that moves in the human breast, all that stirs and works therein, and, generally, to observe and form an idea of himself, to fix before himself what thought ascertains to be his real being, and, in what is summoned out of his inner self as in what is received from without, to recognize only himself. Secondly, man is realized for himself by *practical* activity, inasmuch as he has the impulse, in the medium which is directly given to him, to produce himself, and therein at the same time to recognize himself . . . This need traverses the most manifold phenomena, up to the mode of self-production in the medium of external things as it is known to us in the work of art.[10]

If we remove the idealistic and mystifying trappings of these thoughts, keeping in mind Marx's criticisms, we can see that Hegel set forth two fruitful ideas that would later find full expression in Marxist aesthetics: (1) art is a particular form of practical activity, different from theoretical activity, between the subject and things; and (2) art is a means for man's self-affirmation or self-consciousness in external things. Thus art answers the need of human beings to externalize themselves, to make a human impression on external things; but in the final analysis Hegel perceived this humanization of the external, sensuous world by art as a spiritualization of the world, or as a sensuous manifestation of the Spirit or Idea.

Art for the Spirit and art for man

By virtue of his absolute idealism, Hegel was unable to see the full consequences of these two ideas, whose rational core laid the foundation for an understanding of art and its relationship to the essence of man, to a paramount human need. Marxist aesthetics, on the other hand, emphasizes the specifically human character of aesthetics in general, and of art in particular, by relating them to concrete, real, and historical human beings and their practical, material activity. Hegelian man has a borrowed essence and a borrowed history. That is why Hegelian idealism, after having brilliantly glimpsed the relationship between the aesthetic and the human, is left in the middle of the road. Although Hegel pointed out the relationship of art to man—hence the great value he placed on Greek art—his concept of aesthetics implied that art is made *by* man but not *for* him. Here again, the human being is conceived as a means for the expression—in this case the sensuous expression—of the Spirit. Art operates in the realm of the lofty concerns of the Spirit, and—especially in Greek art—the spiritual content finds its form in the human figure, which art exalts. Aesthetics assumes a transcendental dimension: although art is a human activity, it is in the final analysis only one aspect of the unfolding of the Absolute Spirit.

Hegel asserted that art answers man's need to cast himself in external things, and through this process of objectification to develop his self-consciousness; in this sense, art can be considered part of the work through which man creates himself. Ultimately, however, man is not the true subject of this process of self-consciousness—a process whose manifestations are art, religion, and philosophy. According to Marx, "the subject knowing itself as absolute self-consciousness—is therefore *God—absolute Spirit—the self-knowing and self-manifesting Idea.* Real man and real nature become mere predicates—symbols of this esoteric, unreal man and of this unreal nature."[11]

Thus real man was not the agent in the history of art; instead, this mysterious Idea or Spirit here—as in human history in general—astutely availed itself of human actions. Hegel's considerable understanding of the historical character of art, certainly an advance over Kant's blindness in this respect, fell into the trap of his absolute idealism. The fundamental changes that man has brought about through the history of artistic creation—for example, from symbolic art from classicism to romanticism—changes which artists feel themselves responsible for, were not in Hegel's view the result of strictly human actions but of developments within the Idea itself. Art as a whole was only one aspect or form of self-consciousness of the Idea; a form inferior to religion or philosophy and destined to be superseded, for truth could be grasped only in the realm of abstract thought, where the Spirit, liberated from the chains of sensuousness and concrete objectivity, was in its proper element, like a fish in water. Art, therefore, did not correspond to the true essence of the Spirit and its abstract self-consciousness. For Hegel, the development of art ended with romanticism—that is, at the stage where art historically revealed its inability to express the lofty concerns of the Spirit.

But if art does not correspond to the true essence of the Spirit, neither can it correspond to the essence of man, an essence which for Hegel was defined by its self-consciousness; man is thus "regarded as a *non-objective, spiritual* being."[12] As a result, although man affirms and expresses himself in art and the Spirit requires the human form to manifest itself, artistic activity does not correspond to the "non-objective" essence of man, since the work of art is inseparable from its objectification. That is, art is objectified by human work, even in the abstract-spiritual sense in which Hegel conceived this work. If objectivity is opposed to the real human essence, then art as a creative process through which man objectifies himself will be considered inferior—less burdened by objectivity—to other forms of self-consciousness of the Idea. Hegel therefore never considered art an essential dimension in the history of man; from the summit to which he had climbed, Hegel saw art as a "thing of the past."

By demystifying Hegelian idealism, Marx rid art of the transcendental and metaphysical character Hegel attributed to it. He regarded art instead as an advanced stage in the process of humanizing nature and man himself, an essential dimension of human existence that corresponds to what was for him the very essence of humanity: creative work. Thus, art comes into being to satisfy a specifically human need; artistic creation and pleasure fall within the realm of human needs.

Human needs and man as a creative being

A need is always a need for an object; it requires an object to satisfy it. An object is essential for the externalization and confirmation of the essential powers of the subject. Marx gives this example:

> *Hunger* is a natural *need;* it therefore needs a *nature* outside itself, an *object* outside itself, in order to satisfy itself, to be stilled. Hunger is an acknowledged need of my body for an *object* existing outside it, indispensable to its integration and to the expression of its essential being.[13]

Man is a being conditioned by needs. According to Marx, as a living natural being, man is endowed with natural powers of life—he is an active natural being. His needs direct him toward objects through which he tries to satisfy and externalize his natural powers. But, as a natural being, he is also passive. The objects that are essential to the satisfaction of his natural needs exist outside him, independent of him; they have not been created by him. His passivity is inherent in the dependency of the subject on the object—for these objects are indispensable to him. Man as a natural being is therefore a "*suffering,* conditioned, and limited creature, like animals and plants."[14]

But man is not merely a natural being, he is a "*human* natural being. That is to say, he is a being for himself. Therefore he is a *species being,* and has to confirm and manifest himself as such both in his being and in his knowing."[15] Man manifests his human nature by recognizing himself as a species and as a social being, by using his consciousness to make his social existence his object. His social and conscious character—the terms are inseparable—places on a new plane both the relationship between objects and needs and the relationship between the essential powers of the subject, struggling to be externalized, and the objects in which they find their form.

As a human natural being, man continues to live in the realm of necessity; more precisely, the more human he becomes, the greater the number of his *human* needs. These needs are either natural needs (hunger, sex, etc.) that are humanized when instincts take on a human form, or new needs, created by man himself in the course of his social development—aesthetic needs, for example.

Under the imperative of human needs, man ceases to be passive, and activity becomes essential to his existence. But his activity is not that of a direct natural being. As a human natural being he is no longer driven to and cast upon objects. Far from inserting himself in external objects, he introduces them to his world; he removes the object from its natural state and makes of it an object of his human need. He does not limit himself to circling the object, but instead he subdues it, conquers it, and wrenches it from its natural and immediate state to put it on a human plane. Only thus can it become the object of a need other than natural. It must then adopt a human form, and in this way it emerges as a new object, produced or created through the integration of that which is direct and immediate in the world of man. Human needs, therefore, are needs for objects which do not exist outside of man but which are nevertheless, as Marx put it, "indispensable to his integration and to the expression of his essential being." Human needs characterize man as an active being, and his activity consists of creating a human world that does not exist by itself, outside of him.

The relationship of work to the human essence

The characteristic activity of human beings is therefore the creation or production of human objects through which essential human powers are externalized. Thus, objects which subjugate man as a natural being, and which constitute a reality external to him, become for man as a *human* natural being a reality that is his own, an affirmation of his essential powers, for it is a reality that exists only as a consequence of his work.

> It is only when the objective world becomes everywhere for man in society the world of man's essential powers—human reality, and for that reason the reality of his *own* essential powers—that all *objects* become for him the *objectification of himself,* become objects which confirm and realize his individuality, become *his* objects: that is, *man himself* becomes the object.[16]

Human needs and human creativity or productivity have an indissoluble relationship. The activity that makes this relationship possible is a material, practical activity: human work. Work is the expression and fundamental condition of human freedom, and its significance lies only in its relationship to human needs. Work establishes a distance, which is amplified in the course of social production, between the subject and its needs, or between needs and the objects that satisfy them. With animals, the relationship between needs and the activity which satisfies them is direct and immediate; an animal "produces only under the dominion of immediate physical need, whilst man produces even when he is free of physical need and only truly produces in freedom therefrom."[17]

Work changes the subject-object relationship, which in the natural being is immediate and conditioned, into a mediated and free relationship. Purely natural needs make the subject a slave to himself, and at the same time a slave to the objects with which he satisfies those needs. The distance between the subject and the object is either shortened or obliterated. Necessity casts the subject upon the object with no room for mediation. In work, the subject and the object have a mediated relationship: between the subject and the object to be produced there is the ideal image, goal, or idea to be realized. That is why in *Capital* Marx defined labor as the practical activity of man toward a goal and said:

> At the end of every labour-process, we get a result that already existed in the imagination of the labourer at its commencement. He not only effects a change of form in the material on which he works, but he also realises a purpose of his own that gives the law to his modus operandi, and to which he must subordinate his will.[18]

The goal is the ideal prefiguration of the intended material, concrete result. The product, or object of labor, is an objectified human goal, the fruit of the practical transformation of a reality which had previously been transformed into an ideal in the consciousness of man.[19]

Labor, starting with a given reality, creates a world of objects; these objects are expressions of man—human or humanized objects—in a double sense: (1) as nature transformed by man, they are produced to satisfy needs and are thus useful objects; and (2) they objectify human goals, ideas, imagination, or will, and thus they express the human essence, that is, the essential powers of the human being.

Labor is therefore the humanization of nature. In its transformation of the natural environment, labor expresses a practical and specifically human relationship between man and nature. The products of labor are not only useful; they express essential human powers. Marx pointed out that the expression of man, the realization of his essential powers, had been sought outside the sphere of work, or production; production was recognized only by its external usefulness, not as the objectification of essential human powers. The relationship between labor, or industry, and the essence of man was overlooked precisely because the human essence has been alienated in that relationship:

> The history of *industry* and the established *objective* existence of industry are the *open book of man's essential powers*, the exposure to the sense of human *psychology*. Hitherto this was not conceived in its inseparable connection with man's *essential being*, but only in an external relation of utility, because, moving in the realm of estrangement, people could only think of man's general mode of being—religion or history in its abstract general character as politics, art, literature, etc.—as the reality of man's essential powers and *man's species activity*. We have before us the *objectified essential powers* of man in the form of *sensuous, alien, useful objects*, in the form of estrangement, displayed in *ordinary material industry*.[20]

Art and labor

Labor is thus not only the creation of useful objects that satisfy specific human needs, but also the art of objectifying or molding human goals, ideas, or feelings in and through material, concrete-sensuous objects. In this capacity to realize "essential powers"—to produce material objects that express the human essence—resides the human potential to create objects, such as works of art, that elevate the capacity for expression and confirmation that is already present in the products of labor.

The similarity between art and labor thus lies in their shared relationship to the human essence; that is, they are both creative activities by means of which man produces objects that express him, that speak for and about him. Therefore, there is no radical opposition between art and work. This opposition was postulated by German idealist aesthe-

ticians, for whom work was regulated by the most rigorous
vital needs while art was the expression of the free and creative powers of man. These aestheticians used the opposite
effects of labor and art—misery and suffering from labor, joy
and pleasure from art—to raise an impenetrable wall between
them.

Marx pointed out that an antagonism does exist when
work takes on the form of alienated labor, but not when it
has a creative character, when it produces objects in which
man objectifies and expresses himself. Furthermore, man is
capable of experiencing pleasure not only in artistic creation
but also in labor; in *Capital* Marx described the laborer's
enjoyment of his work as "something which gives play to his
bodily and mental powers."[21]

The common creative character of art and labor should not
lead us to erase the line that separates them, however. The
products of labor satisfy particular human needs, and their
value therefore resides primarily in their capacity to satisfy
those needs. But, as Marx emphasized in *The Economic and
Philosophic Manuscripts of 1844,* these products also function as objects of the essential powers of human beings. A
tension or conflict exists between these two functions which
leads not to the abolition of one for the sake of the other,
but to the predominance of the practical-utilitarian function
over the spiritual or psychological function, which is able to
reveal the relationship between the object and the human
essence. A product of labor that is useless in the material
sense, even if it fulfills the function of expressing or objectifying man, would be inconceivable, for man is interested in
the creation of use values. Clearly, a product can fulfill its
practical-utilitarian function only by materializing specific
human goals or projects, and its material usefulness—its
capacity to satisfy determinate human needs—is of foremost
importance. Such is the law that governs the work of forming
and constructing an object. The human need for expression
and objectification can only be satisfied within a framework
of material usefulness, and therefore the humanization of an

object has certain limits, even when labor has a creative character, because labor is primarily the "production of use values, the appropriation of natural substances to human requirements."[22]

The two functions—practical-material and spiritual—correspond to the two types of human needs satisfied by the product; in human labor, the practical-material has predominated throughout history and will continue to predominate even in communist society. The material utility of the products of labor is a limit on the full spiritual utility of the object—its capacity to express, confirm, or objectify man. Nevertheless, man must take the process of humanizing nature, the material world, to its logical conclusion: he must assimilate matter in a form that satisfies his spiritual need for objectification fully and unlimitedly. The practical-utilitarian limits that labor imposes must therefore be superseded, passing from the useful to the aesthetic, or from labor to art.

Art is the creation of a reality shaped by human goals, as is labor, but in the new reality created by art the capacity to express the human being, without the limits inherent in the products of labor, predominates. The usefulness of a work of art is determined not by its capacity to satisfy a determinate material need, but by its capacity to satisfy the general need that man feels to humanize everything he comes in contact with, to affirm his essence and to recognize himself in the objective world he has created. We see that the difference between labor and art is not, as Kant thought, that one is an interested activity whereas the other is a gratuitous activity, or that labor seeks to be useful and art seeks pure pleasure and play. The difference resides in the type of use to which they lend themselves: narrow and one-sided, in the case of labor; or broad and spiritual, in the case of art. Nature becomes even more human in art, for it has "lost its mere *utility* by use becoming *human* use."[23] But spiritual utility, which is specifically human, is already present within the narrow framework of the material utility of the products of labor: art in effect does no more than express fully and freely, and in an adequate form, the spiritual content that is already present in a limited way in the products of human labor.

This common ground between art and labor as manifestations of the creative nature of man, allowing both similarity and dissimilarity—the predominance of practical-material utility in labor, and of spiritual utility in art—does not exhaust the essential ties between the two activities. We have noted that art is the creation of objects that essentially satisfy merely spiritual needs; that is, these objects are distant not only from direct physical, immediate needs, but also from the practical needs that are satisfied by the products of labor. Art in this sense is the expression of man in response to both physical, immediate, instinctual needs, and practical, one-sided needs. This freedom of art is not something man inherits from nature, but something he has to conquer. And this conquest can only be the result of labor. Man truly produces, according to Marx, when he is free of material needs. Thanks to his labor, not only can man produce objects that are increasingly distant from his physical needs—objects he does not need to consume immediately—but by virtue of this he can produce objects to satisfy material needs that are increasingly distant, and eventually he can produce objects that primarily satisfy exclusively spiritual human needs.

Labor and the origins of art

Before man can produce objects that we can call works of art, the productivity of human labor must increase. In effect, low productivity renders the distance between production and consumption almost immediate; production must exceed consumption to some extent for man to be able to produce objects—such as artistic objects—increasingly distant from a narrow practical-utilitarian criterion, that is, useless in one respect but useful in another. Labor must reach a certain level before it can produce either objects that fulfill both a utilitarian and an aesthetic function, or objects that cut all ties to practical considerations and become works of art.

Labor is thus the necessary condition, historically and socially, for the appearance of art and the development of an aesthetic relationship between man and his products.

In the dawn of artistic creation, in the Upper Paleolithic period, we find that close link between art and labor which tends to disappear in modern societies, especially in capitalist industrialized societies. With the increasingly sharp division of labor, the mind and the hand draw further apart, as do the project and the execution, the goal and its realization. In this way, labor loses its creative character while art becomes a distinct, substantive activity, an impregnable stronghold of the creative capacity of man, and forgets its remote and humble origins. What is forgotten is that work, the conscious activity through which man transforms and humanizes matter, has made artistic creation possible.

When a person carves figures in stone or marble, shapes clay into figures, or paints wild animals on the walls of caves, we can say that he has taken a step that it took human labor tens of thousands of years to prepare for. Art was born, in the Aurignacian and Magdalenian stages of the Upper Paleolithic, from labor, that is, from gathering the fruits of the victory of prehistoric man over matter; and this new activity, which we today call artistic, raised humanity to a new level. Labor preceded by tens of thousands of years an art as advanced as the one found in the Lascaux or Altamira caves. In order for a new reality to emerge in the caves in the Cantabrian mountains or the Spanish Levant, man had to affirm, through work, a constantly increasing control over material nature for tens of thousands of years. The most eloquent measure of this growing domination over nature in those remote times is the ever greater progress in the production of tools.

The first tool man made was no more than a rough piece of flint, violently wrested from its natural state; its very roughness made it adaptable to many purposes, but only in a rudimentary way. Man had just begun to overcome the resistance of matter, and his objectives could be realized only crudely. Hundreds of thousands of years were to pass between the first rough tool and the stoneworker's burin, a tool requiring greater effort in its construction and more dexterity and thought in its use. Since every tool is an extension of the hand, the appearance of a new, more perfect tool always represents an amplification and intensification of man's control over matter, an expansion of the frontiers in the humanization of nature. At the same time, every new tool contributes to making man's hands more precise, flexible, and obedient to his consciousness—in other words, more human.

When man had at his disposal an instrument as subtle, as humanized, as the burin, capable of responding to the most delicate and precise movements of the hand, the conditions were ripe for him to trace the prodigious figures of wild animals found in the caves of Altamira, or to shape small statues such as the Aurignacian Venus of Lespugue. But the development of tools was in itself not enough: the prehistoric artist had to know and recognize the natural qualities of objects—their color, weight, proportions, hardness, volume, etc.—so that he could effectively use them to endow objects with qualities that are not found in nature, with what we today call aesthetic qualities.

The production and use of tools had a practical-utilitarian significance, first and foremost, but it was precisely the practical utilization of matter that created the conditions necessary for man to extend his transformative activity beyond merely utilitarian objectives. It is clear that in the process of working, man had to learn to evaluate an object according to its end result or function. For an object to fulfill its function, matter had to be subjected to a series of changes to acquire the most adequate structure, that is, the form required by the function or goal the object was intended to realize. The discovery that some objects could fulfill their function better than others, depending on their form, or on the best structuring of their raw materials, was of foremost importance in the transition from labor to art. Labor thus became a process of creating objects which existed in a certain hierarchy, determined by their greater or lesser capacity for satisfying specific human needs or fulfilling certain functions. This in turn implied the establishment of a formal hierarchy among objects, and therefore a certain consciousness of the greater or lesser perfection in their realization. Progress in the manufacture of tools, the increasingly greater knowledge of the qualities of different materials, and the accumulation of experience and work habits thus all brought about the development of more perfect forms in the process of creating useful objects: the structuralization of materials became more and more adequate to the task the object was intended for. The achievement of more perfect forms was necessarily accompanied by a certain consciousness of the creative capacity itself, even if it was merely a consciousness of having done a more efficient or more perfect job. Finally, this consciousness of the quality (or efficiency) of a useful object must have been accompanied by a certain pleasure, a certain satisfaction in oneself. This satisfaction must have originated in man's contemplation of an object which gave form to his creative powers and thus assimilated a human content.

From the useful to the aesthetic

The perfection of the form of an object must have led to a branching of prehistoric man's interest in the products of his labor with an interest in their material, practical utility (their greater or lesser capacity to satisfy determinate human needs), and an interest in their spiritual ability (their ability to objectify the creative powers of man or objective human reality). When the latter interest predominates, the form of an object is appreciated for its conformity with its human content, not for its practical adequacy. A product thus acquires a value that goes beyond mere utility, and to the extent that it is contemplated from this new perspective and its new value is grasped, it evokes in man the pleasure we today call aesthetic. This value is found outside the boundaries of a conscious utilitarian standard; we might say that it is arrived at *disinterestedly* with respect to practical-material considerations, but *interestedly* insofar as what concerns man about the object is its capacity to affirm and materialize his creative powers.

In this sense, labor not only antedates art by a wide margin—as Plekhanov demonstrated on the basis of a wealth of ethnographic material—it also made art possible by creating the conditions necessary to arrive at it.[24]

Going beyond practical requirements, the prehistoric artist adorned reindeer or mammoth bones with symmetrically alternating stripes—he introduced decorative themes. The symmetrical placement of stripes on a useful object is not required by the use of the object; therefore the presence of a decorative motif reveals a certain autonomy of the decorated object from its purely utilitarian function.

Starting in the Magdalenian phase of the Upper Paleolithic period, decorative, abstract, stylized, or schematic motifs alternated with realistic, figurative motifs. In the cave art of the Paleolithic period, the representation of the real (of wild animals in particular) reached such a degree of perfection that what we have before us—in terms of the vivacity, dynamism, and realism of the figures—are true masterworks. These cave paintings exhibit the extent to which the prehistoric artist was in control of figuration; a mastery achieved only through the long, tiresome, and patient accomplishments of labor. Abstraction and figuration have been combined and alternated ever since art's first hesitating steps; both must have made prehistoric man conscious of a creativity that was relatively independent of direct and immediate material utility.

It was precisely figuration that made art a powerful tool to compensate for the real and material weakness of man before nature in those hostile times. After a long process that started when the human mind, partly by accident, made the first connection between a piece of rock and the head of an animal, or between the tracing of a hand and a real hand; after having conquered the concepts of identity, similarity, and difference; and after having developed his capacity for abstraction, for separating the essential from the unessential in an object—after all this, prehistoric man began to draw figures that reproduced living animals. The drawing of a bison expresses the knowledge an awed prehistoric hunter had of that animal. If a painter in the Altamira caves drew the outlines of his figures with great precision, it was because he had already considerably heightened his ability to synthesize, abstract, and generalize. Thus, during a phase of human development in which art and knowledge were necessarily connected, man was already able to draw figures that reproduced or duplicated reality. This ability gave the prehistoric artist a certain power over reality itself. Art was able to achieve the splendid figurations of the cave paintings of Altamira, Lascaux, or the Dordogne by going beyond the practical significance of useful objects. This figuration, associated with magic, permitted the development of a realistic art that pursued practical goals. After achieving a certain autonomy with respect to material utility, art, by means of magic, put itself at the service of practical, utilitarian interests: the hunting of wild animals.

From the aesthetic to the useful

Today no one has any doubt about the close relationship between art and magic in the Upper Paleolithic period. The animals represented in the Altamira caves, for example, are the same animals that inspired fear in the prehistoric hunter: bisons, wild horses, etc. We must discard the notion that cave art had any decorative function, for these paintings are found in the darkest and most inaccessible corners of the caves. It is not a specifically aesthetic effect that was sought, but rather a magic one; the animals were depicted with arrows piercing them, in an effort to facilitate the wounding or killing of the real-life dangerous animal.

Art, as a special technique, is integral to the struggle of prehistoric man to survive, defend himself, or obtain food. Like material techniques—and precisely to compensate for their weaknesses—art mediates between man and nature. In pictorial representation, the hunter-painter attempted to anticipate or facilitate what he could not achieve materially with his real weapons and tools. He concentrated his artistic interest on the same objects that interested him as a hunter; that explains why he painted primarily game animals or animals that inspired fear, and why he only rarely drew figures of human beings, plants, or birds.

The relative autonomy of the aesthetic over the practical-utilitarian seems to vanish in this prehistoric art dominated by practical interests. Yet, not even here do we find a complete identity between the useful and the aesthetic. What took place was a peculiar process whereby man, having moved from the useful to the aesthetic, again returned to the useful; but in this return he did not in any way lose what he had won, i.e., the special mode by which art confirms and objectifies man, requiring at the same time a certain autonomy with respect to mere utility. In effect, as we pointed out above, the process in which the aesthetic becomes autonomous started with the introduction of abstract or figurative motifs on useful objects and culminated artistically in schematization and figuration; both, as branches of the same creative activity, enabled the prehistoric artist to develop a consciousness of himself as a creative being. This consciousness was in turn a consciousness of the power to create, in the midst of a hostile natural world, by means of figuration, a new reality that duplicated the existing reality.

The manner in which the painter-hunter connected both these realities was determined by his magical concept of the world, which established a common level of reality: the painted animal was for him as real as the living one. When he painted a bison, the Altamira or Lascaux artist reproduced reality without leaving it; the painted animal was not so much an image as a duplicate of the real animal. What he could do to the former—wound it, kill it—he transferred to the latter, reflecting the power of art as a duplication of reality. The better he could paint the wild animal—that is, the more faithfully he could reproduce or reflect reality—the more completely he would be able to dominate it. The magical concept of the world thus demanded a profoundly realistic art, because the desired effect could be achieved only to the extent that the painted animal resembled the living one. The magical effect of a painting depended on its faithfulness to the reality (of a class of animals, not of an individual animal); to extend the desired effect to all members of a genus, it was necessary to paint generically. This profound, essential realism, together with the vigorous and precise lines of the drawings, implied a high degree of generalization and abstraction.

An understanding of this relationship between the aesthetic and the useful discredits the theory of magic as the origin of art, which has been popular since the turn of the century and has been welcomed by some Marxists. Far from being at the origin of art, magic became intertwined with art long after its first stammerings, at a time when the prehistoric artist already had at his disposal a number of expressive means, at a stage reached after thousands and thousands of years of human labor. Art put itself at the service of magic—it became useful—only after having gone beyond the narrowly utilitarian significance of the objects of labor by means of both abstraction and figuration. Only after having traveled this long and arduous course could the realism required by magic emerge; and only when that level had been reached could art place itself at the service of a magical concept of the world.

Prehistoric man thus made the step from labor to art, from the useful to the aesthetic. Then, converting art into a special technique endowed with magical powers, he integrated art into the sphere of production, specifically to supplement the deficiencies of human labor and technology, to compensate for the low level of the productive forces. Therefore, only a limited autonomy with respect to utilitarian considerations made it possible for art to reach a level that permitted the close-knit special relationship between the aesthetic and the useful so characteristic of magical art. The perfection reached by prehistoric art in its association with hunting magic was made possible by the extent to which artistic activity was autonomous and by the consciousness of himself as a creative being that man had gained. For this reason, although the

Upper Paleolithic cave artist placed himself at the service of practical interests, he must have had some consciousness of the perfection with which he accomplished his magic-utilitarian tasks. In addition, he must have been aware of the goal of his activity: to reproduce faithfully the fearsome animal in order to achieve the desired effect. Likewise, he must have drawn several sketches, selecting in the process lines, colors, forms, etc., until he saw his hands create qualities which had not existed previously—those we now call aesthetic. Paintings as perfect as those in the Altamira caves required a certain sensibility and valuating capacity, a profound mastery over pictorial technique, and an advanced knowledge both of materials and of the object to be represented. Because of all this, one cannot seriously think that these paintings were the product of chance. They must have required a creative self-consciousness accompanied by a certain pleasure, which sprung from a recognition of the degree of perfection in the fulfillment of a utilitarian task. Thus in the very process of producing art as a directly useful activity, the self-consciousness of the prehistoric artist and its corresponding aesthetic pleasure impelled him to transcend the utilitarian boundaries of the magical endeavor and ensure once again, as in the art of all other periods, the relative autonomy of the aesthetic, without which we could not have what we refer to as art.

We have dwelt on the hypothesis of the magical origin of art because since Salomon Reinach proposed it some seventy years ago it has muddled the problem of the sources and fundamentals of art, leaving unanswered the central question of the relationship between art and labor. We can firmly conclude from the foregoing discussion that magic does not give birth to art but instead makes use of it; moreover, the magic-utilitarian function, far from excluding the specific aesthetic nature of art, presupposes it. Magic could make use of art because man, thanks to his labor, had already created the conditions necessary for going beyond the practical demands of the useful object, thus giving rise to the beautiful useful object, and then to the fundamentally and primarily beautiful object. But in a society divided into classes, this latter stage could only be reached by means of the social division of labor into physical labor and intellectual labor. At that point art became a specific form of human activity and the artistic object was appreciated for its specific qualities, its capacity to express and objectify man once he had gone beyond one-sided utility to a universal human utility. Art and labor resemble one another on this universal level, on the basis of their creative character, and reveal an original solidarity that is clear from the dawn of artistic creation.

Human senses and human objects

Transforming external nature, man has made a world to his measure, a human world, and has thus added a human dimension to nature. But he has also had to transform himself, for he was not human at the outset. "Neither nature objectively nor nature subjectively is directly given in a form adequate to the *human* being."[25] As a consequence, man has had to make this double nature—external and internal, objective and subjective—adequate to his humanity; to the extent he humanizes nature and rises above it he creates himself as a human being. Labor permitted man to rise above objective nature by creating a world of humanized objects, at the same time surmounting his own subjective nature and creating a human subjectivity. Man's senses also had to be humanized, for humanity is something that has to be wrested from nature, not something that is given directly. *"Human* objects are not natural objects as they immediately present themselves, and neither is *human sense* as it immediately *is*—as it is objectively—*human* sensibility, human objectivity."[26] This means that the senses also cease to be merely biological and become human.

An animal's senses are purely and simply means by which the organism ensures its physical existence; they are at the beck and call of the immediate, as is all animal life. For animals, there is no distance between need and object, and the senses are designed to ensure the direct and immediate

connection between those needs that require immediate satisfaction and the objects that satisfy them. Animals only hear
or see objects under the imperative of immediate need.
Necessity thrusts the animal upon the object, and its senses
serve to facilitate its submergence in the object. An animal's
eyes are not designed to contemplate an object, for which a
certain distance between needs and objects is necessary. To
obtain this distance, man must free himself from immediate,
physical, natural needs: to contemplate, evaluate, or transform objects, he must first be liberated from an imperious,
vital necessity that forbids any distance between subject and
object. One who is hungry satisfies his need only by plunging
into the object, by devouring it; on the other hand,
contemplation—and the aesthetic relationship it gives rise
to—is only possible if subject and object are separated, because of the specifically human need it satisfies. The subject
can contemplate, transform, and enjoy an object only to the
extent it is not absorbed or enslaved by it.

The humanization of the senses corresponds to the humanization of the object. Human senses confirm themselves as
such in their relationship to corresponding human or humanized objects. "The eye has become a *human* eye, just as its
object has become a social, *human* object—an object made by
man for man.[27] The animal eye becomes human precisely at
the point it is liberated from its natural immediacy; and,
correspondingly, the object can be an object for the human
eye because it has a human significance, because it is a
humanized object, because in it man unfolds and objectifies
himself. There is a correlation between the human character
of the senses and the human sense of the object. "In practice
I can relate myself to a thing humanly only if the thing
relates itself humanly to the human being."[28] Although
human senses take for granted the sensory organs which by
their structure and function constitute the natural and biological basis of the human senses, they are distinguished by
their social character. They have not emerged as a result of
biological or natural evolution, although such an evolution is
a necessary, but not sufficient, condition. Human senses are

the fruit of the socio-historical development of man, of the creation of an objective world; and, at the same time, of the self-creation of man by means of labor. "The *forming* of the five senses is a labor of the entire history of the world down to the present."[29] And this process of forming human senses is inseparable from the process of forming or creating human objects. The human wealth of an object only has meaning for profoundly human senses, but, at the same time, "the objectively unfolded richness of man's essential being is the richness of subjective *human* sensibility—a musical ear, an eye for beauty of form. . . ."[30]

Aesthetic sensibility

We can now understand the important role Marx attributed to human sensibility in general, and aesthetic sensibility in particular. Inasmuch as the human sense of objects exists only for human senses ("the most beautiful music has *no* sense for the unmusical ear—is no object for it"[31]) the senses are a means for man to affirm and know himself in an objective world. That is what Marx meant when he said that "the *senses* have therefore become directly in their practice *theoreticians*."[32] He thus emphasized, unlike Hegel, that man affirms himself not only as a thinking being, but also as a sensuous being. The senses are as human as the intellect; but this humanity of the senses represents a victorious struggle, as does everything human. "Thus, the objectification of the human essence, both in its theoretical and practical aspects, is required to make man's *sense human,* as well as to create the human sense corresponding to the entire wealth of human and natural substance."[33]

The aesthetic sensibility springs from this human process of affirmation. The aesthetic sense appears when human sensibility has been enriched to such a point that objects are, primarily and essentially, human reality, "reality of the essential human powers." The qualities of objects are perceived as aesthetic qualities when they are grasped without a direct utilitarian significance, when they are the expression and essence of man himself. Artistic creation in particular, and the aesthetic relationship to things in general, are thus the fruit of the entire history of humanity, and are at the same time two of the most highly developed means by which man confirms himself in the objective world. The practical activity of man has created the conditions necessary to advance the humanization of things and of senses to the level required by the aesthetic sensibility. By creating new objects, by discovering new qualities and properties in them and new relationships among them, man has considerably extended his senses, and has enriched and raised sensuous consciousness. The aesthetic sensibility is both a specific form of human sensibility and a superior form of this human sensibility, inasmuch as it confirms the essential human powers objectified in the products of human labor.

The aesthetic sensibility places us in a relation to objects which expresses a determinate human content through its concrete-sensuous form. Man creates aesthetic objects by structuring raw materials to endow them with a human expressiveness they do not in themselves possess. Moreover, by virtue of his aesthetic sensibility, man can humanize a nature he has not materially transformed by endowing it with a new meaning while integrating it into his world. Nature by itself lacks an aesthetic value; it must be humanized. Man must penetrate nature to make it expressive. In this way, through its own natural qualities, nature is placed on a human, i.e., aesthetic, plane. The aesthetic relationship to nature and the corresponding appearance of natural beauty emerge from the process of the growing humanization of nature by man. The natural phenomena that startled primitive man and threatened his existence could have held no beauty for him; he saw nature as an alien and terrible power which he could not integrate. The aesthetic sense of nature could only emerge when man could see his essential powers confirmed in it, by integrating it into his world as humanized nature. (It is no coincidence, therefore, that the aesthetic relationship to nature has existed, for the most part, only since the Renaissance.)

Natural beauty therefore exists only in relationship to man; natural phenomena become aesthetic only when they acquire a social, human significance. But natural beauty is not arbitrary or capricious: it requires a material substratum, a particular structuring of sensuous, natural properties, without whose support there would be no human, social, or aesthetic meaning.

The aesthetic sensibility requires the affirmation of the human being in his relationship to immediate physical needs. "The care-burdened man in need has no sense for the finest play; the dealer in minerals sees only the commercial value but not the beauty and the unique nature of the mineral: he has no mineralogical sense."[34] We have seen how immediate needs restrict the subject from developing the contemplative attitude essential for the aesthetic relationship. Immediate necessity imprisons and narrows the senses by blocking their access to objectified human riches, inseparable from concrete-sensuous riches. In the aesthetic relationship, the subject confronts the object not only sensuously but intellectually and emotionally. For its part, the object presents itself as a concrete-sensuous totality that offers itself to our senses; but it does so in an ideologically and effectively meaningful way, as a concrete human reality. Marx stressed the impossibility of entering into an aesthetic relationship with an object, such as a mineral, grasping its mercantile value alone, ignoring its concrete-sensuous whole and its objectification of human forces. Apart from concrete-sensuous form and human content, there is no aesthetic object; for its part, the subject can only enter into a relationship with an aesthetic object when it confronts it sensuously. Object and subject are correlated in the aesthetic relationship: the object has sense for man when it is regarded not in the abstract but in all its concrete human richness; the subject finds its object by grasping it in its concreteness and full human significance.

Particularization of the aesthetic sensibility

By virtue of this correlation, the aesthetic sensibility is

particularized through both the humanized object and the human senses. In an aesthetic relationship, man appropriates the object in which he objectifies himself as much according to his subjective disposition, or sense, as to the object itself. An aesthetic relationship thus becomes particularized, or determinate: there are pictorial relationships, musical relationships, etc. The diversity of art forms reflects the diversity of senses and objects. Each sense has its object, each object its sense. Each of the various art forms thus has limits imposed by the particularities of the terms in this dialectical relationship—limits that cannot be transgressed with impunity. To attempt to turn painting into an art which corresponds to neither its sense nor its object, for example, is to forget these limits. Painting and music are two distinct and irreducible forms.

Let us examine what Marx said in this connection. The objects in which man objectifies himself are his objects, his human reality:

> The manner in which they become *his* depends on the *nature of the objects* and on the nature of the *essential power* corresponding *to it;* for it is precisely the *determinate nature* of this relationship which shapes the particular, *real* mode of affirmation. To the *eye* an object comes to be other than it is to the *ear*, and the object of the *eye* is another object than the object of the *ear*.[35]

Consequently, the manner in which man affirms himself in the objective world through artistic creation, and the particular means of appropriating or enjoying the artistic object are delimited by the peculiarities of the corresponding human, social, objectified sense.

The social character of the aesthetic relationship

The two terms of this relationship—the sense and the object—have a social relation. The senses have become human in a historical and social process, whereby the ear and the eye have become aesthetic senses. But the social character of the aesthetic relationship is due not only to its origin and development: the subject—man—in this relationship is a social being and the object—due to its human, social content—has sense only for this social being.

The subject is man as a social being, an individual who enters into a relationship with nature and with himself through other men. It is only in a social context that man humanizes nature and converts it into the reality of his human powers, into an objectification of his human essence, into a human object. And only in society is man a "natural human being," a subject that corresponds to the human object. Even in his most isolated relationship, solitude, in which man seems to completely fold in on himself, man is related to other human beings. That is why Marx said that "the individual *is the* social being."[36]

Therefore, in production in general, and in that particular production that emerges during a certain phase of social development as a creation "in accordance with the laws of beauty,"[37] the subject-object relationship is a social relationship in which subject and object exist for each other. And it is precisely its social character that maintains this relationship. The social character of the relationship determines the human mode of confronting the object—with a free, conscious, and creative attitude, which, to the extent man appropriates the object, allows him to feel free and independent of it. "Man is not lost in his object only when the object becomes for him a *human* object or objective man. This is possible only when the object becomes for him a *social* object, he himself for himself a social being, just as society becomes a being for him in this object."[38]

This social character, then, must necessarily exist in both the subject and the object. While the aesthetic relationship must have a human, social sense ("the *human* eye enjoys things in a way different from the crude, non-human eye; the human *ear* different from the crude ear, etc."[39]) for man not to lose himself in the object, this relationship also requires that man recognize the social, human character of both the object and himself. In the aesthetic relationship, therefore, man—a social being by nature—affirms himself in all his richness.

The activity of the artist as creative and free work

The artist creates objects in accordance with the laws of beauty, transforming matter into a form which reveals his human essence in a concrete-sensuous object. The artist is wealthy, not in the material sense—the only admissible value in modern political economy—but as a social being who feels an impulse to realize his essence. Inasmuch as man has created himself by affirming himself in the objective world through his labor, the measures of his wealth are his powers of expression and objectification. "The *rich* human being is . . . the man in whom his own realization exists as an inner necessity, as need."[40]

Man appropriates the richness of his being, of his nature, by appropriating material nature. But nature can only be appropriated by entering into determinate relationships with others, within the framework of determinate relations of production, as Marx said in his later works. In the capitalist form of these relations, the sense of human labor is completely inverted. Instead of affirming himself, man loses himself in it and alienates his essence. Instead of becoming humanized, he is dehumanized. "With the *increasing value* of the world of things proceeds in direct proportion the *devaluation* of the world of men."[41] The more man puts into labor, the more he objectifies in it, the more he loses and alienates his being, the more estranged the world he has created with his labor becomes, the richer and more powerful this external world becomes, and the more impotent and poor his inner world becomes. By virtue of alienation, labor, this fundamental human relationship which defines man, humanizes him, and makes him a conscious and free being, robs the worker of his human essence. "Production does not simply produce man as a *commodity,* the *human commodity,* man in the role of *commodity;* it produces him in keeping with this role as a *mentally* and *physically dehumanized* being."[42]

Labor originated as a free activity; man can produce only when he is freed of physical necessity. But now labor is imposed on man, and he cannot refuse because it is his only means of ensuring his physical survival. It is forced labor, alien to the worker, an activity which no longer satisfies a specifically human, inner need for affirmation in the objective world. Its "exteriority" is manifest in "the fact that labor is *external* to the worker, i.e., it does not belong to his essential being; that in his work, therefore, he does not affirm himself but denies himself."[43] In alienated work, man does not find himself in a truly human state. A radical exteriority thus exists between two things that should be indissolubly and internally related: labor and the human essence. "The external character of labor for the worker appears in the fact that it is not his own, but someone else's, that it does not belong to him, that in it he belongs, not to himself, but to another."[44]

The artist directs his energies to fully realize the objectification of the human being. Wealthy man that he is, the artist attempts to unfold his wealth in a concrete-sensuous object, which he creates out of an "inner exigency," an inner need. His activity extends and enriches the essence of human labor, which, under conditions of alienation, is always limited by the material utility required of the products of labor. The activity of the artist therefore aims at a realization of that affirmation of the human essence which is frustrated in alienated labor, and which is limited by the exigencies of material utility even when human labor has a positive meaning for the worker.

But on a fundamental level artistic work is able to respond to the search for a material utility that does not negate what constitutes the real goal of artistic activity: the expression of the "essential powers" of the human being. The artist cannot produce in response to external needs, for he would be converting his activity into an alien, externally imposed activity, which would fail to satisfy his inner need to unfold his human wealth; his activity then would cease to be a goal and would become a means. Only when the artist creates freely—

that is, in response to an inner necessity—can he direct his activity toward the true objective of art: an affirmation of the human essence in a concrete-sensuous object.

Alienation and artistic work

In capitalist society, a work of art is "productive" when it is market-oriented, when it submits itself to the exigencies of the market, the fluctuations of supply and demand. And since there is no objective measure by which to determine the value of his particular merchandise,[45] the artist is subject to the tastes, preferences, ideas, and aesthetic notions of those who influence the market. Inasmuch as he produces works of art destined for a market that absorbs them, the artist cannot fail to heed the exigencies of this market: they often affect the content as well as the form of a work of art, thus placing limitations on the artist, stifling his creative potential, his individuality.

A form of alienation is thus produced, denaturalizing the essence of artistic work. The artist does not fully recognize himself in his product, because anything produced in response to external necessity is alien to him. This alienation becomes total when the sense of artistic creation is inverted, and artistic activity becomes not an end but a means of subsistence. The material utility required of the products of human labor is a necessary condition, for these products are intended for satisfaction of material needs; and it is only within the framework of these needs that man can affirm, objectify, and recognize himself. But the predominance of material utility in the work of art contradicts the very essence of art; for unlike common merchandise its primary aim is not the satisfaction of determinate needs but the satisfaction of man's general need to express and affirm himself in the objective world.

In this manner, capitalist society deprives the artist of creative freedom. In a society where a work of art can sink to the level of merchandise, art becomes alienated or impoverished; it loses its essence. When Marx pointed out in the

Economic and Philosophic Manuscripts that art under capitalism "falls under the general law of production," he was clearly alluding to this degradation of artistic creation; these early remarks formed the basis of his later theories on the contradiction between art and capitalism, between production for profit and creative freedom.

But even under capitalism the artist tries to escape alienation, for alienated art is the very negation of art. The artist does not resign himself to becoming a salaried worker. By seeking to satisfy his inner need as a social being, the artist tends to transcend the alienation that inverts the sense of artistic creation, and thus he tends to overcome the alienation of his own existence. He searches for ways of escaping alienation, refusing to submit his work to the fate of all merchandise, winning his freedom at the price of terrible privations. But the source of this alienation lies outside of art; it is fundamentally a socioeconomic alienation. Therefore, according to Marx, only a change in social relations can enable labor to reclaim its true human sense and art to be a means of satisfying profound spiritual needs. That is why the salvation of art is not in art itself, but in the revolutionary transformation of the socioeconomic relations which permit the degradation of artistic work by placing it under the general law of capitalist commodity production.[46]

The essence of the aesthetic

We may sum up the fundamental aesthetic ideas of Marx's *Economic and Philosophic Manuscripts* in the following terms:

1. A particular relationship exists between subject and object (creation "in accordance to the laws of beauty" or "artistic assimilation of reality") in which the subject transforms the object by giving a determinate form to raw matter. The result is a new object, the aesthetic object, in which the human wealth of the subject is objectified or revealed.

2. This subject-object relationship, the aesthetic relationship, has a social character; it evolves on a socio-historical

basis, in the process of humanizing nature by means of work, and of objectifying the human being.

3. The aesthetic assimilation of reality reaches its most developed stage in art as superior human labor which tends to satisfy the artist's inner need to objectify, express, and reveal his essential powers in a concrete-sensuous object. By freeing itself from the narrow material utility of the products of labor, art raises to a higher level the objectification and affirmation of the human being which, within the framework of material utility, are realized to a limited extent in those products.

4. The aesthetic relationship between man and reality, inasmuch as it is a social relationship, creates not only the object but also the subject. The aesthetic object exists—in its human, aesthetic essence—only for social beings.

5. Art is alienated when it falls under the general law of capitalist production, that is, when the work of art is regarded as merchandise.

Starting with the above theses, we can approach the question of the essence of the aesthetic, and of beauty in particular, in order to establish the fundamental difference between the aesthetic ideas of Marx as expressed in the *Economic and Philosophic Manuscripts* and those of the idealist and pre-Marxist materialist philosophers. At the risk of overgeneralizing, we can distinguish three principal solutions to the fundamental problem of identifying the essence of the aesthetic:

1. The aesthetic as an attribute or manifestation of a universal spiritual being (Plato's Idea, Plotinus' God, Hegel's Absolute Idea, etc.). The objectivity of beauty is recognized in an idealist sense, but the role of material reality as the origin or necessary condition of beauty is denied. Beauty transcends man.

2. The aesthetic as a creation of our consciousness, either in the generic or individual sense, and independent of the properties of objects. The objectivity of beauty is denied, for beauty is regarded as a product of subjective activity, in the

idealist sense of that term. (Aesthetics of "affective projection," etc.)

3. The aesthetic, and beauty in particular, as an attribute of things themselves, manifested in certain formal qualities: symmetry, proportion, rhythm, "golden mean," etc. Beauty is a quality inherent in objects, independent of their relationship to human beings. (Aesthetics of mimesis, Spinoza, Lessing, etc.; pre-Marxist materialists such as Diderot, Chernyshevski, etc.)

In all of these, the essence of the aesthetic is thought to exist in an ideal world, in the subject, or in objects themselves. But Marx's thesis in the *Economic and Philosophic Manuscripts* leads us to a radically different solution. In opposition to those conceptions of aesthetics which maintain the ideal transcendence of the aesthetic, we underline its human character: if man elicits the aesthetic from things, by means of his material, practical activity, giving a determinate form to material nature with the aim of expressing a spiritual, human content, beauty cannot exist outside of humanity. And this human character is determined not only by the human origin of art, but also by natural beauty, inasmuch as it only exists in a humanized nature. Beauty is not an attribute of an universal being; it is created by man in artistic objects as well as in natural beings. Moreover, inasmuch as it is social and human, the aesthetic object reveals its essence only to man, it exists only for "natural human beings," that is, for social beings.

In contradistinction to those conceptions which underline the dependency of the aesthetic on man and deny its objectivity (the aesthetic as creation or projection of the subject), we emphasize that the aesthetic is found only in the dialectic of the subject-object relationship and therefore cannot be deduced from the properties of human consciousness or any particular structure therein, nor from the psyche or biological constitution of the subject. Aesthetic consciousness, the aesthetic sense, is not something given, innate, or biological; rather, it emerges historically and socially on the basis of

practical and material activities—human labor—in a relationship in which the subject exists only for the object and the
object exists only for the subject. Moreover, the aesthetic
object cannot be reduced to the subject; it exists independently of subjective perception or evaluation. The aesthetic is
objective inasmuch as it does not depend on the perception,
values, or representation of one or many subjects. The aesthetic exists only for man as a social being, independent of
the individual subject, but not outside the social relationship
between subject and object. It has its own reality, a human,
social reality, which does not exclude a certain objectivity: it
is always manifested through forms that are objective. And
the spiritual content with which the subject invests it exists,
aesthetically, only insofar as it is materialized and objectified
in a concrete-sensuous manner.

Although the aesthetic object has its own reality, one
which does not let itself be dissolved in the perceptions,
values, or representations to which it is subjected, its objectivity does not imply an independence vis-à-vis social man. It
is one thing to talk of the objectivity of the marble with
which a statue is made—a physical objectivity which implies
an independence from all subjects—and another thing to talk
of the objectivity of the statue as an aesthetic reality, whose
form and content do not exist outside social man. The aesthetic embraces the physical condition of the statue without
being reduced to it. Certainly, the statue could not stand
without the physical reality which it transcends. The physical, the marble, is transcended and absorbed in the statue,
but it is there as a necessary, although not sufficient, condition. If it were destroyed physically, the statue would also be
destroyed as an aesthetic reality.

Let us take a look now at the third type of aesthetic
theory, according to which reality is not the basis of beauty,
but is beauty itself. The aesthetic is found in the object itself.
Beauty is reduced to certain properties of the object, to a
particular structuring or disposition of its parts: proportion,
symmetry, Hogarth's "line of beauty," the "golden mean,"
etc. All of these aesthetic elements have a formal character:

they refer to the form of real objects. They are found in some aesthetic objects and not in others. Symmetry, for example, is classical, but not Baroque. If aesthetic criteria are accepted in one instance, we must then aesthetically disqualify those works of art in which those elements are absent. The problem disappears if these formal elements are seen as functions of a spiritual content. Only thus can we make sense, from an aesthetic point of view, of classical proportion and baroque disproportion. This allows us to conclude that unless objects, and therefore their formal elements, are humanized, charged with a spiritual content, they cannot be called beautiful. Nature in itself, unless it is humanized, falls outside the realm of beauty. Nature as such has no need to be beautiful; it is man that needs beauty; man needs to objectify, express, and recognize himself in beautiful objects.

It is a mistake to search for aesthetic reality in the natural, physical reality that supports it and without which it cannot exist. Mere physical reality must be transcended, transformed, humanized, if it is to have an aesthetic value. And it acquires this value when it ceases to be a separate reality and is integrated in a world of human meanings.

Aesthetic value

Marx stressed the human and social character of aesthetic value, because of the human and social relationships it entails. Beauty, he said, is not independent of the knowledge and will of human beings. Underlining the human and social character of beauty and its relationship to man, Marx asserted that the aesthetic relationship is the product of man, a historical product.[47]

The human, socio-historical character of aesthetic value can be better understood if we establish an analogy between aesthetic value and economic value, as studied by Marx in *Capital.* The economic value of an object or commodity exists not in and for itself, but in its relationship to man. The object has a use value insofar as it satisfies a particular need, and an exchange value under those socio-historical conditions in which the means of production are private property. Although Marx differentiated use value and exchange value, neither has an independent existence as properties or qualities of natural objects outside of their relationship to man. This is clear in the use value of a commodity: an object has value when it has certain specific properties—either natural or created by human labor—which satisfy certain specific needs. The natural properties of a useful natural object exist independently of man, that is, even if they do not satisfy any human need. Their utility, or use value, exists only when the object is an object *for* man. The utility or value of an object is not found in the object itself; i.e., it is not identical to its natural or physical properties. But although its existence requires the presence of and relationship to man, it cannot exist without those natural or physical properties. The use value of commodities does not "float on air," as Marx put it; it "resides in the body of the commodity," but it resides there only for man. Therefore, it exists only in a human world.

The social character of value is manifest, along with other characteristics, in exchange value. While use value resides "immediately" in the thing, and in turn demands a certain relationship between the thing and man, exchange value demands a certain type of relation between man and man—a certain relation of production—without which the use value of an object cannot be transformed into exchange value. In these relations the exchange value is the expression of the abstract labor contained in the commodity, by virtue of which commodities can be exchanged in the marketplace. In this case value, and particularly use value, is determined not by the natural or created properties of things, but by the social relations embodied in those things. In both cases we can see that value, which exists in specific relationships between things and human beings, as well as among human beings themselves, shows a certain objectivity or independence vis-à-vis individuals since it was established irrespective of their wills or personal attitudes; but we cannot say that this value existed previous to or outside of human society.

This is as far as the analogy holds. We cannot carry it any further in the case of exchange value, although the analogy is more rigorous in relation to use value, since both the aesthetic and the useful satisfy a human need, specifically, the human need for objectification, expression, and communication. In this sense, as we have pointed out, the aesthetic object has a human and universal usefulness which is not identified with its material, practical usefulness.

The objectivity of the aesthetic

The comparison between aesthetic and economic value allows us to establish a type of human or social objectivity which is not identical to a physical or natural objectivity, although the former presupposes the latter as a necessary condition. Marx pointed out such a social objectivity in his analysis of the value of commodities in *Capital*. We can conclude that it is indeed possible to speak of the objectivity of the aesthetic, when conceived neither as an ideal objectivity (in the manner of Plato) nor as a material objectivity (in the manner of materialist metaphysics), but rather as the objectivity of a particular reality, human or humanized, which cannot be reduced to its spiritual content, since the human content embodied by the object has an aesthetic value only when it is given shape, unfolded, in a concrete-sensuous object. Nor can this reality be reduced to the material existence of the aesthetic object, for the physical or material does not by itself express man.

We are dealing, then, with an objectivity vis-à-vis individuals, groups, or human communities, but not in relation to society or humanity at large. In relation to the individual who perceives, examines, or evaluates the aesthetic object, this objectivity presupposes a dependency with regard to man as a social being. The aesthetic dimension emerges only in the social relationship between subject and object; consequently, it exists only for and on account of man. Inasmuch as it is a means of expression and affirmation of human beings, the aesthetic has sense only for them. Aesthetic value is not, therefore, a property or quality inherent in things themselves, but rather something they acquire *in* human society by virtue of the social existence of man as a creative being.

The role of praxis in Marxist aesthetics

Idealist aesthetics accentuates the role of subjective activity in the aesthetic relation: Hegel did not regard objectification—inasmuch as it is identified with alienation—as a concern of the human essence (understood as self-consciousness), and consequently did not consider the artistic object a manifestation of the creative activity of man. Pre-Marxist materialist aesthetics emphasized the role of the object, relegating the subject to the role of recreating a beauty which already existed in reality, independent of man and society. In one case the activity is purely spiritual; in the other the practical and creative activity is ignored. As we see from Marx's aesthetic ideas, particularly those expounded in the *Economic and Philosophic Manuscripts,* what fundamentally distinguishes dialectical-materialist aesthetics from idealist and metaphysical materialist aesthetics is the concept of praxis as the basis of the aesthetic relationship in general and of artistic creation in particular. According to this concept, art as a higher form of labor is a manifestation of the practical activity of man by virtue of which he expresses and confirms himself in the objective world as a social, free, and creative being.

Notes

1. This essay is a revised version of "Ideas estéticas en los *Manuscritos económico-filosóficos* de Marx," *Diánoia,* 1961, which does not alter the principal theses of the earlier version. The quotations from *The Economic and Philosophic Manuscripts of 1844* are from the translation by Martin Milligan, edited and with and introduction by

Dirk J. Struik (New York: International Publishers, 1964). Henceforth, we will refer to *Manuscripts*.

2. "The chief defect of all hitherto existing materialism (that of Feuerbach included) is that the thing, reality, sensuousness, is conceived only in the form of the *object of contemplation*, but not as *sensuous human activity, practice,* not subjectively. Hence, in contradistinction to materialism, the *active* side was developed abstractly by idealism—which, of course, does not know real, sensuous activity as such." Karl Marx, "Theses on Feuerbach," in Karl Marx and Frederick Engels, *The German Ideology* (New York: International Publishers, 1970).

3. *Manuscripts,* p. 144.

4. Ibid., p. 138.

5. Ibid., p. 177.

6. Ibid.

7. Ibid., p. 178.

8. Ibid., pp. 181-82.

9. Ibid., p. 182.

10. Georg W. F. Hegel, "Vorlesungen über die Aesthetik," in J. Glenn Gray, ed., *On Art, Religion, Philosophy* (New York: Harper & Row, 1970), pp. 57-58.

11. *Manuscripts,* p. 188.

12. Ibid., p. 178.

13. Ibid., p. 181.

14. Ibid.

15. Ibid., p. 182.

16. Ibid., p. 140.

17. Ibid., p. 113.

18. Karl Marx, *Capital* (New York: International Publishers, 1967), vol. I, p. 178.

19. On the subject of goals as a specifically human category, see my essay, "Contribución a la dialéctica de la finalidad y la causalidad," in *Anuario de Filosofía* (Mexico: Facultad de Filosofía y Letras, UNAM, 1961), vol. 1, pp. 56–64.

20. *Manuscripts,* p. 142.

21. Marx, *Capital,* p. 178.

22. Ibid., p. 183.

23. *Manuscripts,* p. 140.

24. Referring to the relationship between art and labor, Plekhanov develops some convincing arguments in his *Unaddressed Letters* (Moscow, 1957) to prove, in opposition to Bücher's thesis, that the creation of useful objects preceded that of artistic objects: "Labor is older than art . . . man first regards objects and natural phenomena from an utilitarian point of view, and only later does he adopt an aesthetic point of view with regard to them." He adds that use value antedates aesthetic value. Plekhanov was correct in asserting that labor antedates art, and that the transition from the useful to the aesthetic takes place when an object is regarded without any conscious consideration of its usefulness. But the transition from the useful to the aesthetic does not involve only a change of attitude; there is an objective basis for this transition. What is required is a particular structuring of the raw materials, a form that is no longer identified with that required by the utility of the object, although from a socio-historical point of view man can give raw materials this new form only on the basis of what labor has achieved up to that point. Labor not only antedates art but also makes art itself possible.

Plekhanov did not grasp the full possibilities of the Marxist concept of labor, partly because he did not have *The Economic and Philosophic Manuscripts of 1844* and partly because he did not assimilate the rich philosophical content of the concept of work presented in *Capital*. Discussing the art of primitive peoples, Plekhanov viewed work as the "elaboration of useful objects" and art as the consideration of those objects from a point of view which excludes practical utilitarian interests; but he failed to clearly understand what both unites and separates art and labor. He failed to fully realize that art extends labor insofar as it is related to the human essence and that it cannot be reduced to labor inasmuch as it transcends what is fundamental to labor: its practical-utilitarian significance.

25. *Manuscripts,* p. 182.
26. Ibid.
27. Ibid., p. 139.
28. Ibid., p. 139*n*.
29. Ibid., p. 141.
30. Ibid.
31. Ibid., p. 140.

32. Ibid., p. 139.
33. Ibid., p. 141.
34. Ibid.
35. Ibid., p. 140.
36. Ibid., p. 138.
37. Ibid., p. 114.
38. Ibid., p. 140.
39. Ibid.
40. Ibid., p. 144.
41. Ibid., p. 107.
42. Ibid., p. 121.
43. Ibid., p. 110.
44. Ibid., p. 111.
45. ". . . that which determines the magnitude of the value of any article is the amount of labour socially necessary, or the labour-time socially necessary for its production." (Marx, *Capital*, p. 39) Because the work of art cannot be reduced to the socially necessary labor time invested in its creation, its exchange value can be established only according to a category as subjective and superficial as price, fixed in relation to the preferences of the bourgeois public.
46. In the *Economic and Philosophic Manuscripts* Marx did not explicitly speak of artistic alienation, but by pointing out the transformation of the work of art into a commodity within the framework of capitalist social relations, he opened up the way for such an analysis. In our view, this analysis agrees with the later development of Marx's thought, especially with the theory of alienation as "commodity fetishism," in *Capital*.
47. *Marx and Engels Archives* (Moscow, 1935), vol. 4, p. 97.

4. Aesthetics and Marxism

Marxist aesthetics and the sociology of art

In speaking of aesthetics and Marxism, and of the relationship between them, it is not simply a matter of applying the principles that obtain on all levels of social existence and consciousness to a determinate domain. What a Marxist, as a Marxist, has to say with regard to art cannot be reduced to a proposal for extracting the underlying ideology of a work of art, and even less to an attempt to equate its aesthetic value and its ideological content. Nor is it a matter of reducing art to its social conditioning, which undoubtedly opens or closes a vast range of creative possibilities. If that were the case the task would be relatively simple: Marxist aesthetics would be reduced to a sociology of art, and both sociologists and artists would have less to worry about, especially those who erroneously believe that the role of Marxism is not so much to give a greater richness and depth to our existence as to impoverish it and reduce its dimensions.

Marx was aware both of the limitations of a sociological perspective and of the nature of the basic aesthetic problem which he attempted to resolve, in my view unsuccessfully. The problem as Marx posed it does not consist of explaining the relationship between, for example, classical Greek art and the society of those times, but rather in determining how the products of that art, nourished by the ideals, emotions, and aspirations of that society, have value for us, even as canons of beauty. Let us ignore for a moment the fact that Marx, dazzled by the radiance of classical art, tended to regard its values as absolutes. He was nevertheless right in pointing out the difficulty of explaining the permanence of works of art, their capacity (and here we are talking of authentic works of art) to supersede their own conditioning in such a way as to become the incarnation of a certain dialectic of the particular and the universal, the transitory and the eternal. Marx was the first to put us on guard against an aesthetic sociology, that is, the tendency to evaluate art according to the ideology embodied in it, reducing art to the social conditions which engendered it. And he could not have done otherwise. There is, in effect, no full equivalence between one sphere and the other. Art is an autonomous sphere (of course, this autonomy is relative, as we shall see) and all attempts to reduce it to another sphere, whether religious, economic, or political, will end up by erasing what is qualitatively different about art, which as Marx saw it was precisely what enabled Greek art to escape its social conditioning.

We could say then that art, like all autonomous, qualitatively distinct spheres, exists as such to the extent that it transcends the particularity of its social conditioning. This transcendence, which in essence resides in the very bowels of art, is the exact opposite of all sociological reductions. Consequently, if Marx's theory of aesthetics had no other objective than to explain art from the perspective of its social conditioning—expressed, in turn, by its ideological content—it would never amount to more than a sociology of art.

This is not to deny a fundamental Marxist principle, i.e., that consciousness is determined by social existence. Art does not hold a privileged position in relation to man's other spiritual activities in this regard. The art of the Renaissance, for example, is inscribed in a determinate socio-historical context, characterized by a particular concept of man and a particular vision of reality and things. The Renaissance could not produce a vital, truly creative art, prolonging medieval forms, because a new concept of man—bourgeois humanism—had already displaced the theocentric, ecclesiastical-feudal concept of the Middle Ages. Renaissance art did not attempt to infuse medieval forms with a new ideological and emotional content; it successfully attempted to create a contemporary art, one which sought means of expression in harmony with the new humanist conception of man. Consequently, the development of a single perspective in painting, a new way of seeing space, as organized around a vanishing point, in contrast to medieval pictorial space which was a sum of unconnected spaces, was not merely a formal innovation. The world was no longer seen through a divine eye; instead, a human eye organized figures and background to endow space with a continuous character. Clearly it is man who paints in either case, but as the humble servant of God in one and as the center and axis of the universe in the other.

The single perspective enabled the late Renaissance artist to represent nature to his measure, that is, the measure of the Renaissance human eye; correspondingly, he painted a real, natural-human, or humanized, space. In the same manner, Renaissance artists emphasized man's worth as a spiritual being and affirmed his corporeal and sensuous nature. Medieval asceticism opposed the worldly joys of life. How could a Renaissance artist possibly express this rehabilitation of the sensuous nature of man by means of the conventionalism, hierarchism, and geometrism of the Middle Ages, which were developed precisely to express the primacy of the supernatural over the real, the spiritual over the corporeal?

Social conditioning and the autonomy of art

The example of Renaissance art enables us to see that although social conditioning does not fully predetermine the nature of a work of art, it opens up a horizon which makes possible not so much specific works of art, but rather the aesthetic attitude which governs them. Although social conditioning does not exhaust the range of artistic possibilities, it cannot be ignored; by rejecting a strictly sociological concept of art, we clear the way for an exegesis of artistic activity as an autonomous, unique phenomenon. Art is an autonomous sphere, but its autonomy exists only *by, in,* and *through* its social conditioning.

How does this aesthetic differ from one reduced to sociology? Both recognize the importance of social conditioning, but while a sociological aesthetic metaphysically separates autonomy and conditioning, and retains only the latter, we are trying to keep both terms in their dialectical unity in order to enrich our view of art by using its conditionality as our starting point. What is a destination for the sociologists of art is for us a point of departure.

The autonomy of art with regard to its social conditioning does not imply the mutual exclusiveness of the two terms; Engels underlined their dialectical unity as the heart of difference. In the last years of his life he felt obliged to criticize a rigidly determinist conception of the relationship between social conditioning and the superstructure. According to these letters, the action of socioeconomic conditions is not carried out directly but through a complex network of intermediary steps. The complexity of this network, and therefore the degree of autonomy or dependency of the spiritual product, varies according to its nature. For example, political theory depends more on determinate class interests than does philosophy, and much more than does a work of art. The degree of autonomy of artistic creation is greater simply because the entire network of intermediary steps must be filtered through the singular, concrete, and vital experience of the artist; however, his creative individuality should be conceived of not in the abstract, but as the individuality of a social being.

The dual logic of artistic development

Because we are dealing with real human beings, situated in a determinate, historical, and particular context, the means of artistic expression is constantly enriched. This is not a matter of making the creation of forms into an end in itself, because there is no such thing as pure expression, only the expression *of* a determinate human world.

The search for a new form of expression or the improvement of an established form becomes a matter of necessity, imposed by the need to express something that cannot be expressed by the means available. To say that art must constantly invent new means of expression means that all art is by nature an innovation, and that all great art is measured by its power to break with tradition. What is new, creative, and therefore truly revolutionary is a breaking apart, a negation; but not, as is true in other spheres, absolute, radical negation. Every negation, in the dialectical sense, reassumes, assimilates, and absorbs what is valuable from the past. This also means that all creation starts out from the level reached historically by artistic creation.

We cannot speak of progress in art in the same sense we use that term in other spheres, particularly science and technology; it is evident that all great art enriches our human world, our capacity to perceive and express reality, while at the same time it enriches our means of expression and communication. That is why we say that all art has its own internal history, which can only be ignored at the cost of the impoverishment of art. Today one may be able not to write surrealist poetry, but it is not possible to write poetry as if surrealism had never existed. While it is possible to create true realist paintings—and we must underline the word true to differentiate it from those tendencies which in the name of "realism" have actually been the negation of realism and of art itself—in order to be a realist today one must assimilate all the contributions of the most diverse artistic trends, from Impressionism to abstract art.

As Engels writes in his later letters, socioeconomic factors do not act directly on the superstructure, but mold the existing ideological, spiritual material. The history of art cannot be regarded as a series of discontinuous moments, each linked only to the society of its time. Similarly, it cannot be explained by an internal or immanent logic unconnected to historical or social changes. Could one explain the transition from classicism, particularly in its neoclassical form, to romanticism as a merely artistic change, or as a development of certain latent tendencies? Certainly, but there is much more to it than that. Who can ignore that romanticism was the first full expression of a protest against the cold and impersonal logic of bourgeois society and the prosaism of its daily life? Was it not also an attempt, starting with the preromantic Rousseau, to protect and preserve the concreteness, vitality, and individuality of life by means of art? The romantic artist had to create new means of expression to give form to this new attitude, but his creation did not originate in a vacuum—it brought with it the whole weight of the past.

Taking this into account, we see that the attempt to portray the history of art as the development of an internal logic, carried out from an idealist perspective (as done by Wölfflin, for example), is as one-sided as an examination of that history solely as the result of an external logic. In fact, the external logic operates only through the internal logic, and the internal is manifested only through the external. However, the internal logic of artistic development tends to affirm the relative autonomy of art; this autonomy in turn explains why there is no exact correspondence between the internal and the external, that is, between socio-historical and artistic development. This is what Marx analyzed in the last pages of his *Introduction to the Critique of Political Economy*.

If we agree in spirit with this theory of the uneven development of art and society, we can never determine in advance the prospects for art in any given society. But a superior social organization such as socialism opens up enormous possibilities for artistic creation, and, using by analogy Marx's thesis of the hostility of capitalism toward art, we can even go so far as to say that socialism, in principle, is beneficial to art. But in the same way that capitalism, being hostile to art, has known great works of art, socialism does not by itself guarantee an art superior to that created under capitalism; numerous factors, both objective and subjective, have a bearing on this matter. In short, the law of the uneven development of art and society, from a qualitative point of view, always presents a constant need for art to transcend its limits, thus preventing artists from complacently settling down under the shadow of the accomplishments of the society as a whole.

Art as creative labor

When Marx referred to the hostility of capitalism toward art, or when we assert on the basis of this that in a socialist society that hostility is eradicated, we are not referring to a fact determined by subjective factors—such as, for example, a particular official policy of a state with regard to artistic matters—but to the real, objective status of art in a particular society. Marx felt the need to deal with these problems not merely because of aesthetic considerations, but because of the need to expose the radical contradiction between capitalism and man as a creative being. By doing so he pointed up the distinctly qualitative, original character of artistic work, i.e., human creation. Marx discussed these vital aesthetic questions in a treatise on economics, which might explain why certain people in search of a Marxist aesthetic have been thrown off the track looking for a systematic and finished aesthetic which Marx never got to write. A Marxist aesthetic, or, more precisely, those of Marx's ideas which might serve as the source or foundation of a Marxist aesthetic, has to be gleaned from *The Economic and Philosophic Manuscripts of 1844,* or from *A Contribution to a Critique of Political Economy,* written in 1857–1858.

When Marx asserted that "capitalist production is hostile to certain branches of production, and in particular, art and poetry," he saw a contradiction between capitalism and art because of the specific character of art and its domain, not because art expresses an ideology which negates capitalism.

We know from the *Economic and Philosophic Manuscripts* that Marx did not consider art an accidental human activity, but a higher form of labor in which man realizes his essential powers in a concrete-sensuous object. Man is human to the extent that he creates a human world, and art is one of the highest expressions of this humanizing process. We also know that art, as a higher form of labor, raises to a surprisingly high level the capacity for expression and objectification already present in ordinary labor.

The contradiction between art and capitalism takes the opposition between economics and man to its logical conclusion; it is an opposition typical of capitalist society (production for the sake of production, not production for the sake of man). The bourgeois economy and the economic theories which justify its existence are interested in man only as an object, and are interested in the products of labor only as merchandise, not in their function as objectifications of human beings.

This contradiction is not one between capitalism and an art which poses an ideological challenge to the dominant ideology; it is a contradiction between capitalism and art as such. This contradiction does not arise when the bourgeoisie, in its period of ascendancy, is a socially and historically revolutionary force. It grows under the domination of capitalist production, when life becomes impersonal and reified; it is then that artists, without yet being conscious of the true nature of capitalist relations, cease to identify themselves with them. This rebellion began with romanticism and has continued in one form or another into the present. The artist must wage a two-pronged struggle: on the one hand, he refuses to exalt an inhuman reality and searches for artistic forms to express this refusal; on the other, he refuses to let his work cease to respond to an internal need to create and satisfy instead an external need imposed by the laws of the marketplace. Without discovering or understanding the mechanism, revealed by Marx, of the contradiction between capitalism and creation, artists have waged a difficult struggle in modern times, a struggle which also has its heroes: Van Gogh, Modigliani, etc. These artists were heroes because of the incorruptible zeal with which they persevered in satisfying their inner need to create in a world ruled by the laws of capitalist production.

Marx pointed out in the *Economic and Philosophic Manuscripts* that the basis for work resided in the creative nature of man, in his need and capacity to realize his essence in a concrete-sensuous object. He also pointed out that the freer labor is, the more closely it resembles art. In capitalist society there is a tendency to assimilate art to labor, but not labor in the sense of creative work.

The analogy between art and labor does not imply a mutual identity, however. Even when free, labor satisfies determinate material human needs, expressed in the use value of the products of labor; while art satisfies a general human need for expression and affirmation.

Capitalism attempts to treat art as salaried labor, ignoring its role of expressing and objectifying the essential powers of man. In human labor, these powers are materialized in objects which satisfy specific human needs and which have, therefore, human meaning. This labor, which contains a relationship between concrete human beings and concrete needs, between the individuality of the worker and the human meaning of the object, is concrete, vital, and qualitative. But the product itself, in the form of merchandise, has to enter into a relationship with other products having different use values. In order to compare these products one must ignore the human needs which determine their value and establish a quantitative relationship, or exchange value, among them. But this can only be accomplished by completely disregarding concrete, vital labor, making this concrete labor into a fragment of an equalized, undifferentiated, or abstract labor.

Artistic labor is concrete, and as such it produces use values: it satisfies human needs (of expression, affirmation, and communication) by means of giving form to raw materials in concrete-sensuous objects.

Being concrete labor, art has a specific character which obeys the peculiarities of human needs, of content and form. The resulting work of art is characterized by its singularity.

Every work of art is unique and irreplaceable. In artistic labor, as in all concrete labor, quality is foremost. The evaluation of art cannot ignore the quality or specific characteristics of particular works. We cannot compare two or more works of art quantitatively, as if they were fragments of a universal, undifferentiated, and abstract labor, for that would force us to disregard the individuality and uniqueness of creative activity and its products. Moreover, we cannot apply a general criterion of value such as the number of hours of socially necessary labor employed in the production of an object, for this can only be done when a new object can be created to satisfy the same need as another object produced under the same general conditions of production.

Since we cannot apply a quantitative criterion or measure in the evaluation of artistic products, artistic work cannot be reduced to abstract work; its irreproducible nature prevents this. The transformation of artistic labor into salaried labor is therefore a contradiction of the very essence of artistic creation, since its qualitative and singular nature does not allow it to be reduced to a fragment of general abstract labor. Moreover, as an activity that satisfies the human need for expression and communication, the creative essence of art is negatively affected when the artist restrains or limits his inner need to create in deference to external exigencies.

Art as an essential human concern

One of the fundamental principles which the works of Marx more or less explicitly outline and which can serve as the foundation of a Marxist aesthetics is that art is an essential sphere of man.

If, as Marx said in the *Economic and Philosophic Manuscripts,* man is human to the extent that he is able to raise himself above nature to become a *human* natural being, then art is that activity through which he elevates this specific capacity to humanize everything he touches. In other words, if man as a truly human being is above all a *creative* being, then art is one of the spheres wherein he realizes this creative power repeatedly and limitlessly. Because it is a creation, the work of art is always unique and artistic endeavors are always somewhat like adventures; art is not only a reflection of reality, but a creation of a new reality. Thanks to art, that reality

of human or humanized objects created by labor is cease-
lessly extended and enriched and our relationship with reality
is at once enriched and deepened.

That is why there can be no such thing as imitative art, if
by that term we mean a copy or reproduction of reality. True
art has never been a mere reflection or shadow of a pre-
existing reality. When the artist confronts reality, it is not to
copy it, but to appropriate it and give it human significance.
Since it avails itself of the figure only in order to transfigure
it, reference to reality can never be an obstacle to the truly
realist artist. My point is that the polemic between abstract
art and realist art is based on a false premise so long as
realism is not understood in this creative sense; one cannot
decide in favor of what has at times in recent years passed as
realism. But true or creative realism cannot ignore the existence of an art which radically destroys any reliance on the
figure or references to objective reality. This art requires
Marxist interpretation and evaluation such as the recent
study by Fernando Claudin, "The Pictorial Revolution of
Our Times."[1]

The principle regarding the creative essence of art is not
absolute. It grows out of the dialectic interplay between
social conditioning and artistic creation; if we understand this
relationship we will be able to avoid the two dangerous extremes of sociologism, which ignores the specific and relatively autonomous character of art, and aestheticism, which regards art as an absolutely unconditioned and autonomous
activity.

Marxist aesthetics as a science

Starting from an analysis of the place in human existence
of man's aesthetic relationship to reality and of the role of
art as part of the ideological superstructure in a society divided into antagonistic classes, Marxist aesthetics must at the
same time deal with certain problems which are ignored by
sociological aesthetics, such as the structure of a work of art,
the dialectic of its universality and particularity, its dura-

bility, the specific character of artistic objectification, expression, and communication, the relationship between art and reality, the nature of artistic reality, etc. These problems must be resolved on the basis of a recognition of the social conditioning of art, taking into account the thesis that a work of art is a unique totality which can be divided into what we call content and form only by means of abstractions. But when it is a matter of explaining an act—art—we have no other recourse except to abstract from it its essential aspects.

The task of aesthetic theory cannot be identified with that of art criticism. The critic evaluates a particular work and tries to base his evaluation on specific aesthetic principles, although he may not always be fully conscious of doing this. Aesthetic theory is concerned not with accounting for a unique work of art, but with an explanation of the specifically human phenomenon we call art, which occurs in a historical context and is concretized in a store of particular creations.

Aesthetic theory tries to grasp conceptually the essence of art, the structure of all works of art, its categories, its place with regard to other human activities, its social role, etc. It attempts to find the laws that regulate the development of art from its very origins; it attempts to discover the legitimacy of all art, be it primitive or modern, symbolist or realist, romantic or abstract. Thus a Marxist theory of aesthetics cannot reduce itself to realism, without being contradicted by the historical development of art. Neither can it restrict itself to an examination of the problems posed by art in a socialist society. Although this is rightly a question of great importance, Marxist aesthetic theory cannot concentrate its attention exclusively on the art of a particular society, however highly developed the aesthetic and social functions of that art might be; nor should a Marxist aesthetic try to judge the entire history of art in the light of the ruling principles and categories of a particular artistic movement.

Marxist aesthetic theory should strive to be a science, and

as such should be objective, not objectivist. It has a philosophical basis—dialectical and historical materialism—and
cannot consider artistic activity, inasmuch as it is an essential
sphere of human existence, as marginal to the concept of
man as a creative, historical, and social being. Marxist aesthetic theory, as well as Marxism as a whole, would lose its
scientific character if it postulated theses which history,
praxis, or experience contradicted.

We must avoid subjectivism or empty generalizations
which dissolve the specificity of art. Our conception of religion, for example, does not imply that we should ignore the
significance of religion for medieval art. The subject-object
relationship in the process of cognition cannot be mechanically equated with the relationship between the artist and
reality. A critique of bourgeois social relations should not
lead to a rejection of the great art that has been created
within the framework of those relations, namely, art that
transcends the class interests to which it responded.

Against artistic normativism and academicism

Marxist aesthetic theory attempts to give an account of
what is, not of what should be. It does not outline norms or
rules of creation: it is thus incompatible with normativism.

Normativism is the expression of a subjectivism that ends
by congealing or rigidifying the development of reality, of
life itself, and is at the same time the expression of a false
conception of the relationship between theory and praxis.
Because it always implies a loss of touch with reality, an
insoluble contradiction between the unreal road the artist
plots for himself and the reality of the life to which artistic
creation ought to respond, it is the expression of a divorce
between theory and praxis.

Normativism can also have its roots in an attempt to prolong the validity of the principles of an artistic movement
after a substantial change has taken place in the social existence of man, at a time when real, concrete human beings
experience the need for a new art. At such times artists at-

tempt to respond to that need but normativism blocks their way.

The principles which up to that time had aided the artist in his creative work become norms or dictates; but the artist can only create in response to an inner need to express and communicate—freely, not on account of an external demand. This results in a situation analogous to the one Marx pointed out in his discussion of the hostility of capitalism toward art, when artists create in response to an external need imposed by the law of supply and demand, thus subjecting artistic production to the laws of material production.

When an artist creates because of an external need, in conformity with principles, norms, or rules imposed from above, what had been a movement, a vital force, a conscious and sincere reverence for certain creative principles, becomes a formal, external, and therefore false, loyalty. What was alive becomes congealed, inert; this inertia is what exists, like a deadly virus, in all forms of academicism.

When I speak of academicism I am referring not only to the system of ideas historically imposed by the academic world, but also to the academicism that reveals itself as conformism. Art has been among other things a pitched battle against all forms of academicism from the romantic period onward. This nonconformism has clearly been very fruitful, but the academicist tendency which in effect represents the weight of tradition, the gravitational pull of the old and habitual, often appears in the most unsuspected forms. The refusal to conform is not always a sure way of escaping academicism. When negation becomes an end in itself and nonconformism the only value, we find what has been called the conformism of nonconformism, that is, a new and subtle form of academicism.

The roots of normativism

The danger of falling into normativism in the name of a Marxist aesthetic—the substitution of a normative order for an explanation, of a norm for a principle—occurs in art, as in any other field, when the relationship between theory and praxis is inverted. This inversion can have two sources.

One source, which we could call internal, concerns the very nature of theory, inasmuch as it is an abstraction of reality. Whether we are dealing with artistic reality or any other reality, we can only grasp concrete reality by truncating or simplifying a complex and rich totality. Marx considered concrete reality to be the unity of the determinations of an object; but however rich the conceptualization of the concrete might be, it never succeeds in grasping the determinations of reality in all their richness. Some of these determinations must be eliminated in favor of others which are more essential, thus moving from a less to a more profound essence. The result is a concept which reflects with increasing richness and depth the richness and depth of the object itself. The process of knowledge therefore goes from one abstraction to another in an upward movement that has no end. But theory must also change because reality itself is in a process of change, and only by changing, by developing, can it grasp concrete reality with greater faithfulness.

As soon as a theory stops changing, or a particular abstraction is regarded as definitive, or a limited set of determining factors is deemed sufficient to express reality, then theory ceases to have any value; if in spite of this we impose a value on that theory as a guide to action, or praxis—including artistic praxis—we should distinguish between a theory which springs from the movement of reality as an expression of its essential determinations and can therefore help guide praxis, and what is nothing more than a normative doctrine or straitjacket for the creative impulse.

The other source of inversion between theory and praxis is social; the concrete human interests of social groups or classes explain why a decrepit theory is sometimes kept from moving on to make room for a new one. Thus, the classical aesthetic degenerated into academicism in the eighteenth century when the aesthetic principles of classicism were perpetuated to inform an art acceptable to the dominant social classes in deference to political absolutism, although they had lost touch with reality. Theory ceased to be vital and became a collection of rules and prescriptions.

No objective conditions exist under socialism which could bring about such artistic normativism; no specific class interests could serve as its basis. However, bureaucracy and dogmatism in the socialist countries can create (and indeed did create, in the period of the personality cult) conditions which allow the emergence of artistic normativism, manifested in the application of administrative and coercive methods to the field of art.

A Marxist theory of aesthetics must try to avoid this Scylla and Charybdis choice which threatens every theory. It must strive to maintain a close, vital contact with the artistic experience which celebrates the past as well as with modern artistic practice.

It is not easy to avoid the normativist pitfall, thus clearing the way for a real Marxist aesthetic. But it can be done with the combined effort of Marxist philosophers and the fruitful support of artists and writers conscious of the momentous problems posed by their creative labor.

Notes

1. *Cuba Socialista*, no. 30, February 1964.

5. On Art and Society

In a certain sense, each society gets the art it deserves, both because of the art it favors or tolerates, and because artists, as members of society, create in accordance with the particular type of relations they have with that society. This means that art and society, far from finding themselves in a relationship of mutual externality or indifference, either seek each other out or avoid one another, meet or separate, but can never completely turn their backs on each other.

The importance of the relationship between art and society will be denied, or at least minimized, by those who see art as a completely gratuitous or playful activity, those who consider it the manifestation of the most radical individuality, and those who regard it as an absolutely autonomous sphere which escapes all conditioning. While art can have intrinsic value, this need not imply gratuitousness; while art can be an expression of the most profound individuality, it is a real, concrete individuality, not an abstract individuality conceived at the margin of the community; and while art can be an autonomous sphere, this does not deny its conditioning.

The relationship between art and society cannot be ignored, for art itself is a social phenomenon: first, because the artist, however unique his primary experience might be, is a social being; second, because his work, however deeply marked by his primary experience and however unique and unrepeatable its objectification or form might be, is always a bridge, a connecting link between the artist and other members of society; third, because a work of art affects other people—it contributes to the reaffirmation or devaluation of their ideas, goals, or values—and is a social force which, with its emotional or ideological weight, shakes or moves people. Nobody remains the same after having been deeply moved by a true work of art.

But let us pay even closer attention to the relationship between art and society, regarding them from the point of view of the artist. We shall then see how the artist, insofar as he feels the human need to create freely, in such a way that others might share in the fruits of his creation, cannot be indifferent to the nature of the social relations in whose framework he creates, relations which can be either favorable or hostile to artistic creation. We shall also see how dominant social nexuses merge in a unique way in the artist, and how, whether or not he intends it, his work inevitably reflects his sense of himself as a concrete human being living in a given social system.

If the social relations between art and society are of interest both to the artist and to society, it is because artistic activity is an essential human activity. It is essential to the artist who realizes in his creation the essential powers of his being at the same time that he establishes, by objectifying the richness of humanity, a new and original means of communication between himself and others. It is also essential for those who, without being artists, feel the vital human need to absorb the human experience the artist has been able to objectify. And it is just as essential for social institutions which express the interests and aspirations of specific social groups, for these institutions are clearly aware of the social function of art, its emotional and ideological weight.

Art and society are thus necessarily connected: no art has been unaffected by social influences and no art has failed in turn to influence society. No society has renounced its right to possess its own art and its consequent right to influence art. Art is almost as old as man himself; that is, almost as old as society.

But the relations between art and society are not immutably set; they are historical, and as such they are problematic. The attitudes of the artist and society toward each other change because the artist, being a concrete human being, changes, as does the society in which he makes his art, along with its values, ideals and traditions. What has been said about man on more than one occasion can be said with greater reason about art and society: they have no nature, only a history. Therefore, their relations with each other change with history: on the part of the artist, these relations may be characterized at times by harmony and agreement, at times by evasion or retreat, at times by protest or rebellion. And the attitudes of society or the state can be either favorable or hostile to artistic creation, protecting or limiting, to a greater or lesser extent, creative freedom.

The problematic character of the relations between art and society derives from the problematic nature of art itself. Every great work of art tends toward universality, toward the creation of a human or humanized world that transcends historical, social, or class particularities. It is thus integrated in an artistic universe inhabited by works of art from the most distant times, from the most diverse countries, the most dissimilar cultures, and the most antithetical societies. Great art is thus an affirmation of human universality, but this universality is reached through the particular: the artist is a man of his time, his society, of a particular culture and social class. All great art is particular in its origins, but universal in its results. By means of art, man as a particular, historical being universalizes himself; but not on the level of an abstract, impersonal, or dehumanized universality. Instead, he enriches his human universe, conserves and reclaims his concrete being, and resists all dehumanization.

Art has been able to survive and endure to the extent that its origins were in the concrete here and now; only in this way has it achieved true universality. The particular and the universal are united so harmoniously in artistic creation that too much of an emphasis on one or the other term is enough to shatter this dialectical harmony, with dire consequences for the work of art itself. At times it is the artist who breaks this unity, out of a horror of the particular (his time, his class, his society); at times it is society which pushes art down false roads with its anxious attempts to impose its own particularity (its values, interests, and ideas).

The problematic nature of the relations between art and society derives not only from this dialectic of the universal and the particular, but also from the dual character of the work of art as a means and an end, as an ineluctable unity of intrinsic and extrinsic values. The ultimate aim of the work of art is to widen and enrich the human territory. The artist realizes the supreme value of a work of art, its aesthetic value, to the extent that he is able to give a determinate form to matter in order to objectify a determinate human, emotional, and ideological content, as a result of which he extends his own reality.

But this supreme value of the work of art—its ultimate aim and reason for being—is achieved along with and through other values—political, moral, religious, etc.—which in the ideological superstructure of a society are not always on the same plane. The predominance of one or another is determined by concrete socio-historical situations: some express better than others the aspirations and interests of the dominant social class. So long as in a given society the particular dominates the universal, so long as one social class imposes its particular interest at the expense of the general interest of the whole community, such a society will attempt to extend the domination of the particular over the universal to art itself: first, by breaking up the dialectical unity of the particular and the universal; second, by trying to impose the domination of a particular political, religious, or economic value over, or in dissociation from, the supreme value of the work of art, its aesthetic value.

This domination occurred in ancient Greek society, where art, particularly tragedy, was placed at the service of the *polis,* and became a political art par excellence. (Plato clearly expressed the demands society made on art when he excluded from his ideal state poets and imitative artists in general who made no contribution to political or civic education.) Medieval society placed art at the service of religion, and in accord with the dominant ideology the artist regarded people and things as a reflection of a supersensual, super-human, transcendental reality. But in these societies the relations between the artist and society were transparent, so to speak. Exalting the dominant values of his society, the artist recognized and affirmed himself as a member of his community. And society, for its part, recognized itself in an art that expressed its own values.

After the Renaissance new relations eroded the power of the old feudal relations. A new social class emerged—the bourgeoisie—whose power was linked primarily to the growing power of material production as the expression of the domination of nature by man. Production extended not only the power of the bourgeoisie over nature, but also its power over men. Production ceased to serve man, as it had in ancient Greece, and instead began to serve production. Insofar as man ceased to be an end and became a means (transformation of labor power into a commodity), production turned against man. As the sphere of material production grew, everything was subjected to its rigid laws, including art (transformation of the work of art into a commodity). To the extent that the law of material production lengthened its reach, the reification of human existence was intensified. Life lost its concrete, vital, and creative character and took on an abstract character.

In a world in which everything is quantified and abstracted, art—the highest form of expression of everything concrete and qualitative in human life—enters into a contradiction with that alienated world, becoming an incorruptible stronghold of humanity. Art and society thus become radically opposed. Art, representing denied humanity, opposes an inhuman society; and society opposes the artist insofar as he resists reification, insofar as he tries to express his humanity.

Historically, this situation originated with romanticism, and from then on the contradiction between art and society has grown sharper. Great artists have withdrawn from society, as shown by their divorce from the public. Bourgeois society has responded to this rebuff by driving artists to misery, madness, or death. Before the bourgeoisie firmly established its rule—in Greek society, in the Middle Ages, during the baroque or neoclássic periods—artists created in harmony with society. Starting with romanticism, they gradually became isolated and proscribed, especially since the last half of the nineteenth century.

The artist refuses to integrate his work in the abstract, quantified, and banal universe of bourgeois society. Without being fully conscious of his abysmal separation from it, the artist radically opposes bourgeois society simply by remaining faithful to his creative will. Creation comes to mean rebellion. And the more human existence is banalized and robbed of its true richness, the more the artist feels the need to express his human richness in a concrete-sensuous object— outside the dominant social and artistic institutions.

Modern art, in its most heroic moments, is the attempt to escape the reification of existence, an attempt the proletariat makes by other means in its struggle to do away with its alienation. The "accursed" (*maudit*) artist of the late nineteenth and early twentieth century is accursed because of his insistence, expressed through his creative activity, on resisting the inert and abstract universe of the bourgeoisie. By objectifying himself, by making human or humanized objects— works of art—the artist assures a human presence in things and thus helps prevent the reification of humanity. The supreme goal of art, its need and reason for being, thus becomes more imperative than ever, because in a world ruled by quantitative criteria (exchange value), by the alienation of man, art—because it is the creation, expression, and objectification of man—is one of the most valuable means by which to reclaim, assert, and extend the real richness of humanity. Never has art been more necessary, because never has man been more threatened by dehumanization.

In the last few decades a lot of discussion has centered around the concept of the "dehumanization of art," introduced by José Ortega y Gasset. But this discussion has not taken into account the "dehumanization of man" as a process characteristic of bourgeois society by virtue of which, under the rule of surplus production, man was relegated to being a means, a thing, or a commodity. Nor has it been recognized that this supposed "dehumanization of art" was a response—not without risks for art itself—to the dehumanization of man himself. Although these risks were clear, the artist was forced to accept them by the particular conditions surrounding the task of preserving the concretely human. The modern artist thus undertook a task for which his powers were inadequate, for the reconquest of the concretely human, the affirmation of man in an alienated world, could not be carried out by art alone.

The artist has reacted against a society ruled by the law of capitalist material production; he has broken that law, barricading himself in his creative work. He thus asserted his freedom, but as the fruit of necessity. The artist had no choice but to break rules: it was the only way he could remain an artist. The hostility of society forced him to rebel: thus, although he has rebelled in order to preserve his creative freedom, the sources of this attitude are basically social. Modern society has been the only society to endow artistic creation with that heroic countenance we find in the creative life of a Van Gogh or a Modigliani, because only in modern society does the artist realize that as a result of the transformation of the work of art into a thing a terrible chasm has opened beneath his feet. In this realization he has been able to affirm himself as an artist and as a human being.

But while he has affirmed himself he has endangered certain vital aspects of art itself; lengthening distances, cutting ties, and destroying bridges. He has stretched almost to the breaking point what by his essence belongs to him: his capacity to communicate. Art has been able to withdraw from a banal society, an inhuman and abstract universe, by cutting itself loose from its moorings, and has become besieged. That is the terrible price it has had to pay bourgeois society in order to save its creative essence. Modern art has helped save what is concretely human; now it must revitalize this contribution by reestablishing the forsaken communication, by rebuilding the bridges between the artist and the people. This cannot be done by buying an easy intelligibility at the price of a double debasement: that of the work of art and that of the spectator. Communication can only be restored by improving both the quality of the work of art and the artistic sensibility of the public. For this new bridges must be built, for they are indispensable if artistic creation is to extricate itself from the solipsism into which a great part of it has fallen.

A true artist is capable of creating a new language where ordinary language fails. The object he creates cannot be an end in itself; on the contrary, it is a means of reaching people. True art reveals essential aspects of human existence in such a way that they may be shared. An incommunicative art is therefore a negation of an essential aspect of art.

Having cut its ties with an abstract, bourgeois universe which harassed its creative essence, modern art must find new links with people. This search should be mutual, because the public must also seek out art, and must therefore meet art halfway. Thus, while the artist searches for means of expression to make communication possible, the public must search out true art and reject the pseudo-art of a reified and debased world.

In both cases the problem cannot be resolved on a merely aesthetic plane. The communication sought by the artist can only be established when society no longer seems to him to be a completely hostile environment, an abstract universe which can only wither artistic creation. In that sense, the problem of artistic communication is inseparable from the problem of achieving real communication among human beings. Art shares its destiny with the social forces which are struggling to resolve the contradictions, rending both society and the individual, between true community and true individuality. Therefore the heroic rebellion of the modern artist need no longer have the exclusive and impudent character it had when he was considered an outcast.

On the other hand, the public cannot actively seek true art unless it rids itself of the pseudo-art of an alienated human world. Since this cheap and false art exists primarily because of the powerful economic and technological forces which ensure its diffusion, and since these forces are in the hands of social elements which have a vested interest in the maintenance of that abstract and reified world, the liberation of the public is not the exclusive domain of artists and professors of aesthetics, because it is inseparable from the economic and social emancipation of society as a whole.

And thus the destinies of art and society converge once again, in a manner that will prove decisive for both.

* 6. The Concept of Tragedy in Marx and Engels

Tragedy and revolution

All great revolutions are at the same time expressions of sharp class contradictions and radical attempts to resolve those contradictions. When they succeed they constitute true historical leaps: an immense area of humanity, which up to then lay fallow, is suddenly opened to the creative activity of human beings. Historical time flows more rapidly, and the new forges ahead. Marx called revolutions the locomotives of history, and Lenin saw them as true popular festivals. This does not mean that they rest on beds of roses: there is violence and pain, suffering and death, with an intensity that depends on the degree of resistance put up by the dominant classes to the eruption of the new. But what is decisive is the creative action that starts in the first moments of victory. A victorious revolution, by unleashing the creative energies of the people, escapes the prison of tragedy.

But, historically, revolutions are not always victorious; they sometimes plunge into catastrophe or defeat. When a revolution heads inexorably toward its death—its failure means death—it enters into the tragic. It enters in its own specific way, by absorbing through all its pores the substance of tragedy. But not all failed revolutions are tragic. They are tragic only when the character of the revolutionary conflict, the action of the struggling forces, the conditions surrounding them and their resolution, manifest a number of characteristics essential to a tragic situation.

The first incision in the substance of tragedy

With the help of the scalpels of the two greatest thinkers on this question—Aristotle and Hegel—let us make an initial incision into the substance of tragedy.

Aristotle began by trying to rescue tragedy from the low level to which Plato had consigned it. For Plato, the tragic was related to the most ignoble part of man, his passion; consequently, tragedy could not be admitted to his ideal state, for that would imply the displacement of the laws of reason by the dark impulses of passion. Aristotle revealed the greatness of tragedy, its formative and educational value, for in tragedy men are depicted as being "better than they are." Aristotle regarded tragedy as the highest achievement of art, and made enormous advances—although he had no predecessors in this endeavor—in understanding the concept of tragedy. It was already suspected that the intensity of a conflict did not in itself make a situation tragic. A tragic situation is brought about not only by a conflict, but by a crucial conflict in which there is a transition from happiness to disaster. The tragic hero heads toward a disastrous dénouement; things will turn out badly, inevitably so. Tragedy is characterized by that sort of ending, already necessarily foreshadowed in the conflict and struggle.

Hegel profoundly enriched the Aristotelian concept of tragedy. Like Aristotle, he pointed out the presence of a dire ending—for Hegel tragedy was a human situation in which death was inevitable. In addition, he probed more deeply into the nature of the conflict and the character of the goals which the struggling forces try to impose. These goals are universal and the conflict is therefore irreconcilable. The universality of the goals, their essential vital nature, forces those who fight for them to carry on the fight to its logical conclusion: death. The goals are such that man could not renounce them without renouncing himself. Reconciliation is impossible in a true tragic conflict, for it would mean a sacrifice of the universal to the particular, a renunciation of what the tragic hero values more than his own life. A tragic situation is one in which the hero can only affirm his human condition by struggling toward an objective so vital that it calls for his own death. But his sacrifice is not a self-sacrifice; it is a victory, an affirmation of his essence. With his death, the tragic hero affirms the universality of his goals, and thus affirms his true humanity.

Hegel perceived the essential nature of tragedy as a radical and irreconcilable conflict. The character of this conflict is determined by the greatness or universality of the objectives being pursued, which in turn brings about a resolution in which death or failure is inevitable. Any attempt to find a compromise or remedy runs counter to the very nature of tragedy. Any understanding, compromise, or renunciation of the struggle would dissolve the tragedy, and as a result man himself would be lost. Once a tragedy is put in motion, man cannot erase it without erasing himself. His tragic essence is his human essence.

If we sum up what we have discussed so far regarding the nature of tragedy, we find that a tragic conflict is the result of three human inabilities: (1) the inability to reject the objective one fights for; (2) the inability to reach that objective happily (without meeting with death of failure); (3) the inability to renounce the struggle.

Let us now return to the tragedy of revolution.

The interest of Marx and Engels in revolutionary tragedy

However much an author may distance himself from reality, in revolutionary tragedy we are on historical ground, and the conflict is not waged among individuals, or between individuals and the community, but among social classes or forces. The conflict can originate, define, and sharpen itself without necessarily being revolutionary; in a revolution this conflict becomes intense and concentrated, destroying any possibilities for reconciliation. But the revolutionary conflict does not become tragic unless it necessarily leads to death or defeat.

What is the specific form of the tragic conflict which breaks out among concrete human beings who bear the goals, aspirations, and interests of specific social classes? This question captivated Marx and Engels in their consideration of the tragic aspects of revolution in real life and in the artistic tragedy it informs. They dealt with this problem particularly in relation to the idea of tragedy proposed by Lasalle, to which he tried to give form in *Franz von Sickingen,* a play dealing with the tragic fate of a failed revolution.

Marx and Engels had more than a casual interest in this problem. They dealt with it not as mere literary theoreticians, but as architects of the theoretical and practical arms of the liberation of the proletariat. Their theory was a guide to action—hence their interest in the tragic aspects of revolutionary action. Both Marx and Engels were interested in the nature of revolutionary conflict, its historical forms, the conditions which determine its victory or failure, etc. They were bound to be attracted by the problems connected with the revolution seen from the perspective of its failure. The vital problems to which they had devoted their theoretical and practical lives were starkly manifested in the failure of a revolution: the true roles of revolutionary leaders and the people, the nature of revolutionary actions, the manner of solving the contradictions between means and ends, between the possible and the impossible, between the possible and the real, etc.

Lasalle's play was based on a sixteenth-century episode in German history which still cast its shadows on the Germany of Marx's time—even though the sense of time in Germany had been erased to such an extent that, as Marx once said, it still lived in the past, a living anachronism.

Lasalle's concept of tragedy

An insurrection by Rhenish knights in 1522-1523 led by Franz von Sickingen, military and political leader of the lower nobility, and Ulrich von Hutten, their humanist thinker and theoretical spokesman, provided the theme for Lasalle's tragedy. Engels points out in *The Peasant War in Germany* that the goal for which these noblemen rebelled was to bring about reforms leading to a kind of democracy for the nobility, led by a monarch, similar to the system existing in Poland at that time. They were defeated in their struggle against the princes, and their two leaders killed as a result of their inability to attract the peasants to their side.

Lasalle wrote his revolutionary tragedy in 1858-1859, and sent three copies to Marx (one for Marx, one for Engels, and the third for the poet Ferdinand Freiligrath), along with a letter setting forth his ideas on revolutionary tragedy.[1] Marx and Engels answered this letter separately, without knowing the contents of each other's replies.[2] They pointed out the positive and negative aspects of the play, disagreed with Lasalle's views on tragedy, and set forth their own principles, exhibiting an amazing congruence of views regarding revolutionary tragedy.

According to Lasalle, the tragic idea was based on a profound dialectical contradiction inherent in all human actions, particularly revolutionary actions. His idea of tragedy therefore derived from the conflicting, contradictory, yet universal character of all revolutions. What is the nature of this contradiction? Lasalle saw it as a contradiction between ideas and actions, between revolutionary ideas and the practical actions which try to give them life. This takes the form of a conflict between revolutionary enthusiasm and real possibilities, between the infinite ideals of revolutionaries and the limited means at their disposal to carry out those ideals.[3] The limitless revolutionary enthusiasm must resort to limited means if the revolution is to achieve its objectives in a limited reality.

On the basis of that contradiction, Lasalle concluded that revolutionary goals can only be achieved by recourse to inadequate means, necessitating a deviation from the original objectives—a compromise. Lasalle considered this the price every revolution must pay if it desires to go from idea to reality. Philosophically entrenched in idealism, Lasalle thought that ideas were powerful, infinite, expansive, but that they lost all these attributes when they came in contact with reality: realization equals degradation. This is a contradiction with no solution: the realization of objectives requires the adoption of a "realistic" program; from the perspective of the principles being compromised, the "strength and justification of revolutions," this condemns the revolution to defeat. Lasalle believed that revolutionary objectives can only be achieved by means that are not revolutionary, but diplomatic; therein lies the tragedy of every revolution, the conflict which ends by devouring it. Lasalle deprived the revolution of its true sense by proposing that all revolutions inevitably end in compromise.[4]

Lasalle wrote *Franz von Sickingen* in order to illustrate "the formal revolutionary idea par excellence."[5] In the same letter he added, "I have written this tragedy only *in order* to set forth this fundamental idea regarding the revolutionary tragedy."

The two main characters become standard bearers of this tragic concept of revolution. Hutten is the purely intellectual revolutionary who clings to the purity of the revolutionary objectives, while Sickingen is the astute and realistic politician. In contrast are the masses, without whom revolutions cannot be made and whose passionate and ignorant enthusiasm leads them to accept only extreme, absolute, and immediate solutions, and to reject compromise solutions.

Sickingen fails, however, despite his realism, as a consequence of his own faults ("absence of direct moral certainty and conviction in the ideal," and excessive confidence in means that were not truly revolutionary). The causes of failure are therefore subjective, and the socio-historical roots of the conflict are ignored. Furthermore, reality functions as the incarnation of an idea; Lasalle saw tragedy itself as an illustration of the idea of revolution; Sickingen is not so much a representative of his time and class as an abstract spokesman for the idea of compromise; while Hutten is the personification of the idea of enthusiasm. Lasalle thus removes tragedy from real time; his tragedy is an exemplification of something that is eternally repeated. His vision of the revolution is an abstract one, in which characters act in accordance with the ideas they personify. His concept of tragedy is clearly idealist, which is in keeping with his abstract and idealist vision of the revolution.

The objections of Marx and Engels to Lasalle's concept of tragedy

Marx's critical observations in his letter to Lasalle set forth the socio-historical roots of the tragic conflict and the objective causes of Sickingen's defeat. He pointed out that the failure and death of Sickingen was not due to personal mistakes or weak enthusiasm; his astuteness did not seal his tragic fate. "He was destroyed because as a *knight* and a *representative of a perishing class* he rose up against the existing order, or rather against its new form." Without their class character, Sickingen's actions lose their concrete character, and Lasalle's work loses its political and real force to the same extent. Sickingen is a sort of Götz von Berlichingen, the knight whom Goethe pitted against the princes and the emperor—with the difference that Goethe presented him in a true light, as a pitiable hero. Sickingen is the representative of the impoverished lower nobility that rises against the princes; his class goals entail a return to the past. He could not carry out that struggle, given the precariousness of his forces, with his eyes fixed on the past. That is why he had to call on "the towns and the peasants, that is, to those classes whose development signified a negation of knighthood." Lasalle failed to see this conflict. Marx wrote that although he approved of placing the revolutionary conflict at the center of modern tragedy, he did not think Lasalle chose the right subject through which to present this conflict.

What Marx meant was that there cannot be a revolutionary tragic conflict in the absence of truly revolutionary forces. Ignoring these forces, Lasalle was left with a rebellion of knights. Concrete historical reality outpaces the languid reality necessary to illustrate Lasalle's ideas on revolution.

Engels, like Marx, called attention to the necessity of seeing tragic revolutionary conflict as class conflict. The actions of heroes in a revolutionary tragedy cannot be explained on the basis of subjective motivations alone; they must be understood in the context of socio-historical forces, particularly germinally revolutionary forces. When Lasalle lost sight of the true revolutionary element, he deprived the revolution of its tragic content. Engels reproached him for not having given proper emphasis to the role of the peasants and the lower classes. "It seems to me that this neglect of the peasant movement is the reason you have drawn the nationalist movement of the nobility incorrectly in one respect and so failed to see the *genuine* tragic element in Sickingen's fate." The nationalist revolution of the nobility required an alliance with peasants as an essential condition for its success; however, this alliance could not be effected historically. Placing the tragic conflict on an objective historical basis, Engels added: "This, to my mind, was the tragic circumstance: that the basic condition, an alliance with the peasantry, was impossible."

We have said that the nature of tragedy always includes a human disability which seals the fate of the tragic hero; in revolutionary tragedy, the disability is a historical one which the hero cannot overcome. The conflicting forces are conditioned historically with regard to both their aspirations and the possibility of realizing them. Historical exigencies pushed the impoverished nobility of sixteenth-century Germany into a struggle with the princes; those exigencies could not be resolved victoriously because objective reality—the antagonistic character of the class interests involved—prevented fulfillment of the condition essential to such a resolution, namely, the alliance between the lower nobility and the peasants. The nonfulfillment of that condition places this conflict on the level of tragedy; there is no exit. The tragic conflict, according to Engels, is a conflict "between the historically necessary postulate and the practical impossibility of its realization."

Here we have the two poles of the conflict. One, the historical need for certain objectives; unless they are rooted in a historical movement that nourishes them, they do not appear so vital and essential that they cannot be renounced. The other, the impossibility of realizing these objectives which are presented by history as necessary. Engels underlined the importance of that historical impossibility; failing to understand that, Lasalle missed the tragic element in Sickingen's fate. Marx and Engels had every reason to say that revolutionary tragedy had to be based not on an abstract conflict of ideas, but on a historical class conflict. The tragedy of the revolution begins when a movement attempts to realize goals which for class reasons cannot be realized historically.

The abstract conflict on which Lasalle based his tragedy explains why he let the tragic essence of the conflict slip from his hands, why he chose the wrong theme, why he was able to give only subjective reasons for the failure and death of the rebel leaders, and finally, why he was unable to portray these leaders as living, concrete, real beings.

By substituting an abstract, universal, eternal impossibility —the impossibility of achieving a goal without negating it— for the concrete, historical impossibility of satisfying the indispensable condition for the realization of that goal, Lasalle removed the tragic dimension of his knights' rebellion. The heroes of his tragedy are defeated as the representatives of a dying class, but their death, and their rebellion against the existing order, does not have a socio-historical, class content. As Marx and Engels each pointed out, such a content would have required Lasalle to give greater importance to the struggle by the lower classes and to the character of the peasant leader, Münzer.

Lasalle's idea of the tragic flaw

While losing sight of the objective historical bases for the tragic collision, Lasalle turned his attention to the concept of the tragic flaw. He represented Sickingen's cunning realism as the great flaw demanded by Aristotle. The hero's tendency to avoid dealing with the obstacles presented both by the infinite enthusiasm of the masses, clinging blindly to their principles, and by the limited means available and the consequent debasement of the goals, originated in his excessive confidence in the means and lack of confidence in the goals. The hero was to blame.

The question of the hero's culpability is central to tragedy. Can tragedy exist in a framework of total culpability? Are not tragic heroes guilty and innocent at the same time? Doesn't individual guilt imply the guilt of others, in such a way that guilt ceases to be purely individual or merely subjective, acquiring a new dimension by being placed in an objective, historical, and social framework? The question of the relationship between guilt and innocence is related to the question of the nexus between the individual and society, and the relationship between freedom and necessity. Hegel recognized that necessity does not exclude freedom and innocence does not exclude a certain guilt. "Tragic heroes," he wrote in his *Aesthetik,* "are, at the same time, guilty and innocent."

Lasalle severed Hegel's dialectical relationship. He saw Sickingen as culpable because he chose to be cunning, because he considered himself to be superior to the existing order, and because he lacked a conviction in the ideal: the genesis of his culpability is found within him. Lasalle ignored the social, historical, and class origins of his guilt, portraying his cunning not as conditioned by necessity or objective circumstances, but as a freely chosen mode of behavior. Hegel thought just the opposite: the tragic hero's decisions are conditioned by necessity; necessity provides the reasons for acting as he does, not the "subjective rhetoric of the heart," or the "sophistry of passion." A necessity impels the hero to carry out actions for which he then assumes responsibility. One thing does not exclude the other.

Lasalle, a poor disciple of his teacher Hegel, overlooked this Hegelian concept when he ignored the dialectic of freedom and necessity and enveloped his heroes in a net of subjective guilt. Nevertheless, Lasalle claimed that he was giving his tragedy an objective foundation by basing it on an "eternal, necessary, objective conflict of ideas." But this foundation lay outside of history, in the form of an eternally recurrent abstract conflict.

Abstraction vs. reality: Schiller or Shakespeare

In answer to the objections of Marx and Engels, Lasalle defended himself by insisting on his fundamental objective: to illustrate his *tragic* conception of revolution. He rejected the suggestion that he give a more preeminent role to Münzer and the peasant movement. Because he lacked a "realistic diplomacy," Münzer could not have expressed the tragic conflict which Lasalle saw repeated in almost every revolution. Münzer did not lend himself to an incarnation of what Lasalle called "the formal revolutionary idea par excellence." That is perfectly true; however, by not making him the hero of his tragedy in place of the knight Sickingen, Lasalle lost an opportunity to write a truly revolutionary tragedy, as Marx and Engels pointed out. Only Münzer could have personified the revolutionary tragic conflict which Engels defined as the historical necessity of realizing an action which cannot be realized, again for historical and not merely subjective reasons.

The omission of the real interests of the struggling classes, the concrete historical correlations between them, and the real historical roots of the conflict, had grave consequences for the artistic realization of the tragedy. Philosophical idealism turned into an artistic idealism, with negative repercussions on the work of art.

Marx and Engels realized that Lasalle had mutilated historical reality by disregarding the role of the peasantry and the lower classes in order to illustrate an idea. In the name of an idea, he idealized reality. This resulted in a transformation of his characters into standard bearers for an idea, with none of the vitality or concreteness required in a play based on life itself. The false view of historical reality combined with the schematic, abstract characterization of the two heroes as mere instruments of an idea to impoverish the artistic realization of this play. Marx would have preferred a greater *Shakespearization* of Lasalle's tragedy, and saw as its gravest defect its *"Schillerization*, making individuals into mere mouthpieces of the spirit of the times." He added: "I regret the absence of distinctive traits in your characters. . . . Hutten represents, to my mind, a too exclusive 'enthusiasm' which is boring." Sickingen, on the other hand, is the mouthpiece for the idea of compromise. The characters in this play are not concrete men, of flesh and blood, who defend their aspirations and ideas, but who at the same time see themselves as motivated by material, real interests. They are purely and exclusively, as Marx says, ideological mouthpieces, or in more current terminology, mere propagandists.

Marx's reference to Shakespeare and Schiller implied an evaluation of the traditions of historical drama and a clear indication of which of the two heritages he considered the more fertile for revolutionary historical tragedy. Lasalle identified himself with the German tradition of historical drama, and particularly with Schiller. Despite the undeniable artistic merits of his plays, Schiller lost sight of the relationship between ideas and concrete material interests, and saw the historical struggle as a *struggle of ideas.* In Shakespeare's work, not only ideas are at play, but also the passions and interests of the men who stand behind them. His characters are real, living men, and history is portrayed, through them, as full of life. In the face of Lasalle's predilection for Schiller, Marx underlined the need for more *Shakespearization* in response to the requirements of realistic historical drama.

Engels also showed a predilection for Shakespeare, although recognizing the merits of Schiller and of Lasalle himself. He approved, for example, of putting aside the petty individual passions of the characters in order to situate them in the movement of history, whereby they can express the ideas of their time. Following the example of Schiller, Lasalle attempted to impart his tragedy with the greatest ideological profundity and with a conscious historical content. But by forgetting "the real for the ideal and Shakespeare for Schiller" he was unable to realize his objectives. Engels pointed out that Lasalle's concept of tragedy was too abstract and led to the elimination of elements and forces which would have given life to the play. He did not see the need to renounce the ideological content, to completely abandon Schiller, but rather to present that content in the living, concrete form required by true realist drama. The task, in which Engels saw the future of German drama, consisted of fusing "the ideological profundity, the conscious historical content," and "the vigor, the breadth of Shakespearean action." The ideas must be there, and the goals that motivate the characters must be put in the foreground, but in a "living, active and, so to speak, natural manner, by the progress of the action itself"; the "argumentative speeches, on the other hand . . . become more and more useless."

Engels unequivocally situated the role of the ideological content in tragedy. In his view, that content must be embodied in a vital manner if it is not to remain on an overly abstract level. But does the ideological content stand to lose or benefit from being given a living, active, and concrete form, which is the only way by which it can be placed in the foreground of a work of art? "The *ideological content* will be weakened as a result," Engels said, "but this is inevitable." That is to say, because ideas in a work of art are no longer in their own, abstract, milieu they will be weakened as ideas, but the work of art will have its own life. In fact, one cannot speak of a weakening of the ideological content since in the final analysis that content is rescued and strengthened when the characters who express it are real, concrete men, living, distinct characters, and not mere mouthpieces for an idea. That is why Engels explained that "the individual is defined not by *what* he does, but by *how* he does it; and, from this point of view, the ideological content of your play would not have lost anything, in my opinion, if the traits of the different characters had been more clearly delineated and contrasted."

Responding to the critical observations of Marx and Engels, Lasalle clung to his concept of the revolution and defended the right of the artist, in the name of art, to radically separate historical reality and the reality demanded by the need to illustrate an idea. The historical Sickingen was one thing, Lasalle asserted, agreeing in this respect with Marx and Engels, but the Sickingen of his tragedy was a different matter, and he felt Marx's and Engels' criticisms were not with regard to this Sickingen. He asked rhetorically, "Doesn't the poet have a right to idealize his hero, endowing him with a higher consciousness? Is Schiller's Wallenstein historical?"[6] Lasalle's defense of the poet's right to idealize reality concluded the polemic, with everyone maintaining his position: Lasalle insisting on the abstract notion that a revolution is a struggle of ideas; Marx and Engels holding that the tragic revolutionary conflict has real, concrete, historical roots, because tragedy is nourished not by ideas, but by the profound contradictions of real life.

Notes

1. F. Lasalle, letter to Karl Marx, March 6, 1859, in F. Mehring, *Aus dem literarischen Nachlass von Marx, Engels, und Lasalle* (Stuttgart, 1913), vol 4, pp. 132-41; and in *Karl Marx—Frederick Engels:Sur la littérature et l'art*, ed. J. Freville (Paris: Editions Sociales, 1954).

2. Karl Marx, letter to Lasalle, April 19, 1859, and Frederick Engels, letter to Lasalle, May 18, 1859, in *Über Kunst und Literatur* (Berlin: Henschel Verlag, 1949), pp. 111, 113-14.

3. "The strength of the revolution consists in its *enthusiasm*, in this direct faith of the idea in its own strength and limitless nature. But enthusiasm as the *direct* certainty of the omnipotence of the idea is, in the first place, an abstract way of ignoring the finiteness of the means to arrive at an objective realization, as well as the difficulties presented by real complications. Therefore, this enthusiasm must face these real complications and operate with limited means in order to reach its objectives in a limited reality." Letter to Karl Marx, March 6, 1859.

4. Lasalle has been considered one of the forerunners of the opportunist tendency within the German workers' movement. From the beginning of the 1860s, as a consequence of the Austro-Italo-French war of 1859, Lasalle expounded a political position for the working-class movement which was adapted to the interests of Prussia and Bismarck. Lasalle's opportunism extended to fundamental political questions, and this brought about Marx's definitive break with him in 1862. But Lasalle's opportunistic political activities were precisely those he himself had condemned a few years

before in the above-mentioned letter. Political compromise and cunning constitute a great intellectual and moral flaw because they betray "a lack of confidence in moral ideas and in their limitless strength which exists in and for itself, as well as an exaggerated confidence in limited, precarious means."

5. F. Lasalle, letter to Karl Marx and Frederick Engels, May 27, 1859, in Mehring, *Aus dem literarischen,* and Freville, *Sur la littérature.*

6. Ibid.

*
7. A Kafka Hero:
Joseph K.

In this chapter, we intend to penetrate the rich and complex world of Franz Kafka through one of his central characters. Let us begin our journey hand in hand with one of the inhabitants of that world: Joseph K.

But let us first introduce our hero by answering the question: Who is Joseph K.? He is a functionary in a bank in Prague. We know nothing of his past, nor will we ever know anything about it; this is characteristic of Kafka's manner of presenting a central character. As soon as we become acquainted with Joseph K., we realize that his life slips by smoothly, without any abrupt changes, in his job as bank functionary, where he is in fact in his own element. All of a sudden, that gray, routine rhythm of his existence is unexpectedly broken. The cause of this break is apparently a banal, ordinary matter, which is described in a few words, the same words with which we are first introduced to K.: "Someone must have traduced Joseph K., for without having done anything wrong he was arrested one fine morning."[1] Convinced of his innocence, he tries to quickly settle this irksome and ridiculous matter, but a settlement, even one regarding such a banal case, cannot be effected without entering the inextricable mesh of the sordid judicial bureaucracy of Prague in the days of the Austro-Hungarian empire. The settlement, which logically seems to be at hand, becomes increasingly elusive the deeper the accused plunges into the bosom of the pervasive and obscure judicial organization.

One day a year later, two strangers appear before Joseph

K.'s home to carry out the sentence handed down by a court he has never been able to see. Taken to a deserted and abandoned quarry, in a very Kafkaesque atmosphere of phantasmagoria and realism, horror and irony, K. keeps asking himself, without wanting to admit that the legal process is coming to an end: "Was help at hand? Were there arguments in his favor that had been overlooked? Of course there must be. Logic is doubtless unshakable, but it cannot withstand a man who wants to go on living. Where was the Judge whom he had never seen? Where was the High Court, to which he had never penetrated?"[2] But by then one of the executioners is putting an end to his life by stabbing him twice in the heart with a butcher knife. And at that point Joseph K. becomes aware of the inhuman character of his death, although without knowing the reason for it. Perhaps because he has never been aware of the inhuman character of his own life. "With failing eyes K. could still see the two of them immediately before him, cheek leaning against cheek, watching the final act. 'Like a dog!' he said; it was as if the shame of it must outlive him."[3] With these words, with which the novel itself comes to an end, we leave K. dying a death unworthy of an existence which he had always regarded as authentic.

The novel in which this strange story unfolds is entitled *The Trial.* And in effect the entire novel shows us the trial of an accused man who, starting with an accusation whose particulars he never comes to know and which he regards as unfounded, is condemned by an invisible court, after having climbed the arduous, endless, and mysterious rungs of the judicial apparatus. This trial is not presented objectively, but is reflected in the main character through his growing concerns and anxieties, through the innumerable twists and turns of his fate. The novel is therefore also the process or course of a life, which starts from a banal matter that takes on an increasingly mysterious and dramatic significance, and ends by losing itself in the terrible dimension of death. The novel simply traces the movement between two deeds: one is trivial—the arrest of K. for no apparent reason, perhaps the result of an error—and the other is the death of the accused, who attempts to rescue the meaning of his death from the dimension of banality by characterizing it as a dog's death. Between these two events—K.'s detention and execution—there is a necessary, inexorable connection, which Joseph K. never recognizes. Hence his courageous efforts to halt the invisible machine which, with its invisible movements, is digging his grave.

The Trial is a work of only one dimension, monodic. One might say that its main character is not so much Joseph K. as the trial itself. In fact, everything we come across throughout the novel exists only in its relation to this one dimension. And Joseph K. himself, as we shall see, is a man who lives on only one level.

Franz Kafka, the author of the novel, was born on July 3, 1883. He received a degree in law and for several years was employed in a workers' accident insurance company. But his true aspiration was to find enough time to write. Thus he lived a double life, always longing—to no avail—to live only one life, his authentic one.

> I am employed in a social security office. Now then, these two professions can never be reconciled, or contented by being treated equally. The smallest bit of happiness in one is equivalent to a great misfortune in the other. If one evening I write something well, the next day I burn in the office and I can't do anything right. This coming and going becomes more harmful every day. In the office I fulfill my external obligations, but not my intimate obligations, and each unfulfilled intimate obligation becomes a source of endless misery.[4]

This disintegration of existence, which Kafka himself painfully experienced, becomes one of the keys to understanding the abstract fate of Joseph K., as we shall clarify later on.

In the midst of that distressing conflict between what he calls his external and intimate obligations, Kafka wrote some of his most important works: *Amerika, Metamorphosis,* and *The Trial* (the latter in 1914–1915). Three times he fell in love and every time he backed down from marriage, fearing that it would prevent him from meeting the demands of his literary work. This fear grew when his sickly nature became fully evident. His health declined after 1920. In 1923, love again burst into his life; this time he decided to proceed firmly and hopefully toward what he had previously regarded as a threat to his artistic privacy. But in the winter of 1923–1924 tuberculosis further eroded his weakened health and he died on June 3, 1924.

Kafka's works have met an insecure and strange fate. During his life few of them were published, and then not the most important ones. In the will he wrote in 1921, he asked that all his work be destroyed, without exception. Refusing to follow his desires, his intimate friend Max Brod began to publish, little by little, a number of Kafka's works, among them *The Trial* and the twelve notebooks, written between 1910 and 1923, which constitute his *Diaries.* The publication of these texts soon attracted attention in literary circles, but it was especially during and after World War II that his fame reached its zenith, transcending the limits of the small groups of Kafka admirers.

Interpretations of Kafka's world

Ever since his most important works were first published, Kafka has been the subject of the most diverse interpretations. The publication of his *Letter to His Father* gave impetus to a psychoanalytic interpretation. The entire work of this brilliant Czech writer was analyzed in the light of this letter, written in 1919, and it was considered a precious psychoanalytic windfall. This obscure, enigmatic, and complex writer became clear and transparent as his complexity was reduced, or narrowed, by taking him out of his social and historical context. The ambiguity of Kafka's relationship to his father was made to explain everything. This ambiguity certainly existed—and it was Kafka himself who brought it out into the open—but far from being the key to Kafka's world, the ambiguity itself demanded an explanation beyond a schematic application of the Oedipus complex. It is not a mere coincidence that Kafka himself, perhaps fearing such oversimplification, called attention to the limitations of psychoanalysis.

The attempts to see a religious structure in Kafka's work are exemplified, above all, in the biography by Max Brod. According to this interpretation, Kafka believed in an absolute world; the absolute exists, but there also exists an eternal misunderstanding between man and God. Max Brod cites few examples to support his thesis, and the few he does offer have to be twisted in order to infer a religious attitude on Kafka's part.

Existentialists are more successful in their analysis of Kafka, for they do not fail to underline the motifs in his work which find an echo, after his death, in existentialism: the theme of the individual who feels fortuitously "thrown" into the world; the theme of radical individuality; the isolation, insufficiency, and impotence inherent in the human condition, with the consequent and inevitable despair and anguish. But the theme which resounds most vigorously is the senselessness or absurdity of existence, a theme of central importance to existentialism. Kafka foreshadowed, in the field of literature, what Heidegger, Sartre, and Camus later postulated on the level of philosophy.

What about the Marxists? They can clarify what others consider enigmatic by placing Kafka in a determinate sociohistorical context and establishing a relationship between his work and his world outlook. Although this does not provide an explanation for everything in Kafka's world, it does open up horizons which make such an explanation possible. Some Marxists, however, have seen in Kafka only an expression of a decadent bourgeois world and, in condemning that world, have also condemned Kafka. They have fallen into the trap of abandoning Kafka's work to the bourgeoisie, as if Kafka belonged within the narrow framework of the bourgeois world. Kafka certainly expresses, in a brilliant and unique way, the decomposition of the bourgeois world, but his expression is such that the characters in his works seem to be saying to us: behold what men have made of themselves, how they dehumanize and degrade each other. It is also true that Kafka tends to regard this degradation or dehumanization from a timeless, abstract perspective, as we shall see. It will be enough, however, to discover the real foundations that support this world of illusion and nightmare to reveal the full critical power of Kafka's description of the bourgeois world, a critical description which leads to a rejection of a society which creates the kind of person typified by Joseph K.

But let us return to our first question: Who is Joseph K.?

Joseph K., or the abstraction of real man

The first thing that strikes the reader of *The Trial* is the name of its main character. Why are we only given the first letter of his last name? To the reader who is not familiar with Kafka's characters we can say that this technique is not limited to *The Trial*, and that in another of Kafka's novels, *The Castle*, the reduction of the name goes even further; the hero's full name is K. But such an answer begs the question. Let us remember that in *The Trial* almost all the other characters are referred to in the usual way: Mrs. Grubach, the landlady; Miss Bürstner, fellow boarder; the officers who arrest Joseph K.; his uncle; the lawyers to whom he goes for help; etc. Even characters who make brief appearances have names. Only the executioners are ironically called "gentlemen," as if to underline the total alienation among the accused and the accusation, the court, and the enforcers of the sentence.

Kafka wants to remind us, on every page of the book, that the fate of K. is not the fate of a privileged person; it is the fate of every man. On the other hand, he is not really a man of flesh and blood, as Unamuno would say, but an abstraction of real man; K.'s concrete and vital essence lies outside the scheme of social relations through which he is presented. He is first seen as a bank functionary—Kafka does not reveal any previous level to his existence—and then as an accused man, converted into a judicial *case*. Kafka presents his main character exclusively on that level. By refusing to call him by his full name, he emphasizes the abstract character of human existence when it loses itself, when real man relinquishes or is robbed of his concrete, vital content and becomes an abstraction to be expressed by a cypher or initial.

The abstract nature of the main character is manifested by the lack of individualization in Kafka's description of him. What do we know of his childhood or youth? Nothing. What do we know of K.'s life before or after work? Nothing. We only know his present, but it is a present restricted to two levels: his job and the judicial process.

With such a one-dimensional existence, real man is impoverished. K.'s life manifests a universality which is a caricature of true universality; it is one in which men recognize each other by their hollowness or depersonalization. Hegel would have called this universality formal or abstract. But this abstract being Kafka places before us is not an invention in the sense of being unrelated to reality. These human beings exist in reality, and Kafka drew his characters from reality. Because of this faithfulness to reality, we do not hesitate to call Kafka a realist, although some think that his proper domain is one of unreality, strangeness, and paradox. In fact, men exist in reality whose lives are so hollow and depersonalized that they move on the same level of abstract universality or formal commonality as Joseph K.

The bureaucratic world of Joseph K.

The men who live on that level, with the consequent loss or mutilation of real existence, are those who live buried in the world of bureaucracy, a world in which the formal and abstract levels smother all personal and vital impulses. In this impersonal world, in which all real human relationships vanish, Joseph K. feels at home, for he is unable to understand to what extent that world has turned against him and against all human beings. But in this formal and formalized world a crack appears, which at first seems insignificant but which becomes deeper and deeper. Joseph K. begins to feel threatened; the security he had managed to find in his bureaucratic world begins to crack; it ceases to give him support, leaving him up in the air without a hold on reality, and K. will end up by being devoured by the judicial variety of bureaucracy. Joseph K., who was not a human character to begin with, but an abstraction of human characters, finds himself cast into a judicial mesh from which there is no escape.

We were speaking previously of Kafka's faithfulness to reality. And in fact, he has simply described certain real human relationships, characteristic of capitalist society in general, in the particular form that these relationships took under the reactionary Austro-Hungarian empire of his time. These relationships are found in one form or another in every capitalist state, and they can occur even in socialist states where a false conception of centralization and democracy weakens the relationship between officials and the people.

Marx pointed out the corrosive role of bureaucratism in his criticism of Hegel's political philosophy and of the important role Hegel assigned to bureaucracy as the embodiment of the lofty goals of the state. In his *Contribution to the Critique of Hegel's Philosophy of Right,* Marx pointed out the falsity of that attempt at a defense of universality: according to Marx, bureaucracy becomes a particular interest within the state. Hegel identified the interests of the state with those of the bureaucracy; in doing this, he inverted the relationship between the formal and the material, the abstract and the concrete, the real and the unreal. "The real being," declared Marx, "is treated according to its bureaucratic being, its unreal being." It is this treatment of concrete human beings according to their abstract being, their unreality, that is found in Kafka. Thus in *The Trial,* real man is turned into a judicial "case," treated according to his abstract being, by taking away from him all those human attributes which are of no interest insofar as he is a judicial "case."

Marx pointed out another characteristic of bureaucracy which is sharply portrayed in Kafka's novel: its secrecy, its air of mystery. Joseph K. never gets to know what he is accused of. Nor does anybody else. The bank employees he comes in contact with have no information to give him. "We are humble subordinates who can scarcely find our way through a legal document," they tell him.[5] The accused keeps asking questions, but he runs into insurmountable walls. "What authority is conducting these proceedings? Are you officers of the law?" But the officers repel any intrusion into their domain and limit themselves to answers such as: "You are under arrest, certainly, more than that I do not know."[6]

Secrecy is what assures the rigidity of that inscrutable wall. And even if occasionally a crack lets in some light, the wall goes on for as far as the eye can see. "The ranks of officials in this judiciary system mounted endlessly, so that not even the initiated could survey the hierarchy as a whole. And the proceedings of the Courts were generally kept secret from subordinate officials, consequently they could hardly ever quite follow in their further progress the cases on which they had worked."[7]

What Kafka says about judicial bureaucracy was pointed out by Marx as characteristic of the bureaucracy of an oppressive state. "The bureaucracy," he said, "keeps in its possession the essence of the state." Now then, where there is private property there is also a tendency to erect walls around possessions; the bureaucracy fences in its domain, shuts itself in, and tries to keep out everything which in its opinion is an unwarranted intrusion into its territory. It never opens itself outward or downward, but it is always well disposed toward those higher up in the bureaucratic hierarchy. Secrecy defends the bureaucrat against any incursions into his sacred precinct. That is precisely why Marx said that "the general spirit of bureaucracy is one of secrecy and mystery."

Kafka presents Joseph K. in an endless and fruitless struggle to uncover this mystery, but K. never succeeds in breaking through the wall surrounding the judicial bureaucracy. Everything conspires to strengthen that wall: the silence of the officials, the secret proceedings, the impenetrable language of the law books, the subtleties of protocol, etc. Mystery opens an unfathomable chasm between accuser and accused, between law and concrete facts; and this mystery mystifies all relationships.

The world of the absurd

By losing their transparency, human relationships become irrational, unreal, and absurd. It is clear why Albert Camus saw in Kafka's work a confirmation of his own philosophy of the absurd. He felt that Kafka corroborated his conception of the absurd character of our existence: Is there any logic in being persecuted and condemned by people one has never seen, for reasons that are never made clear? And is there any sense in this struggle that leads only to failure?

Just as we cannot criticize Kafka for showing us the unreal, abstract, and bureaucratic existence of man, but only for presenting it in an abstract and timeless manner—that is, without revealing the real roots of that abstract existence— neither can we criticize him for revealing the irrationality and absurdity of human existence. Kafka did not invent the absurd and irrational nature of human relationships—their irrationality exists in real life. Kafka helps us see that irrationality by showing us the absurdity in the mysteriousness of bureaucracy and in the sentence meted out to K. by unknown judges for an unspecified crime, as well as the absurd, because futile, nature of K.'s struggle to break through the inexorable walls which narrow or besiege his existence. All this is absurd, as are many other elements of capitalist society: the fact that the worker, the creator of riches, is impoverished, and those who do not create riches, the capitalists, become richer; the fact that things acquire so much power that they end up by dominating man; and so on.

At other times in history certain natural phenomena have seemed irrational which are today perfectly clear to us, and it was left up to religion or magic to endow them with a sense which the light of reason had not been able to discern. However, the absurd or irrational does not exist by itself, but only in connection with a phenomenon that cannot be integrated in a context or totality which could explain it. When it is said that Kafka's world is the world of the absurd, what relationship is established between the absurd and the real or rational? The events Kafka describes pose a number of questions: Why does K. act the way he does? What is the reason for this invisible trial? Everything is or seems to be real, and yet it makes no sense to us. If we try to make sense of what happens on the level of appearances, we will fail, and therein lies the absurdity. When one is unable to explain events that take place in real life, one must make their absurdity absolute, or look for their meaning on an eternal, transcendental level: this is what Max Brod attempted. Thus the key to K.'s behavior is sought outside of the real, concrete world, struggling to make sense of human absurdity by appealing to a superhuman logos. According to this interpretation of Kafka, absurdity and reason both exist, but in different worlds: the former in the human world, the latter in a divine and transcendental world.

Human alienation and absurdity

It is now more than a century since Marx pointed out the mystified, irrational, or absurd nature human relationships acquire when they adopt the form of relationships among things. Marx also showed, starting in *The Economic and Philosophic Manuscripts of 1844,* that we must look for the source of these relationships in man himself, in specific social systems. We have known since then that the cause of human absurdity lies in the alienation of man, which appears when work, the very essence of man, far from affirming him, reifies or dehumanizes him. This real, economic alienation manifests itself on the level of political or social relations as the division of concrete man into an individual and citizen who leads a double life: public and private. The relationship between individual and citizen is an external one. The individual does not recognize himself in the community. When he acts collectively, as a member of the state, he makes an abstraction out of his real existence. True individuality and true universality are thus found in an insoluble contradiction, and a solution is sought in the sacrifice of one to the other. Thus Joseph K., for example, has sacrificed his individuality to the false or formal universality of his bureaucratic role. His life acquires an irrational and absurd character, but the roots of his condition are to be found in an alienated human world.

Absurdity and rationality exist, therefore, not in two separate worlds—human and superhuman, respectively—but in the same human world; however, they exist on separate levels. Human absurdity is only the phenomenological aspect, the organized appearance of a deeper reality. Absurdity and irrationality are the masks of an occult rationality, which has been turned against man, a rationality which in fact exists on the level of specific concrete, socioeconomic human relations.

The alienated existence of Joseph K.

Returning to K., we see that he lives a characteristically alienated life. We have said that alienation is manifest in all real human beings as the division of life into private and public, individual and universal sectors. Real man is thus converted into a veritable battlefield, especially as long as he refuses to let what is truly personal be dissolved in an abstract universality, that is, as long as he refuses to sacrifice his specifically human qualities to an empty or formal universality with which he does not identify. The process of alienation reaches its culmination when all awareness of the schism is lost, that is, when the process of reification is so advanced that all true individuality is erased. Man's existence is then no more than an abstraction of his real essence, so that it becomes depersonalized and unreal.

Joseph K. embodies this culminating point of human alienation. K. has reached such an extreme of alienation that he no longer experiences his life as fragmented or torn. He no longer notices a conflict or schism between his private and public life because he no longer has a private life. His entire being consists of his role as functionary. Nothing exists, nothing interests him beyond this one dimension. His alienation is so profound that he feels strong or "prepared" only in his abstract, empty, bureaucratic capacity; in other words, he identifies with his alienation. Like a man condemned to always seeing himself reflected in a concave mirror, he only recognizes himself when he sees his deformed image. Furthermore, he feels secure only in his alienated self. The bank is for Joseph K. the only solid ground. When he confronts the new and unexpected situation presented by the trial, he feels weak, insecure, unstable. The rupture of his daily world undermines the ground he walks on. Joseph K. is not prepared to confront a new situation with the decisiveness and self-assurance with which he deals with events that fall within the framework of his alienated existence.

> But one is so unprepared. In the Bank, for instance, I am always prepared, nothing of that kind could possibly happen to me there, I have my own attendant, the general telephone and the office telephone stand before me on my desk, people keep coming in to see me, clients and clerks, and above all, my mind is always on my work and so kept on the alert, it would be an actual pleasure to me if a situation like that cropped up in the Bank.[8]

Joseph K., bank functionary, is in his own element in the bank and therefore feels secure there; he never loses his "presence of spirit." Precisely because he has reduced his existence to an abstract dimension, he can move within it with firmness and self-assurance, since all life and all individuality is excluded from it. His existence becomes problematical only when he is shaken by a unique event which affects not his abstract, bureaucratic self, but his real, individual self. Joseph K. cannot integrate this event into his abstract universal existence, and thus his bitter recognition of a terrible truth: "One is so unprepared." In effect, K.'s monochromatic and one-dimensional life must come to grips with an unexpected event, his indictment. From that moment he must divide his attention between his job and his attempts to defend himself. His life is no longer entirely taken up by his role as bank functionary; something begins to develop outside of it, which starts as a trivial event occupying an empty hole in his vacuous existence, but ends by taking up his whole life. Moreover, the sphere in which he had felt secure becomes an obstacle to the resolution of something he must resolve as an individual, outside his bank life.

One might expect that Joseph K., to the extent that he reduces the time he devotes to his job and increases the time he dedicates to solving something which affects him personally, would become conscious of the split in his existence and take refuge in the sanctum of his private life. But Kafka had more sense than to look for a solution—so typical of bourgeois individualism—in a mere change of levels; it is not a matter of sacrificing the individual to the general or vice versa. Joseph K., in confronting a problem which affects him as an individual, does nothing more than make clear the extent to which he is imprisoned by his alienation. For him, the abstract general sphere in which his bureaucratic self lives continues to be his real existence, and the judicial proceedings appear to him as a disturbance, albeit an increasingly grave one, of that existence. The need to defend himself—to extirpate himself from his abstract world—disgusts and embitters him. "Every hour that he spent away from the Bank was a trial to him; true, he was by no means able to make the best use of his office hours as once he had done, he wasted much time in the merest pretense of doing real work, but that only made him worry the more when he was not at his desk."[9]

Marx has pointed out that one of the forms of the alienation of labor takes place in the act of work itself, in the worker's relationship to himself under the conditions of alienated labor. Work appears then as something external which mortifies and negates him, which does not form part of his essence. Thus the worker feels stifled because he does not develop his physical and spiritual faculties in work. Joseph K. leads such an alienated life that he cannot have a truly human relationship with himself, and in that sense, objectively, his bank activities are as external to him as manual labor is to the factory worker. However, subjectively, far from feeling oppressed, he takes pleasure in his alienated existence as officer of a bank, for he sees it as his real life.

Kafka describes K.'s fate without giving us a key to its understanding. Joseph K.'s complacency with his alienated existence is precisely what seals his bitter fate at a point in his life when a crack develops in the wall of alienation through which he might have gained his personality. The world K. is forced by circumstance to deal with is the exact opposite of the world he feels firm and safe in. It is a world in which every injustice is permitted, a corrupt and mercenary world, in which "innocent persons are accused of guilt, and senseless proceedings are put in motion against them."[10] That is the way Joseph K. sees it. But what he does not see is that this world—in which the bureaucratic spirit appears in a more subtle form—is only a part of the alienated world in which he lives his life as bank employee. Therefore he wages a struggle against this unjust world without breaking with his abstract, impersonal life, a life he continues to regard as authentic. And not only does he not break with it; he tries to defend it in his struggle. That is why the time he spends in his self-defense is, in his view, time that has been robbed from his essential activities. He wages this struggle against abstraction, but he does so as an abstract individual. The problem is that the bureaucrat knows no other form of community than this abstract community which is based on the deprivation of truly human qualities; that is why Joseph K. decides to carry on his defense by "putting himself completely in the power of the Court."[11]

The futile struggle of Joseph K.

What is the nature of the struggle Joseph K. wages against a powerful judicial bureaucracy which constantly strengthens its grip on him? It is a struggle which does not go beyond a verbal protest against the judicial proceedings or an attempt to reach higher officials who might favorably influence the outcome of his case; it is a futile struggle, which cannot prevent a verdict of guilty and a sentence of death.

Kafka shows us the pointlessness, absurdity, and failure of

the struggle K. wages as an individual against the organized injustice of judicial bureaucracy. He depends exclusively on his own resources, and that is the reason for his impotence. Because he knows no other form of community than the formal and empty bureaucratic one, he is unable to make his struggle part of a collective struggle, and he undertakes a futile and solitary campaign.

Kafka shows us the sterility of individual struggles, but there is no other recourse in his world. For that fight to be fruitful, it would have to be directed against the socio-economic structure which makes possible both K.'s alienated existence and the judicial organization which condemns him. That is, in an alienated world, the struggle is sterile as long as it does not express a consciousness of the socioeconomic roots of alienation, and as long as it does not take the form of practical collective action to change those socioeconomic conditions.

Individual and community in Kafka's world

Kafka was aware of the need to resolve the principal problem: the question of the relationship between individual and community. *The Trial* shows that he was aware not only of the problem but also of the falseness of some attempts at solving it. But he did not see—could not see from his vantage point—the real solution to a problem as old as man himself.

Joseph K., with his abstract universality, his bureaucratic existence in which the personal is absorbed by the general, embodies those human relationships in which true individuality disappears. By describing the depersonalized existence of Joseph K., Kafka exposed and unequivocally condemned that false community so characteristic of capitalist society. But Joseph K., because of his sterile solitary struggle and his failure to involve himself in a true community, is also the embodiment of a false individuality.

Kafka thus shows the falseness of two equally one-sided positions: that of the formal community—expressed by the abstract, bureaucratic existence of K.—and that of abstract individuality, the individuality of an isolated, self-involved man—expressed by the failure of K.'s struggle. One cannot confront bureaucracy, which is an expression of total alienation, in isolation. Joseph K. establishes by his death the futility of such a solitary struggle.

The image of Kafka as a poet of loneliness is derived from an exaggerated and farfetched identification of Kafka with Kierkegaard, a similarity which does not really exist, although some passages from Kafka's *Diaries,* if incompletely understood, might give that impression. Let us not forget, in this regard, that Kafka said in those same diaries that "being alone is nothing but a series of punishments." Kafka felt the need for a true community of men, and he denounced vigorously the inhuman character of that abstract community which is bought at the price of total depersonalization. But by not placing the question of the relationship between individual and community in a concrete, socio-historical context, he left the solution to this problem up in the air. He saw a determinate human condition—the alienation of man, the domination of things over man—outside of a social and historical context, and by doing so he precluded the possibility of finding the social forces which are called by history to the task of putting an end to the reification of human existence.

This does not mean that Kafka was impervious to social questions. He saw quite clearly, for example, the dehumanizing character of capitalist social relations. "Capitalism," he once said, "is a system of relations of dependency, reaching without from the inside, within from the outside, from top to bottom, from bottom to top. Everything is organized hierarchically, everything is in fetters. Capitalism is a state of the world and a state of the soul." And referring to the Taylor system, or to assembly-line production, he said, "We are more like a thing, an object, than a living being."

Kafka's sympathy for the oppressed is always clear, as well as his sympathy for those under capitalism who see their personalities mutilated in jobs which are totally external to them. Kafka himself, as we have seen, experienced the torture which results from the schism between one's real personality and the job which negates it. On the other hand, by working in a workers' accident insurance company he obtained a very clear picture of social injustices, and became familiar with the suffering engendered by the bureaucratic machine. But Kafka saw the oppressed only as men overwhelmed by misery, not as a social force capable of overthrowing that "system of dependencies" in which suffering proliferates. He regarded dehumanization—and the pain it engenders—as a force beyond the control of man, one which cannot be uprooted by changing social relations. As a result, he was skeptical about revolutionary attempts to change the world.

Kafka saw the negative but was not able to go beyond it. It is enough to negate this negativity to reveal all that is positive and fruitful in Kafka's work. We must establish a relationship between Kafka's work and reality; we will then see that the irrational, absurd, and unjust world he depicts does indeed exist, but in the framework of historically determined human relations. And although Kafka did not point out the roots of that inhuman world, nor the means by which to put an end to it, it is clear that by describing it his work entails a profound criticism of it. Those who see Kafka's work on an ahistorical level, as a defense of the absurd or irrational for its own sake, are in fact prolonging the kind of abstraction Kafka himself fought against and are helping to close the way to a solution of the problem Kafka dealt with, which is also a fundamental problem of our time: the integration of the individual in society, the union of true community and true individuality.

Notes

1. Franz Kafka, *The Trial* (New York: Random House, 1969), p. 3.
2. Ibid., p. 286.
3. Ibid.
4. Franz Kafka, *Diaries* (New York: Schocken Books, 1965).

5. Kafka, *The Trial*, p. 9.
6. Ibid., p. 17.
7. Ibid., p. 149.
8. Ibid., pp. 26-27.
9. Ibid., p. 248.
10. Ibid., p. 57.
11. Ibid., p. 166.

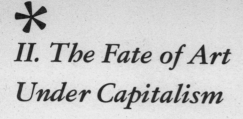

II. The Fate of Art Under Capitalism

"Capitalist production is hostile to
certain branches of spiritual production,
for example, art and poetry."
Karl Marx,
Theories of Surplus Value

8. *The Hostility of Capitalist Production to Art*

Throughout his works, Marx repeatedly dealt with the relationship between art and capitalism. Since the aesthetic dimension was for him an essential sphere of human existence, he was naturally concerned with the fate of art—the manifestation of man's creative faculties—in capitalist society. After exposing the exploitative core of material production under capitalism, he noted that such production "is hostile to certain branches of spiritual production, for example, art and poetry."[1]

In *Theories of Surplus Value* Marx underlined the hostility of capitalism to art in order to prove to Storch, a now forgotten economist of the first decades of the nineteenth century, that the relationship between material production and intellectual production is not as simple as he imagined. Connected as both types of production are to specific forms of social organization, Marx held that material production under capitalist conditions not only does not favor the development of art, but positively hinders it. A more developed form of material production does not necessarily entail a superior art; and if artistic creation flourishes in certain cases, it is not because of capitalist material production, but in spite of it. "It opens the way," Marx adds ironically, "to the illusion of the French in the eighteenth century which has been so beautifully satirised by Lessing. Because we are further ahead than the ancients in mechanics, etc., why shouldn't we be able to make an epic too? And the *Henriade* in place of the *Iliad!*"[2]

In the same work, Marx pointed out the opposition between art and capitalism, but he did not tell us what that opposition consists of or whether, taking into account the character of capitalist production, the opposition is of an essential or inessential nature. Nor did he clarify up to what point that opposition either limits artistic development or is unable to prevent great art from flourishing, even in the unfavorable conditions in which the artist works under capitalism.

However, these questions have answers, although we may not find them explicitly formulated in the work of Marx. We can find these answers ourselves and venture to expound on them in Marx's name, having first gleaned from his various works his comments on the relationship between art and the economy, the essence of capitalist production, the connection between production and consumption, the opposition between creative labor and alienated labor, and the relationship between art and labor.

On the basis of Marx's writings, we shall try to explain in the following pages the origin and essence of the hostility of capitalism to art. But before dealing with this question, we must discard two conceptions regarding the relationship between capitalist production and artistic production which might hide the real nature of the opposition between art and capitalism. These two conceptions make the following assertions: (1) that the above-mentioned opposition is a manifestation of the law, developed by Marx, of the uneven development of artistic production and material production; and (2) that this opposition is ideological: between the ideology of the artist and the ideology of capitalism.

The law of the uneven development of art and economy

Pointing out that capitalist production is hostile to intellectual production, Marx underlined that this is particularly true with regard to art. That implies that this hostility is not expressed with the same vigor in all branches of intellectual production. We can also add, on the basis of comments by the founders of Marxism, that not only is capitalist material production not equally hostile to the various sectors of intellectual production, but that it spares some sectors from this hostility, and even favors some forms of intellectual production. We have in mind the sciences, particularly the natural sciences, which grow and develop in the context of capitalist relations of production. Science, according to Marx, is the intellectual power behind the growth of production, the necessary condition of its development; material production in turn is a determining factor in scientific progress. The demands of capitalist production have provided a decisive stimulus to scientific development. We may say that the nature of modern science is closely related to the practical problems posed by the transformation of nature in the period of the birth and ascendancy of capitalism. We can see then that a branch of intellectual production, science, progresses as a result of the development of material production. The more developed material production is, the higher the degree of scientific development, that is, the deeper the understanding of the workings of nature. Science develops side by side with production, and if there is a discrepancy between them, it is not as marked as it would be in other branches of intellectual production. The congruence is here greater because of the close relationship between science and production.

Art and literature do not respond directly to the demands of material production. Production does not directly determine the content or form of a work of art; nor does production fix the general direction of artistic development or determine whether art will flourish in a given society. We can establish a relationship between the advances made by chemistry in the nineteenth century and the demands of the textile industry, or between the enormous progress of nuclear physics in our time with both the peaceful and warlike applications of nuclear energy. But we cannot establish a direct connection, without falling into the kind of gross simplification Engels criticized, between the romanticism of the early nineteenth century and the conditions of production during that time, or between the emergence of abstract art in our time and contemporary material production.

This is not to say that art has nothing to do with the productive forces; in the last analysis, these forces do have their effect. But although intellectual development is ultimately connected to the economic base, art and literature form part of a complex social totality within which they are intricately connected, not only with the economic base but also with other branches of the ideological superstructure. The result is that art and literature, while they are still conditioned by the economy, enjoy a relative autonomy, much broader than the autonomy of science. The degree of that autonomy varies directly with the number of intermediary connecting links between art and the economic base; consequently, the further removed intellectual production is from material production, the greater the discrepancy between artistic development and economic development. Such a discrepancy can reach the extreme represented by Greek art, which developed within a society characterized by a low level of productive forces.

The reason for this uneven development, which Marx illustrated not only with Greek art but also with Shakespeare, should be sought not in the productive forces but in the nature of the mediations or intermediary links between the base and the superstructure. Among the mediations Marx pointed to with reference to Greek art are a particular concept of nature, and the social relations which by encouraging fantasy gave birth to Greek mythology, "the arsenal and fertile ground" of the art of ancient Greece.

For the same reasons that material production in ancient Greek society did not by itself determine the greatness of Greek art, we should not try to find in capitalist production the causes of either the flourishing or decadence which art has manifested in capitalist society. Here too, the flourishing or decadence of art can only be explained by the particular nature of the mediations between economy and art.

The hostility Marx perceived between capitalist production and art establishes a negative relation between material and artistic production; but, in this case, the negativity is not the result of the specific types of mediations which explain the uneven development of art and economy, but rather the result of the conditions of capitalist production itself. We do not find such negativity in precapitalist conditions of production, such as those of Greek society.

According to the law of the uneven development of art and economy, in an economically inferior society art can flourish to a degree not found in a society with a more highly developed economy. Marx's example of Greek art is quite eloquent in this respect. In no precapitalist society was material production in principle hostile to art, not even at its very origins in primitive society, when art was very directly connected to material production. In principle, the hostility of material production to art is only found under capitalism. According to Marx's thesis, capitalism is by its very essence a socioeconomic formation alien and opposed to art.

When in noncapitalist societies material production entered into a contradiction with artistic production, this opposition did not have an essential character; that is, it was not rooted directly in the nature of their economic organization, but in the complex network of intermediary steps linking art to the economic base.

When Marx asserted that capitalist production is hostile to art, that hostility could be falsely interpreted as simply a manifestation of the law of the uneven development of art and economy; however, the phenomenon is not in any way a manifestation of this law. In fact, the law as expounded by Marx does not postulate that there are specific types of material production which are in themselves hostile or favorable to art; nor does the law specify the conditions under which a particular form of production can influence art one way or another. The only thing we can infer from the law is that, since art enjoys a relative autonomy, it is possible for art to have a degree of development either higher or lower than that of the socioeconomic forces, whatever the predominant type of material production. The thesis of the hostility of capitalism to art establishes a direct relationship between the economy and art; moreover, it proposes that this relationship is negative, that is, that capitalist production, by its very essence, is unfavorable to art.

While this last thesis confirms the law of the uneven development of art and the economy—for example, a superior form of production may exist alongside an inferior art—it seems to be an exception to that law, inasmuch as the discrepancy in the stages of development has its roots in the very character of material production, which would seem to dissipate the relative autonomy of art with regard to its economic base. However, reality has shown us in the past few centuries that despite the fact that capitalist material production is in principle hostile to art, art has nevertheless flourished (Balzac, Tolstoy, Whitman, Poe, Cézanne, etc.) and flourishes today (Mann, Faulkner, Picasso, Chaplin, etc.) under capitalism. This does not mean that art has developed in a way that corresponds to a superior form of production. On the contrary, the uneven development of art with regard to production continues to exist under capitalism because, as we shall see later on, while it is true that art flourishes even when capitalist production is at the height of its powers, it does not flourish on account of the economy, but in spite of it. The fact that such art could exist does not cancel the contradiction between material and artistic production, since we are not dealing here with a transitory, inessential contradiction which can be overcome within the system by means of a superficial modification of the character of capitalist production. On the contrary, we are dealing with an *essential* contradiction; and art, as we shall see, flourishes only to the extent it can elude the grip of capitalist production.

Notes

1. Karl Marx, *Theories of Surplus Value* (Moscow: Progress Publishers, 1963), Part I, p. 285.
2. Ibid.

9. The Artist and Bourgeois Society

Up to now the contradiction between art and capitalism has been presented as an objective contradiction which has its roots in the very nature of capitalist material production, that is, independent of the attitudes of the artist toward capitalist social relations, and irrespective of the ideology embodied in his work or the aesthetic tendencies it reveals. The hostility of capitalism to art we have been dealing with exists insofar as artistic production falls under the laws of capitalist production. What is decisive here is not the attitude of the artist as expressed in his work, but the fact that his creation is subject to the general laws of material production. Later on we shall see what means are open to the contemporary artist through which to escape the domination of those laws, and what price he must pay when he tries to elude them.

This essential, objective contradiction, which exists independent of the artist's attitude, must not be confused with the contradiction expressed by the divorce of the creative artist from bourgeois society, although it bears a certain relationship to it. This contradiction is manifest in the fact that artists do not find their artistic themes in bourgeois reality, or in other words they do not consider it a subject worthy of art. The artist feels no solidarity with the human and social relations spawned by the capitalist system and refuses to integrate his work into that society. He regards that reality as fundamentally hostile to art; he perceives this hostility not insofar as his work is treated as a commodity or thing, but to the extent that human relations, under the domination of the laws of capitalist production and subject to a real and effective alienation, are dehumanized or banalized. Although the artist is not conscious of the alienated character of human existence in the context of capitalist relations, and even less of their socioeconomic roots, he nevertheless notices its vulgarity, its reification; the art which he then creates expresses his nonconformity with, and even his rebellion against, this bourgeois world.

The relationship between the artist and bourgeois society has not always been this way, of course. When the bourgeoisie was an incipient or ascendant social force, it promoted certain aspirations and ideas which were also expressed by artists. Art made its contribution in the struggle against the old feudal order, against the moribund values which the bourgeoisie wanted to abolish. During the Renaissance and in the series of bourgeois revolutions in the seventeenth and eighteenth centuries, art was a spiritual weapon in the hands of the bourgeoisie. By means of a change of artistic themes and the introduction of new ones, art helped to debunk a decrepit world and exalt a new one. In Dutch painting, the simple act of painting a still life or the interior of a house, giving these themes an aesthetic status which up to then they had not had, fulfilled the function of devaluating the pompous, heroic, solemn, or transcendental themes associated with an aristocratic, feudal, and absolutist world. In the Renaissance, Da Vinci's conception of painting as a means of interpreting all of reality, competing in this task with science, expressed the attitude of the Renaissance bourgeois who desired to know nature in order to dominate it, who was conscious of being not a mere serf of God, but master of the world. In the era just before the explosion of the bourgeois revolution in France, the crusade against rococo art and the exaltation of the virtues of the bourgeois family in the works of Greuze or Chardin, formed part of the political and social movement against the *ancien régime.* In the eighteenth century, Diderot was aware of the need to associate a new way of portraying reality in art—realism—and the aspirations of the bourgeoisie, in opposition to the alliance that existed between rococo art and the decadent aristocracy of that time. In order to affirm the new moral values and express the heroic popular vitality of the bourgeois revolution, art returned to classicism, but impregnated it with a new ideological content. The artist, in solidarity with the values and ideals of the bourgeoisie and within the framework of a new classicism, emphasized drawing over painting (thus simultaneously emphasizing puritan simplicity and the heroic revolutionary grandeur) while also avoiding color, lest his work become, in contradiction to revolutionary puritanism, a banquet for the senses or a feast for the eyes, as was the case with rococo art.

But this relative harmony between art and the ideals of bourgeois society could last only as long as the new social relations did not reveal their most vital and profound contradictions, and as long as the new social class in power presented itself not as a particular class, but as the representative of all the people. To the extent that the dream of an enlightened and rational society was dissipated, the supposedly universal reason which was to be its foundation was revealed as a particular class reason which came into conflict with the interests of the rest of society.

Neoclassicism was transformed into an official, cold, and wizened art, intended to serve the ideals of the bourgeoisie at the expense of life, of reality itself; reality was embellished and idealized, its rough edges softened. The academicism of the nineteenth century attempted to prolong, each time more languidly, this scuttling of life and ever increasing idealization of reality.

From the start of the nineteenth century, artists began to develop an awareness that their work could be saved only by breaking with those artistic tendencies, such as neoclassicism, which everywhere stifled naturalness and spontaneity, and which degenerated into a bourgeois academicism. At the same time, artists became conscious of the fact that the prevailing social reality was unacceptable, and took refuge in art as the purest and most adequate means by which to affirm their liberty and individuality in the face of that reality.

Romanticism expressed this alienation of artists from

bourgeois reality. The romantic artist expressed both an attitude of disenchantment with the reality around him and a search for roots outside that reality. He rebelled against the present by taking refuge in the past and by projecting himself into the future. He rebelled against reason because reason was used to justify reality. He exalted his individuality, the unrestrained freedom of his ego, or his radical isolation, thus expressing his opposition to the prosaic and banal reality which harassed his existence. With capitalism, everything became abstract and impersonal, and the romantic, by unleashing an internal subjective volcano, attempted to reclaim everything vital or personal. In both its elitist and popular forms, romanticism expressed an antibourgeois attitude. For the first time, artists regarded social reality—capitalist social relations—as a world hostile to art. Starting with romanticism, through the "art for art's sake" theory, the aestheticism of Keats or Shelley, and the movements which branched out from impressionism, art and capitalism have been divorced.

For a long time, the artist has refused to accept the scale of values offered by the bourgeoisie, taking refuge instead in creative individuality, making his language hermetic, as a means of separating himself from the social reality around him. However, in their zeal to deny that reality, artists have also denied the need to reflect it and change it. They have exalted a radical subjectivity in order to defend themselves from the pressures of bourgeois reality.

When in the middle of the nineteenth century artists such as Balzac or Stendhal returned to reality, they did not let themselves be absorbed by it. In an era of profound social conflicts, characterized by an increasing political and social sensibility, a need developed for a greater understanding of human beings, the motivations for their actions, and the paths they take in carrying out those actions; the human world, in which economic and social factors were becoming increasingly decisive, was observed, described, and evaluated. Realism adopted a critical tone with regard to a social reality in which the power of money had become preeminent.

Although art focused once again on reality, and although

its criticisms did not undermine the foundations of bourgeois reality, art continued to define itself, throughout the nineteenth and part of the twentieth century, by the fundamental principle of romanticism: bourgeois life does not deserve to be exalted.

Since the time of the French revolution—more precisely, since the romantic movement—the bourgeoisie has not been able to count on art of any importance being in sympathy with its class values and ideals. Art which is properly speaking bourgeois, at the service of bourgeois interests, is the anemic prolongation of a formerly vital classicism which became bourgeois academicism, at times idealizing reality by means of a rigid mythology, and at times attempting to reflect objective reality with such attention to detail, with such objectivism, that the artist's interpretation—and his imagination—are made irrelevant, thus dissipating both reality and the subjectivity of the artist. Thus when bourgeois academic art invokes its faithfulness to reality, it is simply trying to justify and idealize bourgeois life as the proper concern of art, which romantic, aestheticist, critical realist, and revolutionary artists reject.

Once capitalist society becomes divided by its fundamental contradictions, the human relationships developed within its framework become impersonalized and take on the appearance of relations among things; the artist, a spiritually rich human being, cannot then be in harmony with a reality which is itself dehumanized. He therefore becomes rootless, a bohemian or a revolutionary, but he can no longer sing the praises of bourgeois reality. Capitalism appears to the artist as a hostile world, because, inasmuch as the artist is a creator of a world designed precisely to manifest the human presence in things, capitalism is an inhuman world not worthy of artistic creation. Therefore, the artist cannot create in harmony with that world; he must create in opposition to it if he is to save himself and his art. The escapism, criticism, or protest revealed in works of art are the means by which artists assert their nonconformity with a dehumanized world, and thus safeguard their creative freedom.

10. The Socio-Historical Nature of the Relationship Between Artist and Public

Our artists live in a specific society: bourgeois society. In that society they maintain concrete, effective relationships with other human beings; they are part of a specific social organization. This means that unless they are content with an illusory, merely subjective freedom, their creative freedom cannot be established outside of their relationships with others and outside of the real, effective relationships characteristic of bourgeois society. As Lenin said, it is not possible to live in a society and be free of it. What is the relationship in capitalist society between creative freedom and the need to enter into a relationship with others, with the public? The artist is a human being who feels an inner need to create; the very meaning of his life resides in the realization of his essential powers in an artistic object. The channeling of his physical and spiritual energies in any direction opposed or alien to his real essence represents a mutilation of his existence. But the artist is a member of a particular society, and he must create and subsist within the range of possibilities offered by that society. In order not to deflect his essential powers from their true course, creative activity must be the artist's means of developing his personality, but it must also be his means of subsistence. His work must ensure his physical survival at the same time that it makes possible the realization of his creative forces.

The material living conditions of artists reveal both the nature of their relationship to the consumer (the public) and the position of the work of art within the given hierarchy of social relations. This in turn is determined by the stage of development of material production and by the relationships which people contract, independent of their will, in the course of the development of material production.

In ancient Greek society, the artist created for the community, for the city-state; there was, strictly speaking, no such thing as a private client and therefore no such thing as producing for a free market. The city-state (*polis*) was a community of free men in which physical labor was considered the primary task of slaves. Freedom had a concrete class content; however, within the limits imposed by its foundation on slavery, a certain harmony existed between individual and community. The slave-democracy of Athens was an attempt to organize individuals in a social community, ruled by a law or reason that transcended those individuals, but which was created by them. There was no greater honor for the Athenian citizen than to be a member of the *polis;* and it was considered a social aberration to place personal interests above those of the community. Aristotle, contemptuous of the ethic of individualism which attempted to place itself above the social ethic, said that he who seeks individual self-sufficiency wants to live like a god, but will in fact live like an animal.

The artist too, inasmuch as he was a member of the *polis,* thought that only in his capacity as citizen at the service of the *polis* could he develop his creative potential. The city-state for its part did not consider art to be either a superfluous activity or a means to material wealth, but rather a means of educating men in conformity with the ideals of the community. The character of artistic production was determined by that of material production. In ancient Greece, as Marx says, man was "always the goal of production," as opposed to the bourgeois world, where "production is the goal of man, and wealth [in the sense of exchange value] is the goal of production."

The art of ancient Greece was nourished by its faith in beauty and the sublimity of the free man, citizen of the *polis.*

(As Sophocles wrote in *Antigone:* "There are in nature many divine forces, but there is nothing stronger than man.") This man, a free citizen, circumscribed by the boundaries of class and city, had the widest range of opportunities to develop his faculties and was the object of both material and artistic production. The city-state encouraged and supported art to the extent that it contributed to shaping the minds and spirits of its citizens. This explains Plato's diatribe against poetry (in the Tenth Book of *The Republic),* for Plato thought that poets, by regarding appearance as reality and by influencing the most negative aspect of the spirit, the passions, did not use their activity as a means of civic and spiritual reform. The importance of the social and political task assigned to art is manifested by the fact that the city-state subsidized the audience and the authors of Greek tragedy. There was no skimping on artistic expenses, which came to be considerable, because art fulfilled a function which Athenian citizens considered essential. And since artistic production had the same aim as material production, production for man—in the case of art, a contribution to the spiritual development of the members of the community—art was regarded as a productive activity. The artist was a producer of ideas, of physical and spiritual beauty, which was what the consumers— the community—sought, encouraged, and appreciated.

In the Middle Ages, the artist and the public continued to maintain direct ties, but the client was no longer the State, but the Church. The political function of art gave way to its religious function, as a means of promoting and spreading the faith, and of forming and raising religious consciousness. Certainly, the Church did not place such a high value on art at first. As is well known, the earliest Christian writers made no attempt to hide their hostility to art, and especially the plastic arts, for they saw in it the danger of idolatry. This attitude accorded with their belief in the great schism between body and soul, which frankly disdained the sensuous and thus any activity, such as art, which could not relinquish the concrete, the sensuous. The fate of art was that of all image cults against which the Church had declared itself in the first centuries of its existence; the most ardent advocates of this attitude within the Church were the iconoclasts, who expressed a repulsion toward sensual paganism and its concomitant idolatry of images; they opposed to this the symbol, which in their view gave more emphasis to the spiritual. It was only much later in the Middle Ages, when the Church felt secure and victorious, that it tried to emphasize the spiritual not through the subtle stylization of the symbol, but through the more concrete and sensuous form of the image. But what convinced the iconoclasts and what finally brought to art the recognition of the Church was the value of art as an educational tool. In an era when those who could read and write were a tiny minority, the visual arts had the capacity to inspire by means of their content, their message, while at the same time they delighted with their harmony of line and color. In this way, an illiterate person could grasp the reality signified by the image. "Painting can be to illiterates what literature is to those who can read," said Pope Gregory toward the end of the sixth century.

From the moment that art was seen as a unique and valuable means of instruction, the Church became the principal consumer of art and placed it at the service of religion. Art did not have a sacred character in itself, but it did serve as an efficient instrument to combat the ignorance of the masses at the same time that it delighted those with a privileged sensibility and culture.

Although the function of art had changed, the relationship between producer and client remained direct and immediate. Artists created to satisfy the wishes of their client, the Church. And since the objective of art was pedagogic, artists abided by the prescriptions of the Church, which determined what themes were consistent with the educational function of painting, thus turning it into a sort of Gospel in images. In spite of its educational function, art remained subject to the ideological content implanted by religion, thus determining the artist's attitude to reality, which was seen only as a reflection of the joy and resplendence of a transcendental reality. Therefore, art was more than realism: it was a form of painting which expressed, signified, or allegorized a supernatural reality by means of the given reality.

We can thus speak of a pedagogic or religious utility in medieval art, but in no way did this art have a material utility. The work of art was considered to be above any narrow utilitarian interest. The work of artists was productive, not in a material sense, but in an ideological and spiritual sense.

The artist was subject to the wishes of his client, but this subjection did not actually entail a conflict, for the artist shared the religious convictions which his public—the Church and the faithful—wanted him to express. Whatever conflicts might have existed between the creative personality and the prescriptions established by the public did not break this ideological and religious community which represented the fundamental commonweal for both artist and public.

Nevertheless, although artists worked directly for the Church, the relations between producer and public were varied. From the beginning of the Middle Ages, the artist entered into a relationship with the consumer by means of the workshop, which fused artistically and technically the work of its members. This eventually became a limitation on the creative personalities of artists; hence the growing need artists felt to free themselves from this intermediary institution, in order to enter into a direct and immediate relationship with the public. But the freedom of labor, when exercised outside the workshop, engendered competition; the artist then had to free himself from competition itself, once again forming organizations to protect his interests. In contradistinction to the earlier type of workshop, this new association did not question the creative personality of the artist; that is, it did not regulate his work by fixing artistic norms but attempted to coordinate the diverse personal interests which were collectively threatened by competition. This new grouping was the medieval guild.

Eventually, the Church ceased to be the almost exclusive client of art; municipalities and courts also patronized the artist and, with the first manifestations of an urban bourgeoisie in the late Middle Ages, individual clients appeared for the first time. However, all this did not alter the relationship between producer and consumer; this remained a direct relationship, the goal of which was to satisfy the wishes of a predetermined client with tastes and needs known to the artist. Artists produced not for an abstract, impersonal, and unknown public, but for a specific client, whether ecclesiastical, municipal, or individual. Production and consumption were in a direct relationship; there were no intermediaries. The artist was not yet subject to the obscure and shifting forces of the market; he still had no idea of what it meant to produce for a free buyer, for a client whose face he had never seen.

What was only a minor tendency in the Middle Ages became the dominant producer-consumer relationship in the Renaissance. The social position of the consumer changed: commissions from churches or municipalities gave way to commissions by concrete individuals, and these were no longer exclusively princes, noblemen, or prelates, but also rich bourgeois. However, the essential character of the relationship between producer and consumer did not change (it continued to be direct and personal), although its particular function began to change from dissemination of supernatural values to exaltation of the worldly glories of a king or a city, to embellishment of the prosaic existence of a rich bourgeois or a glorification of his new social position. The artist was still producing for a particular client. The relationship of course no longer contained the ideological unity we found in the Middle Ages. Moreover, to the extent that the individual clientele grew, the artist had to satisfy a variety of tastes and needs. All this necessarily influenced the artist, for the more he had to satisfy tastes alien to him, the less free he felt. Thus, conflicts arose between the creative personality of the artist and the desires of individual consumers, but these did not become radical because a common agreement still existed between producer and consumer that the work of art was above all a spiritual creation. The relations between producer and consumer were not entirely satisfactory to either party, but this did not upset the fundamental way in which the work of art was appreciated. Although the consumer physically owned the work of art, he did not feel that he really owned it unless he possessed it spiritually, that is, unless he entered into an aesthetic and ideological relationship with it.

The emergence of individual patronage did not essentially change this relationship by virtue of which both producer and consumer saw art as a form of spiritual production which becomes *unproductive* when it is measured by the criteria of material production. The institution of patronage brought about changes in the social status of the artist, but not in the character of his activity. By taking shelter in the benificence of a protector or a Maecenas, the artist once again attempted to extract himself, as he had done in the Middle Ages, from the harassment of the competition which constantly threatened his material existence. The patron assured him a relative material security in exchange for dedicating the products of his creative labor to him.

The artist has always been forced to reconcile the need to assure his material existence with the exercise of his creative freedom. In every period of history, this reconciliation has been problematical. The artist has always attempted, against all sorts of obstacles, to exist or survive in order to create. Subsistence and creation have converged or diverged, without entering into a radical contradiction. For centuries the conditions of existence were for the artist the material conditions of his creative work, but his creation was not the material condition of his existence. By seeking the protection of a patron, the artist tried to put an end to the dangers presented by a problematic existence under the conditions of competition. But this naturally affected his creative possibilities, for it tightened the ties that bound him to the consumer. This relationship freed him from the obligation of having to please diverse individual clients who lacked artistic sensibility, it freed him from the need to divert his creative talents in directions alien to art, and above all it saved him from the constant anxiety that competition subjected him to. But these positive factors had the drawback of the artist having to create for a client—the patron—who had the exclusive right to commission works from him; the artist assured his material existence at the price of a new dependency.

The gravest consequence of private patronage was the reduction of the public and social character of art, that is, the delimitation of the artist's capacity and need to speak directly to society, as the art of the Middle Ages had done, and as the frescoes of the Renaissance continued to do. However, in spite of these limitations, we cannot really speak of a contradiction between artist and society, for artistic creation continued to be considered as spiritual production, and the seeking of subsidiary values in a work of art assumed its value as spiritual production, which lay outside the utilitarian considerations always associated with material production. The patron was able to appreciate the value of art as a means to affirm his social prestige, and although the artist depended on him for his material existence, the patron made his social prestige contingent, in a certain sense, on the artistic prestige of the works created under his tutelage. Consequently, the artist was allowed a certain freedom in his choice of themes and especially in his choice of techniques and means of expression. As far as ideological content was concerned, the artist generally lived in the same spiritual world as his patron and shared the same ideas and values. In those cases where the artist tried to establish a distance or discrepancy between himself and the social milieu on which he depended, the great artist, as exemplified by Velázquez, succeeded in doing this through the greatness of his art and by asserting his spiritual superiority, transcending the boundaries of the dominant social ideas and emotions without endangering the material ties which linked him to his patron.

However, although a genius such as Velázquez may have succeeded in asserting his personality and creative freedom within the limits of the dependency imposed by the system of patronage, it is evident that artists sheltered by the protection of a patron must have experienced their direct and personal relationship to their protector as a limitation on the development of their creative talent. Artists therefore tried to assure their creative freedom by extricating themselves from a direct and personal relationship with a client, that is, by creating in response to their own desires without having to take into account a specific commission. They began to create works which satisfied their personal desires and tastes and offered these finished works to potential consumers. While the artist needed to secure the material conditions of his existence, he tried not to depend immediately on the consumer; he struggled to put the consumer in the background, inasmuch as he did not let a specific commission determine his creative activity. To do this he had to produce a number of works that exceeded, in quantity and economic value, what he needed in order to survive. That is, he had to increase his production in order to be able to offer works of art without the pressure of the need to survive; in this way, he freed himself from the need to create on commission. No longer did the artist adjust himself to the tastes of the consumer as expressed in a concrete and particular commission: in fact, it was the other way around. While in the personal and direct relationship between artist and patron the commission antedates the work, in the new relationship the work antedates its future consumer; in this way, production or creation predominated over consumption. In his creative work, the artist anticipated, when he offered his work for sale, that there would be a demand for it.

But this type of artist-consumer relationship is from a historical point of view a transitional one. It emerged as a form of emancipation from the direct dependency on various forms of patronage; because of its particular social nature, even though the type of patronage (public or private) changed, it represented a transition between the aristocratic, personal relationship which in the sphere of artistic production amounted to a personal dependency (which in the feudal era was also found in the sphere of material production), and the nominally free relationship between artist and consumer that is characteristic of fully developed bourgeois society. With the development of capitalism, these personal ties are eventually broken. In the first stage, the artist produced for a consumer he knew beforehand; in the transition stage, the artist became involved in a personal relationship with the consumer upon offering his work for sale; in the capitalist stage, the concrete, personal ties between artist and consumer are broken; the artist produces for an alien, future consumer, whose face he will never know but whom, in spite of his abstract and invisible character, he cannot afford to ignore in the course of creating his work. Between the producer and the consumer is interposed an inaccessible and strange world: the marketplace. The artist does not even produce for a concrete consumer whom he does not and will not know: he produces, strictly speaking, for something as abstract as the market.

When he ceases to produce for a definite client and therefore to depend on a previously arranged commission, the artist feels he has obtained his freedom to the extent that this relationship is made more impersonal and abstract, that is, to the extent that he produces more and more for the market.

This peculiar relationship was imposed in the middle of the nineteenth century, although the first signs can be found in the Renaissance and, in a more highly developed form, in seventeenth-century Holland. The artist came to think that this relationship was the one in greatest harmony with his desire to create freely, but in reality it was imposed by the specific character of material production; this relationship was destined to become the dominant one in bourgeois society, with or without the approval of the artist. We do not find this relationship firmly established even in the period when, after having secured economic and political power, the bourgeoisie was interested in works of art not as merchandise but as objects which expressed and exalted a new concept of the world, the values and ideas that corresponded to the interests of a rising class, either as objects which adorned or embellished their existence or which made their social position clearly evident. The work of art expressed ideas, feelings, or beauty, and nothing more was asked of it. The relationship between the bourgeoisie and artists in those European countries where the former first gained political and economic power did nothing more than prolong, during this stage, the direct and personal relations which in one form or another had prevailed between artists and princes, noblemen, and prelates. In effect, the old relationship and the new were not different qualitatively: from an economic point of view, artistic work continued to be unproductive labor, and the bourgeoisie accepted it as such, although it recognized its productivity or usefulness in the social and ideological fields.

Between the bourgeois and the artist there did not yet exist the no man's land of the marketplace. The bourgeois buyer did not yet go to the marketplace in search of works of art; rather, he either visited the artist's workshop or invited the artist to his house. Thus, in a social world already dominated by capitalist relations of production, the bourgeoisie was content with art being solely a branch of spiritual production, that is, an ideological or aesthetic tool saved from the domination of the laws of material production.

With the Industrial Revolution of the eighteenth century, material wealth multiplied and the insatiable market absorbed more and more products; its frontiers were opened wider and wider, not only because new sectors of material production were incorporated into the market, but also because certain products which had up to then been regarded as having no commercial value began to enter the market and became subject to its laws. Works of art, which in other times had been considered impregnable fortresses—given the high values they seemed to incarnate—became subject to the general laws of capitalist production and the most revered sanctums were assaulted by the new power, the power of money.

"The bourgeoisie has stripped of its halo every occupation hitherto honored and looked up to with reverent awe. It has converted the physician, the lawyer, the priest, the poet, the man of science, into its paid wage-laborers."[1] These words of Marx's have been clearly confirmed in the past century. At the present time, the work of art is not only a commodity but also a speculative asset. In Paris, thousands upon thousands of artists wage a fierce battle among themselves to gain entrance into the market controlled by powerful art galleries. The artist tries to obey this abstract and impersonal will of the market, and in order to make a living is often forced to seek innovation for its own sake and to introduce into his work so-called shock value. But it is not only new works which open the doors of the galleries: works by the old masters are also welcomed into the fold, and are accepted as safe investments. Living artists must compete with the dead. Artists who were once repudiated, condemned to misery or madness by the bourgeoisie, are among the most fierce competitors. And as far as living artists are concerned, the situation is not free and open competition among equals, in which the fittest win out, but rather a situation where artists are "launched" by galleries which make use of the most varied and advanced advertising and public relations techniques. This situation, characteristic of the more advanced capitalist countries, shows that the artistic production of the large galleries, such as the ones in Paris and New York, has remained subject to the laws of capitalist material production. This subjection of artistic creation to the laws of material production cannot help but have grave repercussions on art since, as Marx pointed out, capitalist production is essentially hostile to art.

The artist is forced to enter into a relationship with the consumer which is objective, independent of his will, and ruled by the laws of material production. Thus a contradiction is established between art and society which is even more profound than the one we presented above, namely, the contradiction brought about by the incompatibility between the artist and a society with whose values and ideals he does not identify. We have already seen that, after having joined the bourgeoisie in the establishment of a new society, when artists expressed in their work the values and ideals of that society in its ascendant stage, artists drew away from it, and in the end cut themselves off from bourgeois society in direct proportion to the banalization and reification of relations among human beings. Starting with romanticism, art expressed its nonconformity or divergence from the abstract, cold, and impersonal world of bourgeois social relations. All authentic artists since the romantics have turned their backs on capitalism, opposed it, exiled themselves from it, or created in spite of it. No great artist has extolled the true interests of capitalist society. No true artist has felt the *inner need* to create in conformity with its ideals or values. Nevertheless, unable to draw the support or praise of artists on the basis of these inner needs, capitalism has forced them to create according to the *external needs* created by the laws of capitalist material production.

When he speaks of the hostility of capitalism to art, Marx refers to the implacable submission of artistic production to the laws of material production. This opposition is even more basic than the contradiction between artists and an inhuman social reality. It affects all art, whatever its ideological content. Even an art that is supported or tolerated by the ruling classes, because of its ideological poverty, cannot escape the hostility. What is the precise nature of this hostility? Why does this submission of artistic production to the exigencies of material production affect art negatively? Can art overcome the negative consequences of that hostility? It is obvious that in spite of the hostility of capitalism, art has not only survived but, in the past century, has also borne splendid fruit. Might this not mean that art is a fortress which, even in the unfavorable conditions pointed out by Marx, does not let itself be overrun? And if this is the case, how valid is Marx's thesis that capitalism is in principle hostile to art? These are some of the questions we shall try to answer in the rest of our study.

Notes

1. Karl Marx and Frederick Engels, *The Communist Manifesto* (New York and London: Monthly Review Press, 1968), p. 6.

*

11. Material and
Artistic Production

What leads Marx to point out, in a work on economics such as his *Theories of Surplus Value,* that capitalist production is hostile to art? Marx is referring to material production; it is a question, then, of the hostility of *material* production to a branch of intellectual production such as art. His interest is not merely aesthetic; he is concerned with showing that what he had clearly established with regard to material production also holds in the case of the privileged domain of art: that capitalist production has become the enemy of humanity.[1] Far from production being at the service of man, man is at the service of production; man disappears behind a world of things, of commodities, and becomes a thing himself. Such is the phenomenon of the alienation (or reification) of human existence.

Marx's study of capitalist material production revealed the extent to which the worker, the producer, suffers a loss of humanity. This is precisely what bourgeois political economists, particularly classical bourgeois economists such as Adam Smith and Ricardo—whose doctrines Marx critically examined—refused to or could not see because of their class bias. Both in *The Economic and Philosophic Manuscripts of 1844* and in *Theories of Surplus Value,* Marx exposed the inhuman character of capitalist economic relations as well as the pretense to scientific objectivity on the part of classical economists. "The ordinary wage, according to Smith, is the lowest compatible with common humanity, that is, with cattle-like existence."[2]

Classical economists thought that it was perfectly natural for workers to receive as a wage, in exchange for their labor power, only what was indispensable to survive as a mere object or instrument of production. By ignoring the contradiction between production and man, classical economics reduced economic relations to relations among things. By making profit, the production of surplus value, the supreme value, it was only interested in the worker as a producer of surplus value. Everything that lies outside that concern (the worker as a human being or the worker outside of the process of production) was left out. Consequently, classical political economy was by its very nature inhuman. Moreover, by remaining on the level of appearances (economic relations as relations among things) and by not getting to the bottom of things (the human relations embodied or crystallized in the apparent relations among things) it offered a superficial, and therefore biased and unscientific, vision of economic relations.

Marxist political economy, by throwing light on the inhuman character of capitalist economic relations, reveals its own connection to a humanist and revolutionary conception of society and of man, and exhibits a scientific character, since, unlike pseudo-scientific bourgeois economics, it can explain the nature of capitalist relations by exposing their reality. Marxist economics is scientific precisely because it reveals the inhuman character of capitalist production (production as the enemy of man, or surplus production). The worker's relationship to the product is characterized by estrangement or alienation: he does not recognize himself in the product, nor does he recognize or express himself in the act of production. "In relation to the worker who *appropriates* nature by means of his labor, this appropriation appears as estrangement, his own spontaneous activity as activity for another and as activity of another, vitality as a sacrifice of life, production of the object as loss of the object to an alien power, to an *alien* person."[3] This alien person, the nonworker or capitalist, also is not involved in a specifically human relationship to the worker, his labor, or his product.

Since the capitalist is only interested in production insofar as it brings him profits, he is only interested in an inhuman form of production which negates the producer. The capitalist adopts as a matter of principle a utilitarian point of view, and any human attitude toward the worker, his activity, or his product is alien to him.

We can therefore see how capitalist material production prevents man from entering into a truly human relationship with the objects of production, such as a relationship between man and the human meaning of an object which both satisfies a specific human need and objectifies essential human faculties.

Under capitalism, material production excludes man from the subject-object relationship. The inhuman relationship between producer and product means that the worker denies himself as a creative or productive being. His labor—alienated labor—is the negation of labor as a vital human activity, as an objectification of his physical and intellectual energies, as an activity in which he affirms himself as a free, conscious, and creative being. Labor is reduced to the production of commodities or surplus value. The inhuman relationship between owner and product means that the infinite number of connections human beings can establish with objects to satisfy a multiplicity of human needs is reduced to only one, the relationship of ownership. Man thus deprives himself of the ability to enjoy in a human way the creations of others. The pleasure or consumption of the object is exhausted in ownership. An inhuman pleasure or consumption corresponds to an inhuman form of production. The worker does not produce in a truly human manner, that is, in a creative way, and the capitalist does not consume or enjoy the product he possesses in a human manner, that is, he does not enjoy the human significance of the object.

Capitalist material production opposes itself to the creative essence of man; it is thus incompatible with free, creative labor and can only recognize work as a forced and uncreative activity, that is, as *alienated* labor in its concrete form of wage labor.

One of the merits of German idealist philosophy was that it revealed the creative, transformative, and active nature of man. Marx recognized this in the first of his *Theses on Feuerbach,* but at the same time he pointed out its weakness: that it showed this active and creative aspect of man in an abstract and speculative manner, as an action or creation of the consciousness. Marx deserves credit for having conceived man as a concrete socio-historical being who transforms external nature, as well as his own human nature, in a real and effective way.

Because of its hostility to creative labor, capitalist material production is all the more hostile to artistic labor, which is creation par excellence. Examining Marx's aesthetic ideas in *The Economic and Philosophic Manuscripts of 1844* (see chapter 3), we find that the common basis and roots of art and labor reside in the creative capacity of man, formed historically and socially and manifested by its expression and objectification in a concrete-sensuous object. This capacity is limited or frustrated in alienated labor, but even in free labor, the creative power, the capacity to endow objects with human meaning, is not realized with as much depth and intensity as in art. This is because the creative objectification of man in the products of his labor is always effected within the boundaries of the material utility of the product. Material production could not sacrifice this material utility to a spiritual utility without threatening the very existence of man. This or that individual, or even a specific social class, can liberate himself of the necessity to undertake practically and directly the productive function (which in class societies is assigned especially to the exploited and oppressed) but society as a whole cannot renounce this type of relationship with nature; that is, it cannot renounce its practical transformation through labor, for it is only through labor that man has been able to rise above nature and thus exist as a human being. Without material production man as a social being would not exist, and since the social dimension is a specifically human dimension, as Aristotle pointed out by defining man as a *political* animal (that is, a member of the community), without it man as a human being would not exist.

The object of labor must have a certain utility; the form given to it by the subject must be adequate to the satisfaction of a specific need. The subject is present in the object inasmuch as it materializes certain goals of the subject. However, on account of the limited nature of the need the object satisfies, man is not objectified in it in all the richness of his subjectivity. But even within these limits, there is a human presence in all free labor, and the products of human beings are a testimony to the creative capacity of man.

From this point of view, art and labor are not identical, but neither are they opposed so radically as Kant thought. The products of human labor are useful in a material sense, and this utility is what essentially distinguishes them; in free labor, material utility is achieved at the same time that the producer feels himself to be affirmed and expressed in his product; in alienated labor, the product retains its essentially useful function but the producer feels negated as a human being, he does not affirm or recognize himself in his product. There is therefore a tension between what we could call the material utility and the spiritual utility of the product, but this tension, especially in free labor, does not result in one type of utility canceling out the other.

Art is labor, but it is truly creative labor inasmuch as in its capacity to humanize objects it does not encounter the limitations imposed on regular labor by its utilitarian function. Its utility is fundamentally spiritual; it satisfies man's need to humanize the world around him and to enrich with the objects of artistic creation his capacity to communicate. In this sense, art is superior to labor. Man feels the need for an objectified affirmation of himself which he can only find in art. And this explains ontologically and historically the human desire to supersede the limits of material utility even with respect to technical objects. If we regard these objects exclusively from a technico-utilitarian angle, whatever beauty they possess seems superfluous or strange. Technology as such does not require beauty. It is man who feels the need for beautiful technical objects, as shown by his zeal to humanize—or aestheticize—everything he touches. The transformation of a technical object into a beautiful technical object is not necessary from a technical point of view; it is not required by the laws of technology. The yearning to beautify a technical object is a yearning to affirm the presence of a human dimension, which is limited by the narrow technical framework of the object. This is not to say that technology is inhuman; it is as human as art. The radical opposition between art and technology, by virtue of which human qualities are attributed to the former and inhuman ones to the latter, is only the prolongation, on a new basis, of the Platonic dualism of spirit and matter. In this concept, art appears as a superior domain, completely spiritual, while technology is an inferior realm. It is forgotten that man has been able to develop himself as a spiritual, conscious, creative being through his capacity to practically and materially transform the world around him by means of his physical labor and technology.

The tendency to oppose art and labor originated with Kant. Having isolated beauty from the practical needs of man with his famous principle of the disinterestedness of beauty, Kant in his *Critique of Judgment* postulated an absolute opposition between labor and art. He defined art as "production through freedom, i.e., through a will that places reason at the basis of its actions."[4] It is activity toward a goal, conscious creation, and in that sense it is distinct from nature. Labor, or craft, on the other hand is not a free activity but a forced one, and therefore unpleasant:

> Art also differs from handicraft; the first is called "free," the other may be called "mercenary." We regard the first as if it could only prove purposive as play, i.e., as occupation that is pleasant in itself. But the second is regarded as if it could only be compulsorily imposed upon one as work, i.e., as occupation which is unpleasant (a trouble) in itself and which is only attractive on account of its effect (e.g., the wage).[5]

Kant here opposes art and labor in general, but in reality the kind of labor which fits his characterization (forced activity that is realized only as a result of external need or force and which entails no satisfaction) is strictly speaking alienated labor. By elevating this type of labor, which is characteristic of capitalist society, to a universal level, Kant opposed it to art, by opposing a forced and unpleasant—or mercenary— activity to a truly free and creative activity. Since Kant viewed labor only in the form it takes in bourgeois society, he opposes it to art in a radical manner.

Marx, as we have seen, started from the common basis of art and labor as different manifestations of the creative essence of man which may oppose each other to the extent that labor, under the specific socioeconomic conditions of capitalist society, loses its creative character. Truly creative artistic production becomes the antithesis of capitalist material production, but not of all forms of social production, e.g., production at the service of man in which labor regains its truly human and creative significance. The contraposition of material and artistic production takes on a socio-historical character and, at bottom, has the same roots as the opposition between capitalist material production and free, creative labor.

To the extent that labor loses its creative character it distances itself from art. At the same time, to the extent that art becomes similar to this form of alienated labor, it ceases to be, as Kant said, "production by means of freedom." The threat which constantly hangs over art in capitalist society is precisely this: that it will be treated in the only way that interests a world ruled by the law of surplus production, that is, according to economic criteria, as wage labor. It is in this sense that Marx speaks of the hostility of capitalist material production to art, a hostility which is manifested as an attempt to integrate a branch of spiritual production, art, into the world of material production. But to what extent is such integration possible? To what extent can art endure this integration without exercising its real nature, that of free and creative activity?

Notes

1. See especially *The Economic and Philosophic Manuscipts of 1844; A Contribution to the Critique of Political Economy* (New York: International Publishers, 1970); and *Capital.*
2. Marx, *Manuscripts,* p. 65.
3. Ibid., p. 119.
4. Immanuel Kant, *Critique of Judgment* (New York: Hafner, 1951), p. 145.
5. Ibid., p. 146.

12. Art as Concrete Labor: Aesthetic Value and Exchange Value

"The wealth of those societies in which the capitalist mode of production prevails presents itself as an immense accumulation of commodities."[1] With those words Marx begins his examination of the process of capitalist production in the first volume of *Capital.* In a society based on the universal exchange of the products of human labor, in which all goods are presented as commodities, works of art cannot escape the fate of being treated as commodities. And since commodities are but materialized human labor, we must examine this world of commodities and human labor in order to be able to understand the fate of artistic production under capitalism.

The commodity is a product of human labor which satisfies a certain human need. In this sense, it has a utility, a use value. The use values of certain commodities are qualitatively different from those of others inasmuch as they satisfy different human needs. But in a society based on the exchange of commodities—in a society in which human beings produce to satisfy neither their personal needs nor those of the community, but those of the market—the concrete qualities of those commodities vanish, and with them their use values. There is thus a leveling process whereby all products of labor become objects of exchange. A commodity has an exchange value, which is the rate of exchange of one class of use values for another. The exchange value of each commodity therefore represents a certain unit of value which is common to all commodities. "As use-values, commodities are, above all, of different qualities, but as exchange-values they are merely different quantities, and consequently do not contain an atom of use-value."[2]

The commodity is thus rooted both in the quantitative and the qualitative. But the latter is erased, as is the use value of an object, by being converted into a commodity, remaining on the outside, showing us only its facade, its exchange value. "Could commodities themselves speak, they would say: Our use-value may be a thing that interests men. It is no part of us as objects. What, however, does belong to us as objects, is our exchange-value. Our natural intercourse as commodities proves it. In the eyes of each other we are nothing but exchange-values."[3] Whereas objects establish relations with human beings, and thus have human significance through their use values, their exchange values appear as attributes of the objects themselves, without relation to human beings. Objects lose their human meaning, their quality, their relationship to man. The commodity, we might say, is a human object, but in a dehumanized form; that is, it is no longer appreciated for its use value, for its relationship to a specific human need.

Whatever transformation is effected on the object when it is converted into a commodity, that is, when its concrete qualities are erased and its ties to specific human needs are cut, the commodity cannot cease to be a product of labor, for it is a materialization of labor. But when the use value of the object is cast aside, a change occurs not only in its relationship to human needs, since strictly speaking its links to human beings disappear, but also in the manner labor itself is materialized in the product.

When a product of human labor is appreciated for its use value, as a useful object, it can be said to be a product of real human labor. Insofar as this labor creates use values, concrete individual objects which satisfy concrete human needs, Marx calls this labor *concrete* labor. In it, a concrete relationship exists between product and producer: between the individuality of the latter, expressed in the objectives and peculiarities of his activity, and the human significance of the object. It is a qualitative labor which can be distinguished by the specific use value it produces, that is, by the specific qualities of the objects it produces.

But in a society where production is aimed above all at the market, products can only be compared by ignoring their useful properties and their human significance. In order to compare the products of labor and make them appear equal, it is necessary to erase their utility, their use values, their capacities to satisfy specific human needs, and establish among them the quantitative relationship of exchange value. Objects are differentiated qualitatively by their use values; each object has its own value, and the use value of another object is of no concern to it. But objects cannot be compared as long as they remain on this qualitative level, because they cannot be reduced to a common denominator. They must be compared quantitatively.

On what basis can this quantitative relationship be established? In other words, what is the essence of exchange value? We already know the essence of use value: concrete, real labor. By virtue of its use value, an object is an embodiment of concrete labor, and is differentiated from other objects. "If we then leave out of consideration the use-value of commodities, they have only one common property left, that of being products of labor ... Along with the useful qualities of the products themselves, we put out of sight both the useful character of the various kinds of labor embodied in them, and the concrete forms of that labor."[4] By ignoring their use values, qualitatively different forms of concrete labor can be homogenized as parts of an identical, indistinguishable human labor, regardless of its form or content, or the specific human meaning of any of its products. Labor thus conceived is *abstract* general labor, and it constitutes the essence of exchange value.[5] In its abstract form, labor is conceived in its generality, as a universal process "in which the individuality of the worker is erased."[6] Likewise, the qualitative differences among diverse concrete, individual kinds of labor are also erased, but the disappearance of the qualitative is what makes possible the leveling of different forms of labor into quantities or fractions of a homogeneous human labor. In this manner, the concrete forms of labor, which by virtue of their specific concreteness are incomparable, can be measured by reducing them to simple, abstract labor, thus acquiring a quantitative magnitude. Consequently, the labor that creates exchange value, the quantitative magnitude of commodities, is abstract general labor.

But if different forms of concrete labor can be compared to each other by means of a reduction to abstract labor, what is it that makes this reduction possible? In other words, how is exchange value measured? "How, then, is the magnitude of this value to be measured? Plainly, by the quantity of the value-creating substance, the labor, contained in the article."[7] The quantity of labor contained in the commodity is measured by the amount of time expended on it, that is, the amount of socially necessary labor under the normal conditions of production, and with the average degree of skill and intensity prevalent in a specific society. "As values, all commodities are only definite masses of congealed labor-time."[8] Labor time thus conceived is also an abstraction of particular or concrete time, which can be greater or lesser than the amount of socially necessary labor time.

The work of art is the product of a particular form of labor. This labor also produces a useful object which satisfies the human need for expression, affirmation, and communication. Human beings produce works of art out of necessity, and these works have specific use values which are determined by the artist's ability to satisfy that need. In this sense there is no such thing as gratuitous art; the products of art have use value by their very nature. Strictly speaking, there is no such thing as art for art's sake, only art in relation to human needs, art for man's sake. The artist transforms raw materials and endows them with certain properties by virtue of which the created object attests to a determinate relationship with man.

Each work of art is unique and unrepeatable. The content

the artist expresses, and the form he gives to his expression in order to objectify and communicate that content, are fused in a concrete and unique totality. As concrete work, artistic work is related to the form and content of the work of art, to its concrete individuality; for it is a concrete man, with all his human richness, who is objectified in the process of artistic work, and the more personal and concrete that activity is, the more it will reveal its creative character and its human content. The artistic work which is embodied in the work of art is concrete work, and we cannot be indifferent to the individual, qualitatively different aspects of a product of this activity. We cannot, therefore, compare two artistic works to each other by means of establishing a quantitative relationship between them, considering them as quantities or fractions of an abstract universal labor. In the same way, we cannot evaluate works of art in disregard of what is qualitative or unrepeatable in each of them, that is, what distinguishes them qualitatively.

Moreover, the reduction of the labor time in artistic work to a homogeneous time—the socially necessary time for artistic creation—makes no sense in the sphere of artistic production since such a reduction is only possible with regard to production under normal conditions and with an average creative skill. To apply such a common denominator to art would lead only to a standardization of creation, to mechanical reproduction ad infinitum, that is, to something totally incompatible with the creative and concrete character of works of art. Furthermore, we must reject labor time as a general measure of artistic labor because in artistic activity time has no value from an aesthetic point of view, either as concrete time or as abstract universal time. The time spent in creation can vary considerably from individual to individual, or even for one individual. While some writers dwell on each line, or even on each word, others produce with amazing speed. These peculiarities may be of interest from a psychological or biographical point of view, but they are of no interest from a specifically aesthetic point of view. The quantification of the creative process by means of its reduction to units of labor time is of no use as a criterion for evaluating what is by its very nature qualitative, that is, the work of art.

This does not mean that the time spent in creation is a matter of total indifference; an artist can sometimes harm his work by not devoting enough time to it, by not having gone over certain aspects of it. As Antonio Machado Ruíz used to say, "Laugh at the poet who does not erase!" But to go over and over the same thing can also frustrate the work of art. That is why Juan Ramón Jiménez cautioned:

> Touch it no more,
> for such is the rose!

For all the above reasons, although the time spent in creation is one factor in the creative process, what is important is the result, the product of artistic work, seen from a qualitative point of view. Moreover, because of its individual and concrete character, artistic work is not reducible to abstract general labor, of which it might be considered a part or fraction. The value of a work of art is determined by its specific characteristics, those qualities which the artist has been able to extract from raw materials and infuse as aesthetic qualities into a new object. The value of this object is in the use value of the created qualities, and in this sense it cannot be compared to other objects.

Nevertheless, the work of art is quantified, an exchange value is attributed to it, when it enters the world of commodities and becomes subject to the laws of capitalist production. Insofar as works of art acquire the ontological status of commodities, their concrete qualities, their use values, disappear, and they become greater or lesser quantities of a common unit of measurement. Converted into a commodity, the work of art loses its human significance. Its value—its capacity to satisfy a specific human need by means of its aesthetic qualities—no longer resides in itself, and therefore in its specific aesthetic qualities, but rather in its capacity to return profits. The exchange value of a commodity, as opposed to its strictly aesthetic value, does not take into account its sensuous properties, the form of the object. The concrete-sensuous aspect of a commodity is a matter of indifference. As Marx pointed out in *Capital*, "Exchange-value transforms each product of labor into a mysterious social hieroglyphic." Aesthetic value, although it cannot be reduced to the form of the object, to its concrete-sensuous properties, bears a direct and immediate relationship to those properties. The human content, the human richness which is expressed in the work of art, necessarily requires a concrete-sensuous form if it is to be objectified.

The exchange value of a work of art, like that of commodities in general, is subject to the laws of supply and demand which rule the market; in this sense it expresses particular social relations, characteristic of mercantile production in its capitalist phase. The aesthetic value of a work of art embodies social and human relations in all their richness and universality. Therefore, while exchange value is inseparable from the fate of a determinate set of social relations—those of capitalist production for a market—aesthetic value, by virtue of its universal character and its capacity to satisfy human needs, has been sought throughout man's socio-historical development, and endures through a succession of different and even antagonistic systems of social relations.

Aesthetic value is the specific value of a work of art, but to the degree that artistic production is subordinated to the laws of capitalist material production, there is a growing tendency to evaluate works of art according to their exchange value, in disregard for their aesthetic qualities. Therefore, there is a tendency under capitalism to make artistic production also production for the market. What characterizes a work of art that has been converted into a commodity is the abstraction of its true qualities. A work of art has exchange value insofar as its true value, as an artistic product, is ignored or denied.

That which befell the products of concrete labor is repeated in the case of works of art, but with even direr consequences. A human object ceases to be appreciated for its human significance. Because the *raison d'être* of an artistic object resides precisely in expressing humanity, in objectively bearing witness to the presence of man, the consequences are even graver, and this is true because artistic work, as we have seen, cannot be reduced to the general abstract labor which is the essence of exchange value.

Neither artistic work nor its products can permit, without denying themselves, a reduction of the concrete to the abstract, of the qualitative to the quantitative. But capitalism is interested in artistic work only in a form which it considers to be in accordance with the fundamental law of production of surplus value—that is, wage labor; it is interested in the work of art only as an object of exchange or a product for the market and acknowledges no other value than the one it has as a commodity, its exchange value.

In sum, under capitalism artistic work and its products are valued in disregard for their specific, qualitative character. This indifference to their true value spotlights the aspect of labor which is of most interest under capitalist conditions of production: its productivity.

Notes

1. Karl Marx, *Capital* (New York: International Publishers, 1967), p. 35.
2. Ibid., pp. 37-38.
3. Ibid., p. 83.
4. Ibid., p. 38.
5. "As exchange-values of different magnitudes they represent larger or smaller portions, larger or smaller amounts of simple, homogeneous, abstract general labour, which is the substance of exchange-value." Karl Marx, *A Contribution to the Critique of Political Economy* (New York: International Publishers, 1970), p. 29.
6. Ibid.
7. Marx, *Capital,* p. 38.
8. Ibid., p. 40.

*
13. The Productivity and Unproductivity of Artistic Labor

From the point of view of capitalist production, there exists only one criterion of productivity: the creation of surplus value. "Productive labour, in its meaning for capitalist production, is wage-labour which, exchanged against the variable part of capital (the part of the capital that is spent on wages), reproduces not only this part of the capital (or the value of its own labour-power), but in addition produces surplus-value for the capitalist."[1]

Surely, artistic labor produces beauty, pleasure, emotions, or ideas in a concrete-sensuous form, but insofar as it falls under the law of capitalist material production it is nothing more than a productive activity. In considering the essential character of capitalist production, Marx perceived the historical nature of this conception of art as productive labor. When capitalist production reaches a certain stage of development it tends to make artistic creation fit within the capitalist economic system, but since this contradicts the very essence of art, artistic creation does not let itself be integrated into that system. Therefore, the effect of the fundamental law of capitalist production is felt only to a limited extent by some branches of art.

The work of artists of other eras, sheltered by the financial aid of their protectors or patrons (as was the case with Michelangelo, Velázquez, Corneille, or Bach), was not productive labor in the capitalist sense, but rather remunerated work, and poorly remunerated at that. In exchange for his labor, the artist received what was absolutely necessary for his sustenance. The patron obtained ownership over the work of art in exchange for his support of the artist, but he did not use the work of art to obtain a value higher than the value consumed by his support of the artist. The same can be said of the labor of the artist when his products were sold to an individual buyer: this transaction did not lead to other transactions. In all the above cases, the artist creates a useful object, which has the capacity of satisfying a specific human need, that is, an object endowed with use value, and exchanges it for a specific sum.

The person who acquired a work of art thus bought a product which had specific qualities, which was the result, in turn, of concrete, qualitative labor and which had a determinate use value. In this direct relationship between producer and owner, the work of art did not pass through the market; it was not merchandise, it was of no interest whether the work might have an exchange value higher than the price at which it was bought. The only point of interest was its real use value, the specific and concrete utility which the artist had been able to materialize in it through his work. But this artistic labor, the value of which does not go beyond its use value and which does not produce an additional value for others, i.e., a surplus value, is unproductive from the point of view of capitalist production.

In effect, so long as the artist only produces objects with use value, the value of which is in their human, concrete utility, his labor is unproductive, precisely because it is a creative labor which satisfies the human need for expression and communication. This labor spiritually enriches both the producer and the consumer, but even so—from the capitalist point of view—it is unproductive as long as it does not materially enrich the owner of the work of art by engendering surplus value. Productivity in this sense exists only for the capitalist, for those who can buy a specific commodity, human labor power, and by putting it in action create a surplus value which exceeds the original value of that labor power. That kind of productivity does not exist for the producer. Therefore, when the distinction is made between productive and unproductive labor, between labor which not only reproduces but also increases the original investment and labor which does not convert that investment into capital, such a classification is made from the point of view of capitalist production, a point of view which is completely alien to the producer himself.

From this perspective, there is no labor or product which could not in principle be productive. And consequently, artistic labor and its products can also be made productive. As Marx pointed out, "Neither the special kind of labour nor the external form of its product necessarily make it 'productive' or 'unproductive.' The same labour can be productive when I buy it as a capitalist, as a producer, in order to create more value, and unproductive when I buy it as a consumer, a spender of revenue, in order to consume its use-value. . . ."[2]

Productivity, therefore, does not depend on the nature of the labor, whether physical or artistic, or on the form of the product; productivity has to do with the specific nature of production in capitalist society, which has as its direct aim not the satisfaction of human needs, but rather the creation of surplus value. Marx gives several examples of the productivity of artistic activities: "A writer is a productive labourer not insofar as he produces ideas, but insofar as he enriches the publisher who publishes his work."[3] "An actor, for example, or even a clown . . . is a productive labourer if he works in the service of a capitalist (an entrepreneur) to whom he returns more labour than he receives from him in the form of wages. . . ."[4] Taking the example of Milton, Marx deduced that when the poet creates in response to a natural impulse, his labor is unproductive, while when he creates books as commodities, in order to increase capital, he realizes a productive labor.[5]

Insofar as the labor of the artist creates a new value or surplus value, that labor is productive from a capitalist point of view. The only condition labor must fulfill in order to be defined as productive, then, is that it create surplus value, either by being converted directly into capital or by serving capital as a means of producing surplus value. Therefore, what is regarded as the productivity of artistic labor "has absolutely nothing to do with the *determinate content* of the labour, its special utility, or the particular use-value in which it manifests itself."[6] As productive labor, artistic labor loses its specific nature as superior qualitative and concrete work, and its products likewise are divested of their specific, qualitative nature to become purely and simply commodities.

When artistic labor loses its specific, concrete, and qualitative nature, what form doe it adopt? What form must it take in order to produce commodities or, more precisely, surplus value? To be productive it must adopt the form of wage labor, the only form which allows it to create an excess value, thus incrementing capital. "Only that wage-labour is produc- tive which produces capital. (This is the same as saying that it reporduces on an enlarged scale the sum of value expended on it, or that it gives in return more labour than it receives in the form of wages. Consequently, only that labour-power is productive which produces a value greater than its own.)"[7]

Since the only labor which capitalism acknowledges as productive is that which produces surplus value, and since labor can achieve this productivity only when it adopts the form of wage labor, artistic activity is productive only insofar as it adopts or approximates that form. But the attempt to subject artistic activity to the laws of wage labor entails both the alienation of the laborer, with all the negative consequences that implies, and the introduction of coercion to the sphere of art, which by its very essence is the sphere of creativity and freedom. When art is made to resemble wage labor (or mercenary labor, as Kant called it), the very future of art as a creative and free activity through which man affirms and expresses himself with all his powers is endangered. Artistic labor can only safeguard its creative and free essence by remaining an unproductive activity from an economic point of view, that is, by extricating itself from the fundamental law of capitalist production. In sum, art can only remain free and creative by retaining its incompatibility with wage labor.

Notes

1. Karl Marx, *Theories of Surplus Value* (Moscow: Progress Publishers, 1963), Part I, p. 152.
2. Ibid., p. 165.
3. Ibid., p. 158.
4. Ibid., p. 157.
5. "For example Milton, who wrote *Paradise Lost* for £5, was an *unproductive labourer*. On the other hand, the writer who turns out stuff for his publisher in factory style, is a *productive labourer*. Milton produced *Paradise Lost* for the same reason that a silk worm produces silk. It was an activity of *his* nature. Later he sold the product for £5. But the literary proletarian of Leipzig, who fabricates books (for example, *Compendia of Economics*) under the direction of his publisher, is a *productive labourer;* for his product is from the outset subsumed under capital, and comes into being only for the purpose of increasing that capital." (Ibid., p. 401.)
6. Ibid.
7. Ibid., p. 152.

14. *Wage Labor and Artistic Activity*

In *The Economic and Philosophic Manuscripts of 1844* Marx pointed out, with reference to Hegel, the ambivalence of human labor. In it the fate of human beings is played out, so to speak; in it man emerges in all his greatness and misery. By means of labor man has risen, has freed himself from his merely natural being to become a *human* natural being; by means of labor man has humanized and transcended himself. Labor as conscious activity is the foundation of the development of human consciousness, and it is also the foundation of human freedom. And insofar as labor implies a constant humanization of nature and of man himself, that is, a transition from a world-in-itself to a human world which exists only as the result of human activity, a transition from non-being to being, labor is creation: creation of a new being. Such is the greatness of human labor. But this greatness, which Hegel glimpsed, gives way to misery, the negative aspect of labor which, according to Marx, Hegel never saw; in the particular conditions prevailing in societies divided into classes, labor loses its original character of conscious, free, and creative activity, to become instead an alien, forced, and devastated physically and spiritually. Such is *alienated* labor, which reaches its fullest expression under the specific conditions of capitalist production and which Marx analyzes.

In a later work, written in 1857-1858, the *Grundrisse der Kritik der politischen Oekonomie (Rohentwurf)*,[1] which Marx left in manuscript form, he again studied the phenomenon of the alienation of labor in the form it takes under the conditions of capitalist production: wage labor. Marx's analysis of capital, particularly in chapter 2 of the *Grundrisse,* gives us a clearer picture of what constitutes, in his view, the radical incompatibility between art and wage labor, whereby we can also gain a better understanding of the roots of the hostility of capitalism to art.

Marx endeavored to establish an analogy between art and labor as free and creative activities, in order to then point out their opposition when labor loses its artistic character, or when art begins to resemble wage labor.

Labor loses its artistic, creative, character when creativity is separated or abstracted from the other components of the process of work itself, establishing an external or indifferent relationship between creativity and labor. The control over the material conditions of production is taken away from the producers, who then adopt a formal or indifferent attitude toward their own activity.

> The objective conditions of labour retain a subjective existence opposed to living labour power, since out of capital there develops the capitalist. On the other hand the purely subjective existence of labour power as opposed to its own conditions gives it a quite indifferent objective form as opposed to them.[2]

Wage labor thus brings about a divorce between the material conditions of labor and the producer's capacity for labor. But indifference or estrangement extends to all aspects of the process of labor.

> The raw material that it works on is alien material; likewise the instrument is an alien instrument; its labour occurs only as an accessory to their substance, and thus objectifies itself in what does not belong to it. Even living labour itself appears to be alien as opposed to living labour power, whose labour it is, whose own manifestation of life it is . . . His own labour (and also its orientation) is thus just as alien as are the material and the instrument. Thus the product appears to him as an alien combination of material, instrument and labour, as alien property. . . ."[3]

The alienation of the worker is so profound that everything becomes alien to him: his labor, the materials and tools of labor, and consequently the product itself. The result is an increasingly greater material and spiritual impoverishment; in order to overcome that impoverishment the worker would first have to recognize that the product, which combines a number of alien ingredients, is his product.[4]

Wage labor thus plunges man into the most absolute human poverty; everything that is alive, creative, and concrete in human beings disappears and becomes instead an abstraction of what is truly alive and real. It is in effect "living work as an *abstraction* of the moments of its effective reality (and, at the same time, nonvalue); total dispossession, lack of any objectivity, purely subjective existence of labor. Labor as *absolute poverty;* poverty not as a shortage, but as a total exclusion of objective richness."[5]

Wage labor emerges, then, as an activity in which the dead dominate the living and the abstract dominates the concrete and determinate. This abstraction and indeterminability pervades not only the relationships between capital and labor and between the producer and his labor, but all relationships among human beings. Individuality disappears, whether of labor, of a product, or of a human relationship.

> Although at each concrete step labor is determinate labor, capital can confront each *determinate* labor; the totality of labor confronts it with all its power, and it is a matter of chance that one form of labor confronts capital specifically. On the other hand, the worker himself is completely indifferent to the determinability of his labor; the specificity of his labor is of no interest to him, and he is only interested in *labor* in general. . . .[6]

Marx also pointed out that the worker has an economic character only when he is involved in labor as such, that is, when he enters into an abstract relationship both with his activity and with the capitalist, in contradistinction to whom he defines himself. "This is not the character of the artisan, of a member of a guild, whose economic character resides precisely in his *determinability* and in his relationship with a

determinate *master.*"[7] This determinate content is characteristic of all truly creative labor, and on that account art resembles labor. Hence, when labor loses that determinability
under the conditions of wage labor, labor and art are divorced and labor loses the creative character it maintained
during the Middle Ages in the work of artisans. The relationship of estrangement and opposition between capitalist and
worker, as well as between the worker and his products, is
translated, therefore, into the separation and opposition between art and labor, insofar as the latter ceases to operate on
the basis of a creative, artistic principle.

> This economic relation—the character assumed by capitalist and
> worker as the two extremes of a relationship of production—
> develops, consequently, in a manner all the more pure and ade-
> quate in proportion *to the extent that labor loses its character of
> art;* that is, to the extent that its particular skill is converted into
> something increasingly abstract and undifferentiated, into an atti-
> tude that is more and more *purely abstract,* merely mechanical
> and, consequently, indifferent to its specific form; into a purely
> *formal* activity or, what is the same thing, a purely material ac-
> tivity which is indifferent as to its form.[8]

We see that Marx defined wage labor by its loss of artistic
character. If we relate this characterization to his theory in
the *Economic and Philosophic Manuscripts* regarding the loss
of creative, human, and spiritual significance by alienated
labor, it becomes clear in what sense we now speak of the
artistic character of labor. By artistic character we do not
mean that the worker, by transforming raw material, is primarily preoccupied with creating an aesthetic object, or that
he forgets that the products of his work must satisfy determinate human needs, possess use value, and fulfill a utilitarian function. The worker cannot refuse to perform this
function, which is essential to him as a creator of material use
values. To the extent that he creates this practical object
freely, without a merely formal, mechanical, or abstract attitude to his work and product, he cannot help but objectify
his essential human powers, thus investing the objects he

creates with a human significance. In this sense, labor is creative; because of this, man cannot remain indifferent to it, and recognizes himself both in his activity and in his products. What Marx called the artistic character of labor refers to its spiritual and free creative character; and, on this level, art and labor are similar.

Labor always implies a transformation of raw material; this transformation can take on an artistic character, even when man does not attempt to create an aesthetic object, as long as he maintains a specifically human attitude toward his activity and his products. In this sense, Marx concluded that "man therefore also forms things in accordance with the laws of beauty,"[9] by considering the object of labor as his product, as *his* reality, as the objectification of his essential powers.

The more the artistic nature of labor is affirmed, the more it approximates art, that is, the more it approximates an activity through which man deliberately realizes and objectifies his human essence. The more labor loses its artistic character, the more it moves away from art, until it becomes a purely formal and mechanical activity which is radically opposed to art. Art then appears as the proper sphere for the spiritual richness which the sphere of labor has lost.

Marx pointed out the original solidarity between art and labor, as well as the opposition between the two under the conditions of capitalist production. What we are dealing with, then, is a historical and relative opposition between art and a socio-historical form of human labor, wage labor. It is capitalist material production which opposes labor to art by divesting labor of its living, creative, and artistic character, that is, when it becomes bourgeois. This opposition should in principle affect only labor, that activity the creative essence of which is denied, not art. In other words, the fact that labor loses its artistic character should not directly imply that art is negatively affected; art should appear as the proper sphere of creativity and freedom.

It was in this sense that both Kant and Adam Smith conceived the nature of art: they both opposed art to labor, as the spheres of freedom and coercion, respectively (a concept of labor as "malediction" and suffering, and of art as freedom and pleasure). Neither Kant nor Adam Smith imagined that art could suffer from the same ills which already afflicted labor. However, art was not able to escape the negative consequences resulting from the transformation of artistic activity into a productive activity, whereby the work of art acquired the character of a commodity, and from the attempt to invest artistic labor with the bourgeois form of wage labor. Consequently, under these conditions the opposition between art and labor does not consist only of the loss of the artistic character of labor, that is, the loss of its creative principle, and, therefore, of the separation of art and labor to the point that their original solidarity disappears; it also consists of the loss by art of its own artistic character, so to speak, whereby art enters into a contradiction with itself insofar as there is an attempt to extend to the sphere of art the bourgeois form of wage labor.

If, as Marx maintained, the transformation of labor into wage labor means that it loses its artistic character, then the extension of the laws of capitalist material production to artistic labor can only mean the negation of artistic activity as such. This means, in turn, that the economic form assumed by labor in capitalist society cannot be applied to artistic creation without destroying it. Artistic labor cannot in any way dispense with its concrete, individual form, for it consists precisely of that form. The artist cannot be indifferent to the determinability of his activity, nor can his creative capacity be converted into something abstract, purely mechanical, and therefore indifferent to its specific individual form. Because of its very structure, art cannot allow this reduction of the concrete to the abstract, the individual to the general, the living to the dead, which is characteristic of wage labor. The determinability of artistic labor determines, in turn, the determinability of its product; all true works of art are unique and unrepeatable; they have their own value, which depends on their specific qualities and on their unique capacity to satisfy the human need for affirmation, expression, and communication.

In this sense, insofar as capitalist production extends its operations to the sphere of art, negating in this sphere the artistic or creative principle which it negates at the same time in the sphere of labor, Marx asserted that capitalism is hostile to art. This hostility reveals that the fundamental law of production under capitalism not only separates art and labor, but also tends to assimilate art and labor under the economic form of alienated labor.

Notes

1. These manuscripts were published for the first time in German in Moscow in 1939 by the Marx-Engels-Lenin Institute under the title *Grundrisse der Kritik der politischen Oekonomie (Rohentwurf)*. They form a thick volume of 764 pages, divided into two large sections: one on money and one on capital, preceded by an essay on the relationships among production, consumption, distribution, and trade, as well as the method of political economy. Portions have been translated into English by David McLellan (New York: Harper and Row, 1972). Subsequently we shall refer to this work as the *Grundrisse.*
2. *Grundrisse,* p. 366; English edition, p. 109.
3. Ibid., English edition, pp. 109-10.
4. Ibid., pp. 366-67; English edition, p. 110.
5. Ibid., p. 203.
6. Ibid., p. 204.
7. Ibid.
8. Ibid.
9. *Manuscripts,* p. 114.

15. Creative Freedom and Capitalist Production

The Marxist thesis of the hostility of capitalism to art allows us to situate on a real base the problem, vital for the artist, of creative freedom. We are confronted with this problem from the moment that art finds itself subject to the laws of capitalist material production, whereby creative freedom is reduced or even annulled.

The creative freedom of the artist, like any other freedom, has nothing to do with freedom in the idealist sense of excluding all dependency or conditioning. It exists, as do all concrete freedoms, in dialectical unity with necessity; that is, it does not imply an absolute dependency, since this would make freedom impossible, nor does it imply a total independence which could only exist in the imagination, ideally, but not in the activity of a real artist who lives in a determinate human world and is historically, socially, culturally, and ideologically conditioned. However exceptional his creative personality, his individuality is always that of a social being. Consequently, his creative freedom has nothing to do with that absolute, anarchic, and aristocratic freedom which only exists ideally, or which is sometimes invoked, as Lenin pointed out, to hide the most profound dependencies.[1]

The creative freedom of the artist exists in an indissoluble relationship with certain needs which assume different forms (social, spiritual, or ideological conditioning; type and level of the artist's relationship with reality; degree of knowledge and mastery of the materials and means or tools of expression; national and artistic traditions; etc.). The artist only affirms himself in this relationship to the extent that he over-comes this diverse conditioning (conquest of universal humanity starting from a historical, social, class, or national conditioning; mastery of the material; transfiguration of the given reality; etc.). Creative freedom, in this sense, is not given; it is a conquest by the artist over necessity itself. From this we can deduce: (1) that this necessity does not contra-dict, in principle, creative freedom; and (2) that this creative freedom only acquires a concrete content when the artist succeeds in affirming himself by overcoming necessity. All great works of art are in this sense concrete, real manifesta-tions of man's creative freedom.

But the relationship between freedom and necessity is not an absolute one. Freedom cannot be asserted before every necessity. Freedom fails, finds itself limited, or is annulled in situations where necessity destroys the subject-object rela-tionship which makes truly free and creative activity possible. Artistic creation implies the transformation of a given mate-rial into a new, humanized object in which the subject is objectified and in which the subject recognizes himself and can be recognized by others. The subject creates, therefore, to satisfy a need for objectification and communication, which he can only satisfy by exercising his creativity in an activity which culminates in the existence of an object for himself and for others. Since the artist creates in conformity with an inner need, his relationship with the object and with his creative activity is an intrinsic, necessary relationship to which he cannot be indifferent; this relationship has a con-crete content for the artist. When an artist creates because of a need to earn a living, and consequently for the market, he creates for another rather than for himself, but this other has an external relationship with him, much as the relationship between worker and capitalist. His activity assumes a formal, abstract character; the more abstract and formal, the more the artist limits his individual creative personality in defer-ence to the tastes and ideals which govern the market. This limitation of the artist's creative personality implies a limitation of his creative freedom, because this freedom can only manifest itself in the realization of this personality and not in the leveling along with other personalities which is necessarily imposed to the extent that artistic labor becomes formal and abstract in response to the exigencies of the market. Creative freedom is a necessary condition for the realization of the artist's personality, but it is incompatible with an extension of the laws of capitalist material production to the sphere of art.

As a young man, Marx was already conscious of this incompatibility between creative freedom and creation for the market, even before he exposed capitalist production as production for the creation of surplus value. In a May 1842 article published in the *Rheinische Zeitung*, he dealt with the problem of creative freedom in relation to freedom of the press, attacking the position of those members of parliament who saw this question from the perspective of the social class they represented. The bourgeois parliamentarians defended a freedom of the press which corresponded with their interests. For them the press was an industry and freedom of the press was a part of industrial freedom. Marx believed that this concept of the press implied its degradation, and that the sort of freedom defended by the representatives of the bourgeoisie had nothing to do with real freedom, because *"the first freedom of the press consists in its not being a business."*[2] In this framework Marx placed the incompatibility between the activity of writing as an end, as labor that satisfies a spiritual need of expression, and as a means, whereby the writer is forced to satisfy the needs of another in order to earn a living. "A writer must of course earn his living to exist and be able to write, but he must in no sense exist and write so as to earn a living."[3] In this case, his labor ceases to be truly free labor, an end in itself, and becomes instead a means of earning a living for himself and profit for others.

In no sense does the writer regard his works as a *means*. They are ends in themselves; so little are they means for him and others that, when necessary, he sacrifices *his* existence to *theirs* . . . The writer who debases his writing to a material means deserves, as punishment for his intrinsic lack of freedom, the extrinsic lack of freedom of the censor; although his very existence is already his punishment.[4]

In effect, the artist who finds himself forced to sell his creative talent to produce for the market experiences a reduction of his creative possibilities. To the extent that the laws of capitalist material production are extended to the sphere of artistic creation, the artist finds himself in contradiction with the economic system into which his production is assimilated.

The artist cannot renounce his creative freedom without sacrificing his own artistic activity, that is, without renouncing the true satisfaction of his vital need for expression and communication. He cannot cease to create in order to escape this conflict, because his silence would be tantamount to a double suicide: artistic and human, since only by creating can he manifest his most profound human dimension. When Rimbaud put an end to his creative existence in his youth, not only was the creative potential of a genius truncated, but the world of alienation—alienation of nonworkers, as Marx put it in the *Economic and Philosophic Manuscripts*—became enriched with a prosperous marble merchant. When Rimbaud ceased to create he put an end to the life of a truly rich man who felt a human need for expression.

In the conflict with a society which vilifies and debases artistic production, the artist cannot choose a life of silence or renunciation without thereby destroying the structure which safeguards his human condition in an alienated world. The artist has another alternative: to try to affirm his creative freedom in a world which militates against it by attempting to convert it into a commodity. The artist then produces for himself and for those whom his message cannot reach because his means of access are closed when he refuses to produce in accordance with an external need, that is, for the market; his work, moreover, comes into contradiction with the tastes and ideals which govern the production of commodities, and therefore he cannot find a buyer. In that situation the artist creates heroically in response to an inner need for expression, without making compromises which limit his creative freedom; his work turns its back on the artistic marketplace and defies the exigencies of that market. This defiance, this incorruptible faithfulness to a vital need to create in accordance with an inner rather than an external impulse, can be associated with Van Gogh, for example. But the rebellion against the implacable laws of capitalist production cannot be carried out with impunity. The history of art in the last third of the nineteenth and beginning of the twentieth centuries shows us the terrible price that the greatest of artists have had to pay for their rebellion: hunger, misery, suicide, or madness.

Sometimes artists try to escape the rule of the law of capitalist production by dividing their creative activity. They produce for themselves, to satisfy their inner need for expression and communication, as well as for the market, to satisfy an external need. The artist thus reproduces in his existence as an artist the schism characteristic of real life in bourgeois society. Just like other people in capitalist society who lead two lives, private and public, without being able to integrate them, the artist splits his artistic life in two: authentic creation and public creation. This is the road chosen, for example, by artists who in order to earn a living decide to do commercial or advertising art. Advertising is in the direct and immediate service of commercial and industrial interests. The artist who puts his talent at the disposal of advertising must abide by a number of exigencies which can only contribute to the depersonalization of his work and the withering of his creative talent, because the characteristics of advertising art end up by creating habits which in time obstruct the course of true creative impulses. The work of a commercial artist must distinguish itself by simplicity, clarity, and lack of complexity in order to facilitate its communication with the public. Everything in advertising art must be easily recognizable—the theme, the intention, etc.—and everything must contribute to a direct, immediate, and unequivocal influence on the spectator. Advertising art must be capable of producing the desired effect of attracting potential consumers to the product being praised, and of influencing consumers without their being aware of how they are being influenced. Apart from the moral and ideological questions which this poses for the true artist and his reputation, the exigencies of artistic realization in this field, which can be satisfied only by dissipating the creative personality, by depersonalizing artistic activity, end up by frustrating the real creative energies of a talented artist. Such are the negative rewards which, in highly developed capitalist countries, advertising art yields to true artists. And such is the painful situation which faces an artist who, in order to escape the transformation of his works into commodities, rends his creative activity in two, because his works, either on account of the limitations of the market or his rejection of it, cannot assure his material existence. The artist thus ruins a number of creative possibilities at the same time that he contaminates the truly artistic work he wants to realize. This is one of the most trenchant and dramatic manifestations of the hostility of capitalism to art.

At times artists try to earn a living by completely separating their creative activity from the exigencies of their material existence. Their creation is not, then, an expression of their concrete, total lives, but rather an abstraction of it, an ivory tower within which they preserve what they identify as their real lives. This is another way in which artists lead a double life: they are painters and bank tellers, poets and diplomats, novelists and judges, etc.; their daily or normal lives are implacable mutilations of their authentic existence. Kafka lived in the misery of such a schism between two lives which never succeeded in becoming one. Many other artists today live this double life in capitalist society, each anxiously wresting from one life the time he needs for his other, authentic life.

In all the above cases, the artist fights to defend his creative freedom and therefore struggles against what represents a threat to that freedom in capitalist society, i.e., the attempt to treat his work as a commodity, to assimilate artistic creation into the alienated world of material production. Inasmuch as the concept of productivity which capitalism applies to artistic labor establishes a radical contradiction between art and capitalism, all great artists who want to create in response to an inner need and not according to external needs imposed by the market necessarily come into conflict with the socioeconomic system which restricts and limits their creative possibilities. This conflict with bourgeois society is manifest in the divorce from that society of the most important and fruitful artistic movements of the nineteenth and twentieth centuries, although artists in those movements may not have been aware, in most cases, of the socioeconomic basis of that divorce. This conflict is also manifest on a purely artistic plane in the distinction between creation for its own sake and creation which does not let itself be ruled by the laws which govern the market and which are an expression of the ideas, tastes, and ideals of the dominant class. But once the artist becomes conscious of the real economic and social roots of that conflict—as a conflict between artistic production and capitalist material production—he becomes convinced at the same time that a solution cannot come from a mere change of direction of artistic creation, but must come from a radical transformation of the economic and social system which by its nature attempts to extend the laws of capitalist material productivity to artistic creation.

Therefore, when Marx asserted that capitalist material production is hostile to art, he emphasized that the sources of this hostility are found in the very nature of capitalist production, which attempts to extend its laws to all spheres of human activity. This hostility is manifested above all in the attempt to reduce artistic labor to a general, abstract labor, as is done to alienated labor under the conditions of capitalist production. However, artistic labor cannot be assimilated into wage labor, and the work of art cannot be reduced to a commodity, without negating the very essence of art. If the hostility of capitalism to art is an essential manifestation of the laws of capitalist production, and if the extension of these laws to artistic creation has harmful effects on the fate of art, what leeway does artistic creation have in a society dominated by this type of material production? And how valid is the Marxist thesis of the hostility of capitalism to art when we apply it to the real state of art in capitalist society?

Notes

1. "There can be no real and effective 'freedom' in a society based on the power of money, in a society in which the masses of working people live in poverty and the handful of rich live like parasites. . . . One cannot live in society and be free from society. The freedom of the bourgeois writer, artist or actress is simply masked (or hypocritically masked) dependence on the money-bag, on corruption, on prostitution." V. I. Lenin, "Party Organisation and Party Literature," *Collected Works,* vol. 10 (Moscow: Foreign Languages Publishing Houses, 1962), p. 48.
2. Karl Marx, "Debating the Freedom of the Press," in Karl Marx and Frederick Engels, *Über Kunst und Literatur* (Berlin: Henschel Verlag, 1949), pp. 427-28.
3. Ibid.
4. Ibid.

16. The Development of Art Under the Hostile Conditions of Capitalism

Marx pointed out two kinds of hostility of capitalism to art: hostility which originates in the very nature of the capitalist economic system, and hostility which affects art *essentially,* insofar as it is qualitative and creative labor. At the same time, he recognized that under capitalism the development of art has not been halted but has reached great heights, as manifested in the nineteenth century by such artists as Balzac and Dickens, not to mention the previous accomplishments of Cervantes, Shakespeare, or Goethe. It is enough to mention these names—to which we might add those of Byron, Shelley, or de Maupassant in literature, Delacroix and Courbet in painting, or Beethoven and Brahms in music—to discard the idea of a retrogression or paralyzation of the development of art under capitalism in the nineteenth century. And as far as our century is concerned, we can both enlarge the list of great writers, painters, and composers, and record the birth of new arts, like film, which would have been impossible without the scientific and technical progress that has come about under capitalism. Does recognition of the fact that art has flourished in the novel, poetry, and symphonic music at the same time that it has broadened its field of activities to include film (which Marx could not have known or foreseen) invalidate the Marxist thesis of the hostility of capitalism to art?

In the first place, let us establish the scope and limits of this thesis. It cannot be extended to all forms of artistic production in capitalist society, but only to those affected by the law of capitalist material production, that is, by the criterion of productivity which rules wage labor. A great number of writers and artists, particularly in capitalist countries with a weak economic development, do not live on their literary or artistic activity because their production does not fundamentally assume the character of production for the market. Moreover, in those capitalist countries where the market is already well established and where a great number of writers and artists practice their creative activity as a profession from which they earn a living, an important group of nonprofessional or amateur artists and writers remain unaffected by the exigencies of their respective markets.

Capitalism attempts to assimilate artistic production under the scope of material production, subjecting it to its laws, but this does not mean that this attempt is fully or mostly successful. If that were the case, the hostility to art would become a mortal threat to its existence, as is true in those cases where artistic creation is subjected to the law of capitalist productivity.

As we have previously pointed out, the degree of subjection of artistic production to the laws of material production depends on the degree of capitalist development in the country in question. Insofar as material production increasingly assumes a capitalist form, it attempts to apply that form to the most diverse branches of intellectual production: science, education, art, etc. A certain degree of development of capitalist material production, which from a historical point of view emerges with the first industrial revolution, is an indispensable condition for the application of the criterion of material productivity to intellectual production, including art. For that reason, to an Adam Smith artistic labor was still unproductive from an economic point of view. In the same way, art and literature do not fall under the laws of material production in any particular country as long as that production does not assume a capitalist form.

We must also point out that not all branches of art are

subject to the laws of capitalist production to the same extent. Some arts suffer the hostility of capitalism to a greater degree than others, but this means that capitalism is more interested in subjecting some arts to its laws than others; for example, film depends much more than dance or poetry on the totality of the economic phenomena of which the film industry forms a part: investment of capital, mass distribution and consumption all create conditions for increased profits, etc. Today it is possible to write lyric poetry with no regard for those economic phenomena, especially if the poet lowers his voice and contents himself with a small number of readers, but it is not possible to produce films without putting in motion a whole complex economic mechanism. Moreover, from the perspective of capitalist production, it is always more profitable to invest in the production of a film than in publishing a book of poems. The more profound the interest in the material productivity of a work of art—an interest which is in turn determined by the amount of capital invested and the amount of profit or loss in question—the more creative freedom is limited, the more the creative process is manipulated in an attempt to assure that its product will be accepted by a mass audience.

This is clearly evident in the film industry. The subjects, plots, styles, and even the language used in films are adjusted in the interest of achieving the highest productivity from an economic point of view. Throughout its history, the American film industry has offered constant proof of this. Today, films produced by two or more capitalist countries under the system of co-production are not in general made to bring together filmmakers of different national origins in a common activity, responding to common artistic and ideological needs, but in order to achieve common economic goals: to make new markets available to both sides, to ensure better conditions for export, to invest free capital which in its country of origin cannot be fully utilized. In sum, international co-production has emerged in order to ensure profits national production cannot guarantee. This imposes a number of demands on the creative process, which affect the theme, style, choice of actors, locations for filming, etc. The application of the criterion of productivity to cinematographic art, reducing it to the condition of *industry*, seals its lamentable artistic fate, since only in a very few cases does the director succeed in overcoming the hostile environment which surrounds his creation. However, the names of Fellini, Buñuel, Antonioni, Visconti, Resnais, and other film directors in capitalist countries are associated with an affirmation of the creative nature of man precisely in this field where the hostility toward the creative impulse is most openly manifested; this exposes the degree to which art is a fortress which capitalist productivity cannot easily conquer. But it is no accident that this affirmation of creative freedom comes from countries such as Italy or France, and not from Hollywood, where film production is most implacably subjected to the laws of capitalist material production—this only confirms, in another way, the thesis of the hostility of capitalism to art. But it is only fair to also mention the fact that in the United States some films manage to escape from a system of production which has been characterized as a "flagrant prostitution of the creative intelligence." It is again no accident that these exceptions that confirm the rule can be found only among the small film companies and independent producers, who have nothing to do with the eight large companies which control 95 percent of the Hollywood film industry.

We have dwelt on the example of film for two reasons: (1) it is the most painful and obvious example of the hostility of capitalism to art; and (2) even in this branch of art artistic creation is not paralyzed; in the works of the European directors mentioned above, to which we could add the names of such Americans as Frank Capra, King Vidor, and Orson Welles, it is possible to transcend the limits of film as an industry.

What we find in film in such a palpable manner we find to a greater or lesser degree in the other branches of artistic creativity. The more the laws of material production are extended to artistic activity, the less propitious are the conditions for creation and the more intense is the effort needed for the artist to resist and overcome hostile elements. That is to say, the relationship between the two terms of this contradiction (the hostility of capitalism to art and the continuity of artistic development) is not immutable. It varies according to the specific historical period of capitalism, the degree of capitalist economic development in the country, and the specific character of the branch of art. But the two terms of the contradiction are in a state of tension from the moment that capitalist material production reaches a high degree of development and attempts to assimilate intellectual production into its world.

In sum, hostility to art appears as a tendency which is nurtured in the very heart of capitalist material production, but it is never so absolute that it can stop the development of art and thereby make its continued existence impossible. The realist novel of the nineteenth century, most of the modern art movements against the official and academic painting of the nineteenth century, and the recent neo-realist movement in film prove the impossibility of stopping the development of art even under the intensely hostile conditions of modern capitalist production. On the other hand, the flowering of the novel, poetry, or symphonic music and the achievement of great artistic successes even in those branches of art as dependent on the exigencies of material production as architecture and film does not exclude in any way the hostility of capitalism to art, for this hostility is an inevitable manifestation of the laws of capitalist production.

Capitalism does not succeed in fully imposing itself on art because of the impossibility of reducing artistic labor to the condition of alienated labor by transforming it into a purely formal or mechanical activity. Even when an artist works for the market, he resists the uniformity and leveling which destroys his creative personality. By the mere fact of realizing his creative abilities he finds himself involved in a struggle against the hostile limits established by the capitalist market. The artist is not always victorious in this struggle, and as shown by the experience of the Hollywood film industry, the criterion of economic productivity repeatedly blocks creative possibilities. But without this struggle to affirm the creative nature of man, the history of art in the past century, especially in certain branches, would be nothing more than a barren field. To this affirmation of creative activity we must also add the heroic struggles of artists who have refused to produce for the market at the cost of the most terrible privations. Finally, capitalist material production does not succeed in extending its laws to all forms of artistic creation because in the societies dominated by those laws artists become conscious of the fact that the fate of their work and of art in general is connected to the fate of society and its radical transformation. Thus a new art emerges which is opposed to the ideas, tastes, and values of the dominant class and which expects nothing from a market ruled by the ideas, tastes, and values which it repudiates; this new art attempts to reach those who share its ideas and values, but without subjecting itself to the laws which govern the capitalist market. But these difficult victories of art, amid the hostile conditions created by a mode of production which is the antithesis of creative labor, do not contradict the validity of Marx's thesis regarding the hostility of capitalist material production to artistic production.

17. Production and Consumption
(Creation and Enjoyment)

Up to now we have considered the work of art from the perspective of its production or creation. But production is not an isolated process or end in itself: it forms part of a greater totality in relation to which it assumes its final form. Within that totality is also the process of consumption, whereby the products "become objects of use and enjoyment, of individual appropriation."[1] Production implies consumption, and the product is related both to its producer and to others whose needs it satisfies. Production thus affirms its social character by requiring a collective effort—particularly in material production—and in the fact that even when it is individual production it is the production of an "individual only in society,"[2] and therefore of a socially conditioned individual. The social character of production also is manifested in the fact that its products are the direct objects of consumption or enjoyment.

Although they are part of the same totality, production and consumption are separated in a temporal sense: production precedes consumption. Consumption can only be actualized when the act of production results in a product which, after having objectified the subject, is separated from the producer. The product then begins its own life, so to speak. While it objectively manifests the appropriation of nature by the producer, it demands a new, different appropriation, which can only be realized in consumption. The product appears as a destination from the point of view of production and as a point of departure from the perspective of consumption. It therefore satisfies two needs, particularly in the case of creative labor or artistic production: a need for expression by the producer and a spiritual need for enjoying or contemplating it. The relation between production and consumption is consequently a necessary, intrinsic one, by virtue of which both processes are implied and rooted in each other.

In the introduction to the *Grundrisse,* Marx revealed the general unity of production and consumption, which is manifested most strongly in the unity of artistic creation and enjoyment. Production adapts matter for consumption, thus making possible a determinate form of appropriation; consumption orients and provides the goal of production.

> The product receives its last finishing touches in consumption. A railroad on which no one rides, which is consequently not used up, not consumed, is only a potential railroad (or is a railway on which no one travels) and not a real one. Without production, no consumption; but, on the other hand, without consumption, no production; since production would then be without a purpose.[3]

If we apply this concept to artistic creation, we will find that artistic production realizes its true essence only when it is shared by others. While the artist expresses and objectifies himself in his product, thus satisfying an intrinsic, concrete need, his manner of satisfying that need demands in turn the satisfaction of the needs of others. The form given to matter in order to reveal the ideological or emotional content the artist expresses must be such that it enables others to *use* it. A work of art can only be consumed, properly consumed, in the domain of reality, as a realized potential. As a point of departure for a new process as well as a point of destination it is not a definitive goal but a road, which upon being traveled places different human subjects, eras, or worlds in relationship to each other. It is a road which is always open, which can be traveled time and again, keeping human communication alive even though the specific human subjects, societies, eras, ideas, or interests may change.

What is Sophocles' *Antigone,* written twenty-five centuries ago in a society based on slavery, if not a bridge between the men and society of that time and the men and societies of other times, by which they can find and communicate with each other time and again? It is a firm and enduring road which human beings will be able to travel at all times. An object created two and a half thousand years ago in faraway Greece continues to be not a thing-in-itself but an object for others, a living language.

Products in general, and artistic products in particular, demand this transition from potential to realization which can only be accomplished in consumption. "A dwelling which is not inhabited is really no dwelling; consequently, a product, as distinguished from a mere natural object, proves to be such, first *becomes* a product, in consumption."[4] A work of art is a message, has a human meaning for others, and is a real product, not a merely possible one, only when others appropriate its meaning.

Artistic creation is an objectification of the subject, but not all objectifications are valid. "Production is a product, not as the material embodiment of activity but only as an object for the active subject."[5] An artistic object is such only as it relates to a human subject, that is, only through its enjoyment or appropriation by others as a means or instrument of communication. Inasmuch as the artist creates not only by objectifying his activity, but also by creating an object *for a subject,* he cannot dispense with the needs of others. The artist takes those needs into account before really and effectively satisfying them, that is, before his objectification has reached its goal. Renaissance society wanted an art which satisfied its new aspirations, ideas, values, or interests; it therefore needed a new type of production. In this case consumption determined production itself. "Consumption produces production by creating the necessity for new production, i.e. by providing the ideal, inward, impelling cause which constitutes the prerequisite of production."[6] Therefore, consumption gravitates around production, determining its purpose, its *raison d'être,* before and/or during production. Consumption determines production in the sense that it *ideally* supplies the purpose or object of production. Production in effect produces objects which to a certain extent already have been *ideally* produced as goals drawn by the needs of consumption. As Marx stated:

> Consumption furnishes the impulse for production as well as its object, which plays in production the part of its guiding aim. It is clear that while production furnishes the material object of consumption, consumption provides the ideal object of production, as its image, its want, its impulse and its purpose. It furnishes the objects of production in a form that is still subjective. No needs, no production.[7]

We can see that consumption does not play a decisive role; instead it influences production by establishing the goal toward which the objectified activity of the producer is directed. It is not external to production, however, but in an indissoluble relationship with it, since it is only by virtue of consumption that a product is truly a product, that is, an object for a subject. Consumption, both of products in general and of artistic products in particular, therefore determines the social character of production as an activity which from the outset requires the enjoyment or appropriation of its objects by other subjects. The product responds to the needs of both producer and other subjects, of both present and future subjects; it therefore responds to needs which are never exhausted and which are unlimitedly reproduced through the enjoyment or consumption of the object throughout history.

Although consumption determines production by creating its purpose and consequently creating the need for a new type of production, this does not in any way mean that production is passively subordinated to consumption or that it plays a secondary role in the intrinsic relationship. On the contrary, we will shortly see that production is primary in this process since it makes real, effective consumption possible and creates both the subject who satisfies a determinate need in the act of appropriating (consuming or enjoying) the object, as well as the very mode of enjoying or consuming it.

Marx indicated three ways in which consumption is determined by production. First, production supplies the material or object of consumption: "Consumption without an object is no consumption, hence from this point of view production creates and produces consumption."[8] Although consumption traces the ideal purpose of production and thus influences it, it is only the real, effective existence of the produced object which makes possible its appropriation, its enjoyment or consumption, in a real and effective manner. As far as art is concerned, it is equally clear that without artistic creation there would be no enjoyment or contemplation. Second, production produces consumption by supplying it not only with its object but also with its mode of consuming the object. The produced object is not an object in general but a determinate object which must be consumed in a determinate manner; the object satisfies a determinate need, and in addition the determinability of the object, the form given by the producer to the material, determines in a certain sense the form of consumption.

> Hunger is hunger; but the hunger that is satisfied with cooked meat eaten with fork and knife is a different kind of hunger from the one that devours raw meat with the aid of hands, nails and teeth. Not only the object of consumption, but also the manner of consumption is produced by production; that is to say, consumption is created by production not only objectively but also subjectively. Production thus creates the consumers.[9]

The relationship between the product which answers a need and the manner of satisfying that need by consuming the produced object is manifested as an adaptation of the mode of consumption to the determinations of production. It is in this second sense that Marx precisely affirmed that production produces consumption, but this also is manifested in a third way. Production determines consumption by creating the very needs which are satisfied in consumption, that is, by creating subjects which are adequate to the objects. By creating needs for its products, production enriches the forms of human appropriation. "The object of art, as well as any other product, creates an artistic public, appreciative of beauty. Production thus produces not only an object for the subject, but also a subject for the object."[10] It is no accident that Marx gives this example. He would not have done so if his entire dialectic of the relationship between production and consumption were not applicable to the production and consumption of works of art. He underlines the creative essence of artistic activity on a new level. If production were passively subordinate to consumption, artistic creation would be reduced to supplying an object to a subject, and the manner of enjoying the beauty of the object would be defined in advance. If that were the case, artistic creation would always have to keep up with or be a step behind the needs of a pre-formed audience, with previously established tastes, values, or categories, and the great artistic innovations would have to wait for the emergence or maturation of a new mode of consuming—perceiving or enjoying—artistic objects. While a change in the ideological climate of a society or an era demands innovations and thus creates favorable conditions for a new aesthetic attitude, the history of art and literature shows that changes in aesthetic sensibility do not come about spontaneously, which explains the persistence of aesthetic criteria and values in contradiction to profound changes in other spheres of human life. A new sensibility, a new audience, a new aesthetic attitude have to be created; they are not fruits of spontaneous processes. And among the factors which make a decisive contribution to the creation of a new subject for a new artistic object is the object itself.

This point, which we can infer from the passage quoted above, reveals the twofold creative capacity of artistic production: it both supplies objects capable of satisfying human needs and creates new modes of enjoying the beauty of those objects. In the same way, it creates an audience capable of assimilating what can no longer be assimilated by those who continue to abide by old forms of aesthetic enjoyment.

Notes

1. Karl Marx, *Grundrisse der Kritik der politischen Oekonomie* (Moscow: Marx-Engels-Lenin Institute, 1939), p. 10; English edition (New York: Harper & Row, 1972), p. 22.
2. Ibid., p. 6; English edition, p. 17.
3. Ibid., pp. 12-13; English edition, p. 24.
4. Ibid., p. 13; English edition, p. 25.
5. Ibid.
6. Ibid.
7. Ibid.
8. Ibid.
9. Ibid.
10. Ibid., p. 14; English edition, p. 26.

18. Aesthetic Creation and Enjoyment as Forms of Human Appropriation

Production and consumption are two different types of relationship between subject and object; they are also two different types of appropriation.

All productions, material or artistic, are appropriations of matter by human beings, who in that way make nature their own and create new objects, human or humanized products. Nature, or matter, is here the object of production; when man puts into action his physical and spiritual powers, that natural, given object ceases to be an object in itself and becomes a human object. Man humanizes nature and his own nature at the same time. Appropriation is thus twofold: of external and internal nature.

The product is not only witness to the appropriation of nature by the producer; it is also an object of consumption, since it appears in order to satisfy a need. In consumption or enjoyment one establishes a relationship with an object which satisfies a specific human need; one enters into a specifically human relationship as one appropriates an object for its human significance. To enjoy or consume a painting means to appropriate the human significance, the beauty, the spiritual content which has been objectified in it by its creator through a determinate form.

The relationship between subject and object in both production and consumption is not direct and immediate but is established within the framework and through the mediation of a determinate society. Both the producer and the consumer are socially conditioned. Because individual production or consumption does not exist outside of society, appropriation varies from one society to the next in accordance with the relations human beings contract among themselves. As far as production is concerned, there is certainly a difference between appropriation of its products under conditions of free and creative labor (by virtue of which man enriches his human essence in objects to the extent that he humanizes his own and external nature), and appropriation under the conditions of alienated labor under the domination of the means of production by private property (by which objects become strange and alien to the subject, along with his own activity and his relations with other human beings). In the second case, the more the subject appropriates nature, humanizing the world around him, the more he is impoverished and robbed of his human essence. Appropriation then loses its human sense, because the products of labor cease to be for the worker objects with human forms.

We have noted that while artistic production represents a highly developed form of specifically human appropriation, this appropriation or artistic assimilation of the external world is harassed under the conditions of capitalist society by the tendency to apply to it the laws of capitalist material production. What happens to consumption as a form of appropriating objects in a society in which a human being is essentially defined by what he owns? And what happens to that specific form of consumption, artistic enjoyment, in a society which tends to reduce the complex network of human relationships to a relationship of ownership?

Ownership of objects and aesthetic enjoyment

In order for man to *be,* he must appropriate both his own and external nature. But in capitalist society appropriation presents itself as the possession of objects, which in turn implies a dispossession in human terms, an impoverishment of the subject's humanity. Deprived thereby of his specifically human essence, the subject ends up by becoming yet

another object. *Having* dominates *being* in the capitalist
world and truly human appropriation gives way to private
appropriation, or ownership of objects. Being and having are
equated: he who does not have, who does not own, does not
exist. Man thus appropriates his essence and the human
reality of the object in a one-sided and abstract way, since his
own being and the object have been reduced to an abstraction: a being which owns and an object which is owned.
"Private property has made us so stupid and one-sided that
an object is only *ours* when we have it—when it exists for us
as capital, or when it is directly possessed. . . ."[1] We perceive
objects in only one sense: "*All* these physical and mental
senses have therefore—the sheer estrangement of *all* these
senses—the sense of *having.*"[2]

To humanly appropriate an object is to make it truly ours,
to appropriate it as a human product; to enjoy an artistic
object is to appropriate it as the work of and for man, to see
ourselves confirmed in our human reality in the process of
making that object ours. I can enter into a relationship with
an aesthetic object as an object of and for man only insofar
as I affirm and realize the essential powers of my being. And
an artistic object exists as such for me only when it appears
before me as a humanized object and not as a mere object.

As far as the subject is concerned, in the relationship of
ownership the object loses its human meaning, all its objectified human richness, and is reduced to its material wealth.
The many meanings of the object are reduced to one: its
material utility. All the qualitative riches of the object are
dissolved in the relationship of ownership and the human,
concrete object thereby becomes an abstraction. But when
the object is dissipated as a concrete-sensuous entity in which
determinate spiritual riches are objectified, it loses its aesthetic condition to become purely and simply an object of
possession. The relationship of ownership, seen from the perspective of the object, is incompatible with a truly aesthetic
enjoyment or consumption. But this incompatibility is also
manifest from the point of view of the subject. In effect, in

the aesthetic relationship the subject can only grasp (consume or enjoy) the object by realizing his spiritual powers—intellectual, affective, and sensuous—as a unique totality, in indissoluble unity, and in all their richness. In the ownership relationship the subject suppresses this internal richness and gives free rein to his egoistic nature, his sense of ownership, and this is revealed in his behavior toward the object in its narrowly utilitarian sense. Thus an impoverished subject with eyes only for material utility corresponds to an abstract, mutilated object in which the human richness—expressed in a concrete-sensuous form in the work of art—is dissipated. The subject can only affirm his egoistic reality, his sense of ownership, insofar as he dispossesses the object of its human richness and sees in it only its material richness. And the object can be only a confirmation of the egoistic reality of the subject insofar as it is appropriated purely and simply as a useful object, dissolving everything that is consubstantial with the aesthetic object—its concrete-sensuous richness, its human meaning, and its concrete individuality.

The relationship of ownership thus blocks the way to an aesthetic attitude or enjoyment by preventing man from appropriating the object in a human manner, as a total man, not as an abstract and mutilated being. Moreover, the more highly developed the aesthetic value of the object—that is, the richer in human significance and the more complex and profound the human world objectified in the work of art—the more hostile will be the utilitarian attitude to the aesthetic object.

For the capitalist *qua* capitalist, the appropriation of a work of art is exhausted in purchase and ownership. The subject enters into a relationship with the object on the basis of his *having*, not of his being. In a society in which works of art become commodities, in order to possess a work of art one does not need to have the artistic taste or sensibility which allows one to discover the spiritual wealth objectified in it. The fact that one is not cultured, sensitive, or capable of perceiving beauty is not an obstacle to the appropriation of a work of art in the capitalist sense. In a society where being is identified with having, what I am, my qualities, my individuality is determined by money.[3] Money enables me to possess even beauty. But it is one thing to *possess* beauty and another to enjoy beauty, to make it truly ours, to appropriate it in human terms.

In his analysis of the relations between production and consumption, Marx did not regard the enjoyment or consumption of the object to be external to the process of production, since the product is not only an objectification of the subject but also an object for another subject. If we apply this to artistic creation, we can see that the artistic product is a human product in a twofold sense: as an object in which the artist realizes and objectifies his essential powers and as an object in which other subjects see their essential powers confirmed, thus dissolving the new objective reality of the product into a new reality which is actualized in the relationship of enjoyment or consumption.

Art is individual creation destined by its nature to supersede the limited sphere of its creator in the form of creation for others. Art is social in a twofold sense: (1) it is the unique creation of a socially conditioned individual, and (2) it satisfies both the creator's and the consumer's need for expression. The latter can only satisfy that need by entering and sharing the world created by the artist and engaging in a dialogue with the artist. The created object is therefore a bridge or means of communication; the artist expresses himself of necessity and his expression, once objectified, will be shared of necessity.

Art is essentially dialogue, communication, an open sea in time and space. Because artistic production by its nature demands doing away with all walls which limit its capacity for communication, the adequate consumption or enjoyment is open and social. This type of consumption converts the work of art into a constant source of contemplation, criticism, understanding, or valuation; it maintains the dialogue after each individual communication with the work of art, which makes it possible for each individual to make the work of art his, humanly his, but in such a way that his individual appropriation gives way to other appropriations. In sum, by integrating these individual appropriations through time, this consumption reveals the entire human richness objectified in a work of art by virtue of its many-sided and rich appropriation.

When I appropriate a work of art individually I affirm myself in this act with all the powers of my being. It is my concrete individuality which is involved here, and all great works of art are characterized by this capacity to shake or move our entire beings. This impact affects me insofar as I am human, concrete, and individual in the sense of a node of social relations, but it is not and cannot be an exclusive impact. Today or tomorrow, even after the disappearance of a whole series of concrete circumstances which were related to the creation of a particular work of art or to my contemplation, enjoyment, or consumption of it, other individuals will appropriate the works of art, and the limitless open dialogue which began with its creation will proceed. My appropriation has nothing to do with the exclusivity of ownership and joins with other appropriations as participants in the same dialogue, a dialogue which is required by the social nature of art itself.

Private appropriation in the form of ownership of works of art completely changes the social nature of the work of art, suppressing or restricting its possibilities for establishing a dialogue. Although the owner of a work of art may want to appropriate it in a relationship that is more than mere ownership, it is clear that no matter how much he tries to supersede its narrow and one-sided framework by allowing others to enjoy or consume *his* work of art, his private ownership of that object will limit its capacity for communication and dialogue.

With regard to other products, the act of consumption is in general an individual act. The owners of those products can appropriate them in a human sense insofar as they satisfy specific needs, that is, by entering into relationships with their use values, not their exchange values. But the work of art is a product which not only demands this human, real appropriation of the object, a relationship with its use value which is manifested in the individual act of enjoying or consuming it, but also requires a vital link between it and human beings which can never be severed; it demands an infinite number of individual appropriations. Private ownership stands in contradiction with art because it both prevents one from establishing an adequate relationship with the object, possessing it in a full sense, but also because it prevents that object from realizing its proper destiny, that is, its social function as a particular instrument or means of communication, as a human work for human beings. Of course, the number of buyers and owners can be increased; the owners can temporarily give up the works which they control as private owners and offer them to galleries or museums, thus enlarging the vital links between the artist and the public. In the first case, the principle of ownership is spread by increasing the number of owners; in the second, there is some broadening of true appropriation within the framework of private ownership, but the radical contradiction between private property and the social and public function of art will persist under capitalism as long as artistic products are made into commodities and ownership of them is restricted to a minority.

The extreme consequences of the application of the principle of private property in the artistic sphere include not only the limitation of the artist's freedom of expression and the restriction of what we might call the freedom to enjoy or consume, but also the total curtailment—temporary or definitive—of that freedom.[4] This is manifested by the fact that in advanced capitalist countries with large artistic markets certain paintings are removed from circulation by large galleries for the purpose of speculation. They are kept hidden for the time needed to increase the profits they can bring to their owners—although not to the artists—making them mute and inert by preventing them from realizing their social and artistic destiny.

Notes

1. *Manuscripts,* p. 139.
2. Ibid.
3. "That which is for me through the medium of *money*—that for which I can pay (i.e. which money can buy)—that am *I*, the possessor of the money. The extent of the power of money is the extent of my power. Money's properties are my properties and essential powers— the properties and powers of its possessor. Thus, what I *am* and *am capable* of is by no means determined by my individuality." Ibid., p. 167.
4. The fate of Diego Rivera's mural *Sueño de una tarde dominical en la Alameda Central,* painted for the dining room of a luxury hotel in Mexico, is well known. In this case the principle of private property upheld its rights and prevented the general public from seeing this work. Another example, even more brutal and mortal for art, was the destruction in 1933 of the mural painted by Diego Rivera for Rockefeller Center in New York, in the name of private property rights.

✷
19. Art and the Masses

The principle of private property stands in contradiction to the social function of art, which must be based on an extensive interconnection between the artist and the public, that is, on the effective possibility that aesthetic enjoyment cease to be the exclusive property of a minority and become instead an increasingly profound and human enjoyment. This enjoyment is not fortuitous; it is essential for artistic creation inasmuch as it fully realizes itself in that enjoyment, and it is essential for the consumer inasmuch as art is one of the most rewarding means which human beings (not just artists) possess to deepen their humanity. Apart from the limitations on the relationship between artist and public which might result from the language employed by the artist or from the inability of the public to understand that language, limitations inherent in the work of art or in the public, the principle of private property divorces the artist from the public.

But what force does this principle have in capitalist society? If it is understood in the sense of a relationship of exclusivity between owner and work of art, particularly in the form of individual ownership, it is currently restricted to painting, especially easel painting, as well as sculpture and architecture. The principle of private property in the other arts—literature, theater, film, music, etc.—essentially is manifested in the use to which property rights are put, which in many cases results in a limitation of creative freedom.

When private ownership of a work of art is capable of

returning high profits, the interests of the owner require that the product be enjoyed not exclusively by a private person, but publicly by the masses.

This mass enjoyment or consumption could not exist as long as consumption involved a unique and unrepeatable work, as in earlier periods of history, although access to it could be extended by exhibits of paintings, public readings, concerts, theatrical presentations, etc. To be massively and unlimitedly consumed, the unique and unrepeatable work of art had to be standardized and mass produced. This reproduction or mechanical standardization of a unique work was and is not an aesthetic problem, but a scientific, technical, material problem. It was necessary that science and technology progress, as they indeed did within the very bosom of capitalism, in order to create the technical means which have made possible the mass distribution of works of art.

The invention of printing at the dawn of capitalism introduced the possibility of mass consumption by making possible the unlimited reproduction of a single work. However, it is only in our time that technical methods have been invented which make possible the truly mass consumption of artistic products. For example, printing methods have been perfected to the point that it is now possible to make magnificent reproductions of paintings, which allows us to familiarize ourselves, in our own homes or in schools, with the artistic masterpieces of the most distant museum. The reproduction of works of art has multiplied their relations with human beings to an unforeseen extent. Of course, the drawback of this enormous technical advance is the fact that a reproduction, no matter how faithful, can never be a substitute for a direct relationship with the original. But from the point of view of the need for art to be unlimitedly open so that it can realize its social function, this approximate, relative, and somewhat unfaithful contact is always to be preferred to an absence of any relationship. The same can be said about recorded music, which by disseminating a good performance beyond the narrow boundaries of the concert hall makes a piece of music available to an unlimited number of listeners.

Public concerts, as well as exhibits of paintings, already marked a new stage, introduced by bourgeois society, which represented an advance over the private concerts or exhibits held in the palaces of aristocrats. However, it is only through the advances of modern technology that large-scale public consumption of literary, graphic, or musical works is possible, especially through the use of such means of communication as the radio, newspapers, and television.

Our era also offers a new art, film, whose products demand from the outset a mass consumption never before required by any other type of artistic production. The number of spectators who see a film, especially when distributed internationally, is counted in the millions, at times in the tens of millions. Radio and television also have audiences that number millions of listeners and viewers.

What can we deduce from all this? That while private appropriation, as a relationship of ownership of artistic products, prevents art from fulfilling its public, social function as a means of communication, the development of productive forces, among them science and technology, has created the most favorable technical and material conditions for the realization of the social function of art; it has done this by extending the enjoyment of art to an enormous audience, thus establishing links more extensive and diverse than could ever have been imagined by artists of other times.

As I have pointed out elsewhere,[1] technology is ambiguous; it does not have an intrinsically determined destiny and therefore can contribute either to the development or degradation of man. But since it is man who endows technology with its value and power, it is man who decides to what *use* it is to be put and who decides whether it will be a source of good or evil for society. Of course, when we speak of man we are referring to social man; therefore, the use of technology is socially determined, inseparable from the dominant social relations within whose framework it is applied. Naturally, the application of technology can be potentially either a benefit or a misfortune for human society, but that potential is converted into reality by means of con-

crete human relations—relations of production—in a determinate society.

With regard to art, technology has the potential of being
applied in either direction and thus has the potential for good
if it is used to multiply the opportunities for artistic consumption. But the realization of this potential and the concrete content of that vast consumption depends on the relations of production and on the specific character of the
fundamental law of material production that governs those
relations. In capitalist society that law is the creation of surplus value, that is, the law of profits. We have seen in previous chapters the difficulties of extending that law, which
governs material production above all, to cover artistic production. Those difficulties result from the impossibility of
reducing the concrete artistic labor to a general, abstract
labor, that is, to the conditions of wage labor. However, because modern technology makes possible both the large-scale
reproduction and mass consumption of works of art, it becomes possible to apply on a large scale the law of capitalist
material production to this sphere. The necessary condition
for this is that art, by taking advantage of the opportunities
offered by technological and industrial development, be
organized as an industry, and that consumption be structured
commercially in order to be truly mass consumption, since
only consumption on that scale can ensure the realization of
the fundamental law of capitalist production. The aesthetic
qualities and ideological content of artistic products can exist
only insofar as they do not conflict with the law of the
maximization of profits. This does not exclude the possibility
that the means of distribution be put at the service of great
art; this is particularly so in the case of literary, musical, or
graphic works which already enjoy the prestige of being
masterpieces by virtue of having resisted the action of time,
that is, a prestige that can be translated into an economic
value. But under capitalist conditions the utilization of mass
means of distribution results in the distribution not of great
art, but of inferior, banal, routine art which corresponds to
the tastes of the empty, hollow and depersonalized mass man

of capitalist society, whom capitalism itself is interested in maintaining in a condition of spiritual hollowness.

More than a century ago, Marx pointed out in *The Economic and Philosophic Manuscripts of 1844* the historical, economic, and social conditions of capitalist society which bring about the alienation of the worker by transforming his creative labor, which is the essence of man, into alienated labor, in which man negates himself, no longer recognizing himself in the products of his activity, in the activity itself, or in his relations with other human beings. Insofar as man does not recognize himself in his products or as a creative subject, thus losing his human essence, he becomes himself an object, a thing. His existence is reified, it becomes a tool, a means, or a commodity. But in capitalist society the phenomenon of alienation proliferates until it includes, in different ways, even the capitalists themselves, with the result that human relations in general assume the form of relations among things, and everything becomes abstract, impersonal, and dehumanized.

This thesis of the alienation of man, which is one of the cornerstones of Marx's critique of capitalist society and of his conception of man, has been confirmed by the growth of monopolistic state capitalism and the fortification of its bureaucratic organization. The powerful development of technology, turned against man under alienating social conditions, makes the "reification" or "depersonalization" of human relations even more apparent. The phenomenon of alienation is today so evident that the great majority of bourgeois thinkers of our time have attempted to deal with it (of course without reference to Marx), in the form of a critique of "mass man," the "one," or "Don Nadie" ("Mr. Nobody"), whose inauthentic existence opposes itself to the authentic existence of the "gifted minorities" (Ortega y Gasset), or the critique of man as "being for death" (Heidegger). What is an essential characteristic of the capitalist system—insofar as it can only affirm itself to the extent that it maintains the "reification" of human existence in general—is converted by these thinkers into a category of human existence in general, or into the consequence of any advanced industrial society, no matter whether its socioeconomic structure is capitalist or socialist, thus ignoring both the concrete, economic, class roots of that reification and the revolutionary way to extirpate it. However, as we have tried to show, in opposition to a number of philosophical conceptions currently in vogue in the West, the phenomenon of "depersonalization" or "reification" of human existence inheres in capitalism, by which we do not mean to deny that it can also be found in socialist societies.[2] Indeed, manifestations of this phenomenon can be found in socialist societies precisely insofar as they apply methods of state control which are alien or contrary to the principles of socialism; this phenomenon, which is an *essential* characteristic of capitalism, can emerge in a socialist society only as a deformation of its very essence.

That the depersonalization or reification of human existence forms part of the very heart of capitalism can be shown by the fact that this phenomenon has grown and assumed even more monstrous characteristics in societies, like that of the United States, ruled by capitalism in its most advanced stage, monopoly capitalism. It is precisely in that form of capitalist society that we find the most refined, and at the same time the most repulsive, forms of manipulation of individuals and consciousness, a manipulation whose purpose is to achieve, by any means, the most extensive and profound transformation of man into a thing, an object.[3] The capitalism which Marx knew carried in the core of its being the tendency toward the reification or massification of existence; but never has that tendency been as fully and threateningly developed as in modern American society. For voracious capitalism the ideal man is the man which it has itself engendered: a depersonalized, dehumanized, hollow man, emptied of any concrete, vital content, a man who tamely allows himself to be molded by any manipulator of consciousness; in short, mass man.

What sort of art or pseudo-art can this mass man digest or consume? What sort of art does capitalism, which is already in a state of decomposition, have a fundamental interest in

encouraging, especially in a highly developed industrial society under conditions which facilitate an extension and
deepening of the process of depersonalization or massification? The answer is art which we can justifiably call *mass
art*.[4] By mass art we mean art whose products satisfy the
pseudo-aesthetic needs of mass or reified man, who is himself
a characteristic product of industrial capitalist society. The
mass consumption of this art is ensured by the existence of a
quantitatively enormous potential audience, as well as by the
possibility of making those artistic products available on a
mass basis through the powerful means of distribution (the
press, radio, film, and television). These products are, in the
literary field, stories of the *True Confessions* variety, popular
romantic fiction of every sort (including radio and television
serials), and the great majority of crime and detective novels;
in music, the great majority of popular songs; and in film, the
great majority of commercial films. In this type of pseudo-
artistic production the great human and social problems are
cast aside for the sake of an alleged need to satisfy a legiti-
mate desire for entertainment; and even when any of these
problems are dealt with, it is always done superficially, with
solutions which do not undermine confidence in the existing
order. In this type of pseudo-art, ideas are emasculated, feelings are stifled, and the most profound passions are cheap-
ened. Mass art is nothing but false or falsified art, a banal art
or a caricature of true art, an art produced entirely to the
measure of the hollow and depersonalized people to whom it
addresses itself. If there is such a thing as total congruence
between production and consumption, between object and
subject, or between work of art and audience, we find it in
the relationship between mass art and the tastes and needs of
its consumers.

The existence of this trivial art which leaves man on the
periphery is therefore undeniable; it is characterized by an
artfully facile language which corresponds to its lack of
human depth; a language which can be understood and com-
municated all the more extensively the more superficial and

hollow its content and the more banal, impoverished, and feeble its means of expression.

In the face of this pseudo-art, we can understand the vehement unrest, malaise, and displeasure expressed by those who truly love art; at times, the criticisms against this mass art lead to an exaltation of elite art, which is offered as an alternative to degraded or reified art. But those criticisms will simply make ripples so long as the economic, social, and ideological sources of the mass art of modern society are left unexamined. For example, there is a tendency to explain this pseudo-artistic phenomenon which sees in it the same characteristics we have seen, but which completely distorts the dialectic between consumption and production. According to this view, the object corresponds to the demands or needs of the subject (the public), and the producers simply satisfy those needs; the product simply adapts itself to the requirements of the consumer. This explanation is generally given by capitalists when they are asked to account for the low aesthetic and ideological quality of their products. They thus make mass art seem to be a product of the masses themselves, which they demand or impose, and therefore to be an inexorable fact, given the relations between supply and demand.

An important theoretician of contemporary art, Wilhelm Worringer, even speaks of the "dictatorship of the consumers" in justifying the need for an art created by artists free of the dictates of consumers.[5] Such a theory endows the consumer with absolute power, able to impose his tastes and desires on the producer insofar as the producer is presented as a solicitous person who only lives to satisfy the needs of consumers. But the profound reality is different: the relations between production and consumption in capitalist society are mystified, since production under capitalism is not at the service of man, or directed to the satisfaction of his needs, but is directed to the creation of surplus value. Thus while consumption or enjoyment appears to determine the direction and extent of production, it in fact is directed and organized to satisfy the requirements of production.

Normal relations between production and consumption, those which can and must be established in a society where the economy serves man, of course assign an important role to consumption or enjoyment, since consumption motivates production and its relationship with production is not therefore external or fortuitous. But we also pointed out that even though consumption plays an active role, the primary role in this relationship belongs to production, since it produces not only objects, but also the subject and the mode of consumption. When Marx declared that the object also creates a subject capable of enjoying it, he revealed the demystified relationship between production and consumption: it is not a dictatorship of producers which in the sphere of art would mean an exclusive production by the artist *for himself,* as an expression of his needs, whereby he would be cutting his ties with others whose needs for appropriation must also be satisfied by the work of art; nor is it a dictatorship of consumers, which would make the inner need to create into a mere external exigency, thus limiting the creative freedom of the artist. In short, consumption does not completely impose itself on production, nor does production have such absolute power that it denies consumption any influence.

In mass art this natural, human relationship between production and consumption is broken. On the level of appearances, the exigencies of consumption—"the public in command"—determine the character of artistic production; the consumer or masses seemingly determine the motivation or purpose of production, obliging the producers to satisfy their needs. We would thus find ourselves in a dictatorship of consumers, to use an expression of Worringer's, but in fact there is no such thing, while there is indeed a dictatorship of producers. In a society ruled by the fundamental law of maximum profits, production produces objects which not only satisfy specific needs but also create those needs and with them the consumers. Through techniques of *persuasion,* advertising and one-sided and reifying education, people desire what they do not need or what does not correspond to their real human needs. When man is divorced from his real needs his desires no longer aim at the satisfaction of his own needs but at those of others. Such is the situation of mass man in a highly developed capitalist society, reified through the techniques of persuasion and thought manipulation by the dictators of production, who are also the lords and masters of consumption.[6]

This situation, which is quite evident in the sphere of material production, is also extended to the type of production which we have called mass art, above all with regard to film and those artistic and pseudo-artistic products which are distributed through the press, radio, and television. If the public prefers a trivial, hollow art of low aesthetic and human quality, it is clear that the preference has been induced, fabricated, or produced from without. The producer no longer limits himself to falsely and enticingly exalting the qualities of his product; in order to ensure the widest possible consumption of his commodities, he disregards their objective qualities and, on the basis of imaginary qualities, artificially creates a desire for consuming them, even though the product in question may not satisfy any real needs of its consumers. In an alienated society the relations between production and consumption become so mystified and alienating that both products and needs, objects and desires, become artificial from a truly human point of view. Man becomes so alienated that not even *his* enjoyment, his consumption, is properly his.

Film offers eloquent proof of the adaptation of the tastes and needs of the public to the needs of the producers. The "star system," for example, which is the basis for the capitalist film industry in general and the American film industry in particular, is artificially created by the producers in order to ensure maximum profits, which are in turn related to the number of spectators who can see a particular film. And along with the star system there is the preference on the part of the audience for certain themes or genres—a preference fabricated or induced from without—which then become the themes or genres which the public *needs,* although actually it is not so much their need as the need of the producers them-selves.[7]

So while for the first time in history the development of science and technology offers art the possibility of being enjoyed by a public which can potentially number millions upon millions of human beings, for the first time this enjoyment or consumption is frustrated in the concrete conditions of capitalist society. Enjoyment of consumption conflicts with its own nature as the truly human assimilation or appropriation of the object, insofar as it is manipulated or "prefabricated," but this form of consumption is the one which most adequately corresponds to the type of artistic or pseudo-artistic production which we have called mass art. How could a subject appropriate in a human way, in all the richness of its aesthetic and human manifestations and meanings, a product which is impoverished and dull from an aesthetic and human point of view? How could we possibly enter into a relationship with a pseudo-art which slides off our skin, which does not require that we give full rein to our essential human powers, which does not deal profoundly with any problem, which does not penetrate the deepest fibers of our being and which instead of deeply rooted hopes offers us the lure of false or one-dimensional solutions and narcotic illusions?

Notes

1. See my work "Mitología y verdad en la crítica de la época," in *Memorias del XIII Congreso Internacional de Filosofía* (Mexico City: Universidad Nacional Autónoma de Mexico, 1963), vol. 4, particularly the chapters "Crítica de la cultura y la técnica," and "Un nuevo fetichismo: el fetichismo de la automatización."

2. See ibid., particularly the chapter "La crítica de la 'depersonalización' o 'masificación' del hombre en nuestra época."

3. See Vance Packard, *The Hidden Persuaders* (New York: David McKay, 1957). The importance of this work is not so much its

analysis of an extremely important aspect of the "American way of life" as in the amazing facts presented. The author reveals the enormous effort, intensified in the past few years, by professors of social science, psychiatrists, psychologists, and specialized personnel of large corporations, to shape the consciousness of Americans both as consumers and citizens, in order to destroy their psychological and ideological defense mechanisms and make them passively accept proposals and decisions in the interest of large American monopolies. All means are acceptable to reach this goal—to persuade consumers to consume products which they neither need nor want—for only in this way can the ghost of economic depression which constantly haunts American industry be driven away. That explains why, because of the enormous stakes involved, this task is not assigned exclusively to the usual heads of the propaganda and advertising departments of companies. According to Packard, for example, special seminars have been organized at Columbia University in which social science professors teach public relations experts the best methods of manipulating consciousness. Mr. Packard timidly complains about the "anti-humanist implications" of these techniques of persuasion, without understanding the gravity of their consequences for man; ultimately techniques of alienating or reifying human existence, consciously and coldly devised, for economic, political and ideological reasons, to maintain men in that state of depersonalization and dehumanization described by Marx at a time when alienation was spontaneously engendered by the capitalist and did not yet assume the monstrous forms manifested in modern capitalist society.

4. The word "mass" in terms such as "mass man" or "mass art" has only a pejorative meaning, since the massification of human existence is characteristic of capitalist society and applies to Marx's concept of the "alienation" or "reification" of man. Marx saw this man-thing who does not recognize himself a human being either in his products or his actions in the relationship which establishes between the worker and his products. Marx also found this phenomenon in the nonworker or capitalist. That is why an alienating society such as modern capitalist society, especially the very eloquent example of the United States, tries to extend the process of reification to the entire community. Hence the use of manipulation tech-

niques which aim at reducing man to the condition of an object and at keeping him in that condition. The deliberate application of these techniques by the capitalists means that not only do they enter a relationship of alienation with respect to other men whom they see as their objects, but they consciously attempt to strengthen their economic and social position by fixing other men in a condition of objects. The process of keeping others in a condition of alienation is a manifestation of the capitalists' own alienation. Insofar as he lacks class consciousness, the worker finds himself defenseless against this attempt to shape his spontaneous consciousness. But the revolutionary proletariat, guided in its public and private actions by consciousness of its class interests and its historic role (a consciousness which it develops to the extent that it assimilates its class ideology, Marxism-Leninism), can successfully resist the massifying endeavors of professional consciousness-manipulators. The proletarian himself, in the alienating conditions of capitalist society, grasps himself as a subject, as an active, creative subject, with the power to bring about not only his own emancipation but also the emancipation of all mankind. The worker, on account of his consciousness of his own alienation and his organized and conscious struggle to abolish this alienation both in his own mind and in practical life, is already the very negation of mass man, who lets his fate be passively shaped. The working "masses" who struggle for their emancipation in a new society in which man will be the goal and not the means, the subject and not the object, struggle because they do not want to be treated as masses; precisely through their revolutionary struggle they create the conditions to end the massification of human existence which prevails in capitalist society. Thus we use the term "mass art" in a pejorative sense, defining it as a pseudo-art deliberately produced by the dominant class to be enjoyed and consumed by mass men. The revolutionary proletariat, because it is the class which revindicates the human essence, deserves a superior art, not artistic by-products which numb the senses, mutilate the mind, and misdirect creative energies.

5. Wilhelm Worringer, *Problemática del arte contemporáneo* (Buenos Aires: Ed. Nueva Visión, 1958), p. 9.

6. In *The Hidden Persuaders* Packard presents numerous examples which show the extent to which consumers are manipulated. Accord-

ing to his data, the consumer obeys external suggestions; his motivations are an autonomous and internal expression of external suggestions and commands. Although he believes that when he decides to buy a particular product he is operating spontaneously and fulfilling his own desires, he is in fact only satisfying the wishes of the manufacturers of those products. The transformation of external desires into *autonomous* desires is carried out in accordance with the research and methods of institutions which specialize in that process (Institute for Motivational Research, Color Research Institute of America, etc.). In managerial or executive conferences, according to Packard, there is talk of a new "revolution of the market" by virtue of which the problems of consumption have come to the foreground; the question today is how to convince and stimulate the consumer to buy things he does not need, how to instill a blind and irrational desire to buy an unnecessary product.

Additional material on manipulation of consumption and the application of techniques to create artificial needs and desires includes: David Riesman, *The Lonely Crowd* (New Haven, Conn.: Yale University Press, 1950); William H. Whyte, Jr., *The Organization Man* (New York: Simon and Schuster, 1956), and a "manual of public relations" written under the direction of Edward L. Bernays, whose title, *The Engineering of Consent* (Norman, Okla.: University of Oklahoma Press, 1956), is quite revealing.

7. The importance of the "star system," from the point of view of the interests of capitalist production, is undeniable. In effect, the average spectator "chooses" to see a film not on the basis of the reputation of its true creator, the director, not because the subject or theme interests him, and even less because of the opinion of a film critic, but more than anything else because of the name of his favorite star who heads the cast. This is no accident. Nor is the fact that in a survey in France (according to data furnished by the Centre National de la Cinématographie), 89 percent of viewers asked what made them decide to attend a particular movie responded that it was the presence of their favorite star. A film producer addresses himself to a potential public formed by millions of people of different national and class backgrounds, with different cultural, aesthetic, and ideological levels of sophistication; in principle, these differences would lead people to see movies for a variety of different reasons. The fate of a

particular movie would then be determined by a number of unfore-
seeable circumstances imposed by the diversity of interests, tastes,
and inclinations. To assure the widest possible consumption, the
producer must do away with this uncertainty; he must bring uniformity to the process of production in order to bring uniformity to
the preferences of the public. He thus emphasizes one of the film's
many elements, the director, the star, the theme, etc. The element
emphasized in capitalist production of films is the star. Because the
star can bring together a vast public which other elements in the film
might differentiate, the star system answers an imperative and objective economic need. The financing of a film is at times accompanied
by special clauses which require the inclusion of a particular star in
order to guarantee that the borrowed or invested capital will return a
profit.

20. Capitalism and Mass Art

Each week in the capitalist countries almost a billion people consume the artistic or pseudo-artistic products offered by movie houses, radios, or televisions. The numbers involved are truly awesome: tens or hundreds of thousands of spectators—at times, millions—for a single picture shown in thousands of theaters throughout the world; millions of listeners for a single radio program broadcast by a single station, which sometimes joins other stations in a network, forming a chain which shackles the docile and defenseless minds of their hollow consumers; television programs which thanks to videotape are internationally distributed, thus extending more and more their circle of influence. This enormous potential for communication is put at the service of the distribution of artistic or pseudo-artistic products; whom does it benefit or harm? Who stands to lose or to gain from it? What is discouraged or encouraged in man when such powerful and efficacious media are put in the service not of real art but of mass art? The one who stands to lose is mass man himself, the reified man who absorbs the products of mass art; for his enjoyment or consumption, often presented as an innocent distraction or diversion, only affirms him in his spiritual hollowness, in his miserable position of object, instrument, or man-thing.

Even when it is presented in the most banal form, or when it glosses over the most profound human problems, concealing their underlying real and living contradictions, mass art plays a well-defined ideological role: to keep mass man in his place, make him feel at home in his mass being and close the windows through which he might catch a glimpse of a truly human world—and with it the possibility of becoming conscious of his alienation as well as the means of abolishing it.

But it is not mass man alone who suffers; it is a loss for all men, more precisely for all men who are consciously struggling to establish a truly human social order. This is a loss in turn for authentic art as an expression of what is specifically human, the creative nature of man, insofar as mass consumption or enjoyment prevents a truly aesthetic and human appropriation. There is in effect a total lack of communication between true art and mass man, because mass man cannot enter into the type of relationship demanded by the artistic object and consequently cannot appreciate it. This deafness or blindness of mass man with regard to true artistic creation is a widely acknowledged fact, although it has been inadequately explained; statistics are extremely revealing in this matter. We can at least say, on the basis of these statistics, that there is no relationship between quality and popularity. In the conditions characteristic of mass consumption, the general public almost always prefers the products most perishable from an aesthetic point of view to those that offer higher aesthetic values.[1] Of course we recognize the existence of a certain sector which rejects these products and seeks others of higher value, just as we recognize the positive role of film clubs, certain publishing houses, listener-supported radio and television stations, and cultural or academic institutions which attempt to satisfy real aesthetic needs. But in spite of the efforts of these institutions and in spite of the lofty desires of a more demanding sector, the general public prefers pseudo-artistic products or works of low or dubious aesthetic quality.

This is necessarily so, because, as we pointed out, the tastes or aesthetic criteria of consumers are shaped to appreciate certain products and reject others, specifically those which have a higher aesthetic value or those which offer an ideological content opposed to the impoverished and narrow mold in which their minds have been enclosed. The kind of works which are appreciated are thus conventional, with cardboard characters, false solutions, and cheap sentimentalism, while any attempt to penetrate the fundamental problems of concrete human beings is rejected in the name of pure entertainment. The abstract, fleshless man who consumes these artistic products measures them by the yardstick of his own abstract and fleshless existence, in which there is no room for a properly aesthetic relationship since such a relationship can only exist when man manifests himself with all his essential powers, when his entire being is moved. In this mass consumption or enjoyment, the loss suffered by art cannot be more dramatic: the subject does not behold truly aesthetic objects, but those artistic products or pseudo-products offered by mass art. On the other hand, even when true art is offered to the subject, he is incapable of recognizing it because he cannot establish a properly human, aesthetic relationship with it.

The consumer has nothing to gain from this form of artistic consumption, since all it does is confirm his abstract, reified human existence, and prevent him from establishing the sort of relationship required by a true aesthetic object. If art and society, insofar as art is a social phenomenon, also have nothing to gain from this type of mass consumption, since it establishes an inadequate relationship between the subject and the aesthetic object, whereby the order of values is subverted and true art is denied the consumption or enjoyment which corresponds to it, who gains from the mystification of this relationship, a mystification which manifests itself in all its gravity in mass consumption? It can only be the producer, not in the sense of an individual creator of an artistic product, but rather a producer of a consumption or appropriation which is inadequate to the object, that is, the capitalist.

The capitalist is interested primarily in mass art; in principle, nobody is more interested than the capitalist in the mass consumption or enjoyment of mass art, for two essential reasons: one economic, the other ideological. From an economic point of view, only mass consumption of artistic products can ensure the highest possible profits. This implies that mass art is fundamentally an industry and its enjoyment or consumption is evaluated according to economic considerations. Film consumption is manipulated to ensure the greatest possible number of spectators, that is, the highest possible profits; the same objective guides producers in other forms of mass art. But as we have previously pointed out, this objective can only be realized by means of a leveling process which affects both the object and the subject, that is, by means of leveling both the specific characteristics of different artistic products and the tastes, desires, and needs of consumers. A *standardization* of both the object and the subject is necessary, because without it there could be no mass consumption and therefore no large profits. If qualitatively diverse products were to be offered to one-dimensional consumers, incapable of absorbing that kind of diversity and wealth of products, consumption would be limited; such limitation would run counter to the interests of capitalists, who can increase production and therefore profit sources only to the extent that the number of consumers is increased. But if one-dimensional, leveled, and uniform artistic production were to be offered to consumers who demanded a diversity of artistic manifestations to satisfy their own spiritual diversity and wealth, the limited and uniform character of production would act as a brake on consumption itself. There is a third possibility: a rich and diverse artistic production for a rich and diverse public. From the point of view of capitalist productivity none of these possibilities is acceptable. In the first two cases, the discordance between products and consumers results in a limitation of consumption and therefore of profits; in the last case, the discordance disappears and consumption, even on a large scale, is guaranteed, but because that consumption would be achieved on the basis of a diversified and rich production in the spiritual sense, in response to the most varied and diverse tastes, it would not be economically advantageous. This type of relationship between production and consumption could only exist in a communist society, particularly in its higher stage, when the individual can develop fully within the framework of the development of society itself. This type of relationship is certainly what Mayakovsky had in mind when he called for "many good and different poets!"

Capitalism is therefore interested in leveling both artistic production and the tastes which determine its enjoyment or consumption, primarily for economic reasons, since mass consumption yields the highest profits, and secondly from an ideological point of view, since it is one of the most effective ways of preserving the alienating, reifying relations characteristic of capitalist society. Under present conditions in capitalist societies, when the manipulation of consciousness on a massive scale has become vital to capitalism, from both an ideological and economic point of view, the production and consumption of mass art corresponds so fully to the reifying objectives of those societies that we can say that mass art is a truly capitalist art. It is the antithesis of true art, and by virtue of its ideological content, its affirmation of the condition of man as a thing or instrument, it opposes itself to the theoretical and practical struggle currently being waged to demystify and disalienate human relations. The ideological effectiveness of this mass art is determined by these two factors: first, because it has at its disposal mass means of distribution, its ideological message can reach areas to which true art has no access, and second, because it corresponds to the need of the depersonalized masses, it is, at the present time, the only art which can hope for mass distribution. Even an ideological message which is openly sympathetic to capitalism, but which is expressed in the form of a novel, for example, can never achieve the distribution of a radio drama which expresses the same attitudes and themes. From the point of view of capitalism, mass art with its vulgar and simplistic products is therefore much more effective than any other form of artistic creation which attempts to realize specific ideological objectives without renouncing determinate aesthetic exigencies. Moreover, it is the only art suitable for mass distribution since it is the kind of art which can be consumed by human beings who have been robbed of their spiritual riches and the kind of art which speaks the only language which depersonalized and massified men can understand.

The millions of spectators who see vulgar movies which excite their base passions or help to enlarge their spiritual vacuum find themselves in *their* element, they hear *their* language, a language easily understood by those who inhabit an alienated world, and they share the spiritual poverty and mystification of human relations and values because they themselves lead a spiritually poor, hollow, and mystified life. It would be useless to offer them a different sort of artistic product, for they would reject it; it would serve no purpose to speak to them in a different language, for they would not understand it. In mass art they have *their* art; in its language, their own voices. Therefore, once capitalist society is ruled by the alienated relations which capitalism is interested in maintaining, mass art emerges as one of the most adequate ways of reaching the mind of reified man and with the aid of the powerful modern means of distribution, it is a real industry. The mass art of our times best suits the interests of capitalism from both an economic and ideological point of view.

Notes

1. It often happens that a good film is shown for a week or two while others of extremely low quality are shown for months and months. Sometimes a film of undeniable artistic value obtains a more enthusiastic following, but this is on account of extra-artistic factors (eroticism, star system, sensationalism, etc.). Similarly, polls taken to determine the tastes and preferences of radio listeners or television viewers in general register more votes for programs of the lowest artistic quality.

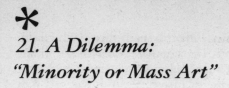

21. A Dilemma:
"Minority or Mass Art"

In present-day capitalist society, especially in countries like the United States where the law of material production gains so much power that men are robbed of their autonomy both in the process of production and when they consume its products, the production and consumption of artistic works result in an even wider gap between art and vast sectors of the society.

The artist who objectifies his essential powers creates a product which requires in turn a real appropriation, a human and aesthetic assimilation; however, this appropriation is not as large as it should be because a whole sector of society remains outside the aesthetic relationship—alienated human beings, whose consciousness is manipulated by others and who lack that human integrity and richness necessary to artistic enjoyment and consumption. In capitalist society there are millions of people with whom real artists cannot establish a dialogue. For millions of people the bridges between them and art have been broken. While few would deny this, many simplistically blame either the creative artists of our time or the present-day public. The guilt does not lie with artists who speak a truly human language—the language of creation—nor with the readers or spectators who remain deaf or blind to those artists, since their eyes and ears are capable of consuming or enjoying only a mass art. Nor should we try to place the blame on the individual person or flesh-and-blood capitalist who offers them those products of mass art. The blame—or more precisely, the cause—has to be placed on the socio-

259

economic relations embodied in the capitalist, which by turning against art harm both the creator (the artist) and the consumer (the public). Those relations harm the artist because they lower the volume of his voice, limit the reach of his words, and thus block his access to larger and larger audiences; and they harm the public because they keep men in a reified, alienated state, which keeps them from properly enjoying true human products such as art. In a society in which a vast number of people—workers and nonworkers, as Marx put it—live an alienated existence, there necessarily exists a gap between artists and a large sector of society, a gap from which both art and society stand to lose a great deal, as the artistic experience of our time shows.

A profound manifestation of the hostility of capitalism to art is the fact that in bourgeois society the artist is *necessarily* divorced from the masses because he cannot descend to their level, and the masses do not want to raise themselves—nor can they—to the level of art; artists today cannot hope to share their art with the millions of human beings kept by capitalism in a reified state. From the fact of this historical divorce between art and the masses, there are those who deduce that the art of our time must necessarily be a minority art, only for the initiate or the chosen few.

Such is the view of José Ortega y Gasset in *The Dehumanization of Art,* which from the time it was published thirty years ago has represented this manner of conceiving the relations between art and the masses. The theories of Ortega y Gasset are well known in Spanish-speaking countries, but it is worthwhile remembering them. In his words: "Modern art . . . will always have the masses against it. It is essentially unpopular; moreover, it is antipopular."[1]

Ortega's thesis is based not only on the recognition that art is divorced from the public (the masses), but also on the assertion that this divorce is insurmountable; modern art only reaches a "specially gifted minority." Since for Ortega the concept of the masses does not have a concrete, sociohistorical character, for he includes under that category everything that does not belong to the "gifted minority," modern art is by its essence minority art, or as he says, "the art of a privileged aristocracy of finer senses."[2] This art is not, in principle, for everybody, but "for those who understand"; however, Ortega does not even try to explain how one might gain access to this privileged circle, or how people go from one level to the other. His artistic categories—elite and mass art—are inexorable: "This implies that one group possesses an organ of comprehension denied to the other—that they are two different varieties of the human species."[3]

This is in perfect harmony with Ortega's aristocratic concept of the division of human beings into two orders or classes, elite and common; modern art is proper to the former. What ensures its being understood and well received by one and not understood and refused by the other, is its lack of realism, as well as its dehumanization or rejection of art as an expression or representation of humanity.

We are not concerned here with undertaking an analysis of modern art as such. We will simply reiterate that in our view there is a divorce between art and the public, and one of the reasons for this is that the artist, in his endeavor to assert his independence and subjectivity in a reified world, has ended up by destroying the bridges which could have made communication possible. And with regard to the consumer, because of the profound alienation into which he has fallen as a human being, the opportunity for true aesthetic assimilation is denied to him. The people who oppose modern art and its valuable accomplishments are the same people who oppose all true art. The same factors which prevent a man drowned by spiritual misery from establishing a truly human relationship with a painting by Picasso, a poem by Paul Eluard, or a film by Fellini, also prevent him from establishing such a relationship with the works of Velázquez, Góngora, or Tirso de Molina.

We cannot, in general, speak of an absolute lack of communication, but only of two extreme cases of incommunicability: when the artist does not succeed in making himself understood because he has not wanted or been able to develop an appropriate language, and therefore has not succeeded in objectifying his expression in forms which ensure an indispensable degree of communicability; or when man, transformed into a thing, dehumanized, deaf or blind to human richness, has no possibility, in principle, of establishing communication with a work of art. But even these extreme cases—the solipsism or radical subjectivism of the creator, or the numbness of mass man to real aesthetic enjoyment—are cases which historically occur only in particular societies, such as present-day capitalist society, and even there they do not account for all of art or all of society.

The dilemma between true art (minority art) and inauthentic art (majority or mass art) is false when posed in absolute terms, although in an alienating society the latter may enjoy the support of the majority of people. Art may reduce its capacity for communication as a result of socio-historical factors, such as the ones that cause the hermetism of artistic creation or the inability of large groups of people to enjoy art, but this particular condition of art in a specific society and of the reified men who live in it cannot be elevated to the category of an absolute principle, as Ortega tries to do, because art in essence is neither elitist nor hermetic, nor does the majority necessarily or essentially have to turn its back on art. The art of our times will eventually supersede the limitations imposed by a hermetic language which prevents it from realizing its social function; and the masses, now estranged from art, will return to it, but this turnabout will at the same time be a sign of the abolition of their alienation. Art will then truly fulfill its social function. A situation in which art is directed to *all* men, because everybody needs to affirm himself as a human being in order to appropriate the human riches offered by art, will only exist in a future society in which human relations have a truly human character. This accessibility of art in all its complexity and richness to great numbers of people will not be a symptom of the spiritual impoverishment of humanity, as is the case with the mass consumption of mass art in present-day society, but a sign of the development and enrichment of human sensibility in general and aesthetic sensibility in particular. The artist will not feel then that the accessibility of his art to vast numbers of people constitutes an incursion of the "masses" into the sacred precincts of art; rather, he will feel that such a situation fulfills the true destiny of art.

We can see that in the conditions of capitalist society the economic and ideological interests of the dominant class are linked to a mass aesthetic consumption or enjoyment of what generally can be only banal art, since true art tends to become a privileged art, to which vast groups of mass men have no access. This objective situation must be felt by the artist as a limitation on the reach of his work. Hence his destiny is objectively bound up with the destiny of the social forces which are struggling to put an end to the alienating human relations which keep large sectors of society away from art by destroying or deforming their capacity for aesthetic enjoyment or consumption.

The problem of reestablishing truly aesthetic relations between artist and public, a fundamental problem of our times, cannot be posed without taking into account the profound, radical changes required by the irreconcilable contradictions of capitalist society. We cannot hope to broaden and enrich truly aesthetic consumption without extensively deepening and enriching the human sensibility, a task which is also indispensable to the radical transformation of social, political, economic, and spiritual relations. The attempt to establish a large-scale dialogue while passively submitting to the prevailing aesthetic sensibility leads to a search for a facile means of communication, thus limiting the enrichment of the means of expression and lowering the aesthetic value of art. Because production creates the mode of enjoying or consuming the product, the artist cannot passively wait for society to change and thus create favorable conditions for a radical change in sensibility. No; the artist must help bring this change about by creating a public capable of enjoying his work, as Marx said, without overestimating his own power and without forgetting that his power to create a public is not direct and immediate, but developed within the framework of social conditions which can either impede or favor his efforts. In capitalist society, the powerful technical means of distribution and communication are not under the control of the artist and he thus cannot use them to create a public capable of consuming true works of art. The potential for mass consumption or enjoyment of art is a problem which exceeds the limits of the capacity of art to create a public to its measure. In order to tear reified, alienated people away from the mass art which they consume every day and get them to enjoy an authentic art, it is necessary first to pull them out of their reification or alienation. Although art can also make a contribution to this, the fundamental task is of a different nature: it is a critical revolutionary task which must be realized on the level of real, material relations, and the realization of this task is the responsibility of that social class which has the greatest interest in putting an end to all alienation, the proletariat.

Capitalist society poses this dilemma: minority or mass art, privileged consumption of artistic works or massive consumption of artistic sub-products. Although some theoreticians of modern art respond to this dilemma by asserting that it is inexorable, rooted in the very nature of modern art, we have tried to show that the deeper roots are socio-historical in nature. Keeping in mind that every true work of art by its essence establishes a human dialogue across boundaries of time, class, or nationality, once one becomes aware that those roots exist the response to the dilemma must be a rejection of the dilemma itself: neither minority art nor mass art, but *art for all;* that is, for all who feel the need for a human appropriation of things and who find in the aesthetic relationship a way of profoundly satisfying that need and in the aesthetic object a human utility. Temporarily left out of the category "all," that "immense minority," are the people-things of capitalist society, who as long as they do not recover their humanity cannot establish a truly human and consequently aesthetic relationship with objects. This once again makes manifest the hostility of capitalism to art, in this case with regard to aesthetic enjoyment or consumption.

The artist creates for men who feel a need for a totality of vital human manifestations, as Marx pointed out, although present-day capitalist society engenders for the most part a type of mass man who at present does not feel that need. In order to create for all men, although that "all" does not effectively include all men, on the one hand he produces for a wide consumption or enjoyment of his product without giving in to the exigencies of mass consumption, and on the other hand he maintains the highest aesthetic standards in his work, without reducing it to a creation for elites or privileged groups.

Therefore, the dilemma between "minority art and mass art" which capitalism endeavors to maintain is a false dilemma from an aesthetic and human point of view. It has nothing to do with the real interests of art and man. But while it is difficult under prevailing conditions for the artist to reject that dilemma, he can avoid it by struggling to make an art which is neither elite and for the initiated, nor a mass art which obeys the economic and ideological demands of capitalism and is interested only in mass consumption. An art suitable for a public capable of a human or aesthetic appropriation of its products must address itself neither to a privileged nor an alienated public, but to the people, because it would be the living language of man. Only art of that nature, a truly popular art, could transcend its socio-historical conditioning and establish a dialogue in the here and now, with both the disalienated men of today and men of the future, totally free of all alienation. This art alone will be able to survive its circumstances and continue to live when current conditions become only a dim memory or a forgotten matter.

Notes

1. José Ortega y Gasset, *The Dehumanization of Art* (Princeton, N.J.: Princeton University Press, 1968), p. 5.
2. Ibid., p. 6.
3. Ibid.

22. Truly Popular Art

The expression "popular art" is increasingly the object of the most crude mystifications; hence the need at this point to reestablish the real meaning of that term. One of the most hackneyed mystifications is based on identification with what we have called mass art, or art which corresponds to the reified and alienated man of industrial capitalist society. As a result of this identification of popular and mass art, there is a tendency to characterize the true art of our times as a privileged, *antipopular* art. Regarding true art as essentially minority art discards the possibility of an authentic art, since this concept is based on the gratuitous premise that art can hope to be understood by the majority only to the extent that its own means of expression are perverted. There is no room left for an art that is neither a minority nor a mass art, that is, for a truly popular art which does not let itself be imprisoned in the stifling framework of the dilemma so dear to Ortega y Gasset: distinguished minorities, or undistinguished masses. Sometimes, with the noblest intentions, the opposite view is held: that it is possible to bridge the two poles of this dilemma by cultivating a popular art, popular not in the sense of art for the people but that of art about the people, or populist art. Those who hold this view believe that in order to have a truly popular art it is enough to make the people the object of artistic representation and color the artistic means of expression with a "popular" hue by recording popular language and customs. But this notion, in spite of its good intentions, is false. While the previously mentioned idea contemptuously rejects any relationship between art and the people, and sees popular art as an inferior art which is opposed to authentic or "artistic" art, this new idea limits itself to establishing a superficial relationship between art and the people, which can only lead to a populist, folkloric, or regional art, not to a truly popular art. In one case popular art is conceived in a quantitative, massive sense, popular in the sense of "popularity," which can only be guaranteed by artistic inauthenticity; in the second case popular art is viewed as art which focuses its attention on the people, but this attention is superficial. Just as we should not confuse popular art with best-selling mass art, neither should we equate popular art with provincial, folkloric, or regional art, or populist art.

Under the conditions of capitalism, which is interested in encouraging a privileged, elite art and in impeding the distribution of true art, it is possible to create an art which addresses itself to the majority, not to the masses, that is, a truly popular art, in both a quantitative and a qualitative sense. There are quite a number of examples of this. But the hostility of capitalism to art can create a situation in which truly popular art is not "popular," not accepted by the majority, while an art that is actually antipopular, mass art, is "popular" by virtue of the conditions under which production and consumption are carried out in capitalist society.

Once we have discarded the false concepts which equate popular art and mass art or popular art and artistic "populism," we must select a qualitative criterion in order to define what we mean by truly popular art. This can be none other than the depth and richness with which art expresses the desires or aspirations of a people or nation in a particular historical stage of its existence. We therefore agree with the concept of popular literature expressed by the great Italian Marxist Antonio Gramsci: "Question of how or why literature is popular. 'Beauty' is not enough. What is required is an intellectual and moral content which is the elaborate and complete expression of the most profound aspirations of a determinate public, of the nation-people in a certain phase of its historical development."[1]

Gramsci asserts that "beauty" is not enough when it is not sparked by a profound ideological and moral content. This beauty in itself, nourished by itself, would have such an uncertain status that Gramsci puts it in quotation marks. But while he rejects self-subsistent beauty, at least in a truly popular literature, Gramsci is very careful not to regard the content as self-subsistent, that is, as sufficient to guarantee the popular character of art. Gramsci is very careful on this point, being conscious, perhaps, of the fact that the best intentions have led to disastrous results in the name of Marxism, in the much-discussed question of the relations between content and form. What Gramsci says about this question serves to clear up the ambiguities with regard to the definition of truly popular art. "While agreeing with the principle that in a work of art we must only look for artistic quality, this does not in any way exclude . . . the attitude towards life which infuses the same work of art."[2] This attitude of a people toward life is what is expressed in the ideological and moral content of popular literature. Art is not realized purely and simply in the "beauty of the content" nor in that self-subsistent "beauty" which originates in the form alone, but in the form "in which the abstract content has been forged and identified."[3]

Popular art is a profound expression of the aspirations and interests of the people in a given historical stage, and as such it maintains a certain relationship with politics. This relationship is neither external, imposed from without, nor direct and immediate. Because of this relationship, the work of art is tendentious, and in this sense, as Engels wrote in his letter to Minna Kautsky on November 26, 1885, all great art is tendentious. "The father of tragedy, Aeschylus, and the father of comedy, Aristophanes, were both powerfully tendentious poets, as were Dante and Cervantes, and the main merit of Schiller's *Cunning and Love* is that it is the first German political tendentious drama."

The most representative contemporary theoreticians of

bourgeois and idealist aesthetics regard gratuitousness and irresponsibility as cardinal principles of modern art. However, the above letter reminds us, truly popular art has always had an intimate relationship with human life, with the people, and therefore it reveals a profound ideological content. Popular art is tendentious. Far from being a dominant force throughout the history of art, artistic gratuitousness and irresponsibility, which today are elevated to the category of ruling principles of creation, appear only in a late stage of bourgeois society, as a refusal of the artist to serve bourgeois morality, politics, or religion.

Popular art in the sense Gramsci speaks of it is tendentious, as according to Engels all great art has been since man created art in societies divided into classes. There are two things which concern us in this regard: the emergence of a consciousness of that tendentious character, and the hopeless attempt to evade the spirit of tendentiousness which is intrinsic to the work of art.

Popular art is profoundly tendentious precisely because it expresses the highest interests of a people in a determinate historical stage, but this does not mean that art can be reduced to its intention or that the artistic can be dissolved in the political. Neither art nor politics would have anything to gain from this dissolution. A political criterion can be applied to art as long as we understand the limitations of art. Such a criterion can be useful, as Gramsci pointed out, "to demonstrate that somebody as an artist does not belong to a particular political world and that—since his personality is essentially artistic—in his intimate life, in the life that is peculiar to him, the world in question is not operative, does not exist."[4] But we must be very careful not to transform a political criterion into an artistic one, for that would mean using the same yardstick to measure activities which can never be identical, even though they are related. Moreover, while both art and politics bring us in contact with the human reality, we must not forget that politics justifies itself by its capacity to transform that reality in an effective, real way, whereas art transforms that reality, transfiguring it in order to create a new reality, the work of art. The transformation realized by politics is transitory; the transformed reality gives way to a new transformation, and this series of transformations which politics effects on reality, consciously directing human action toward determinate objectives, is for the most part identified with the movement of history itself. The transformation which the artist effects on a determinate reality, reflecting or transfiguring it, is unique and unrepeatable in each creative act and remains fixed, enduring through the real-historical process. Politics and art are two ways of overcoming time, but the victory of politics over time is transitory, because politics itself will be overcome in the future, in a communist society after the withering away of the state. But because of its permanence, art is one of the most reliable means man possesses, once he has been freed from the illusion of physical or spiritual immortality, by which to overcome time and resist the inroads of caducity.

Popular art is the true art of its own time; because of that, it is also capable of conquering or overcoming time. Because it is faithful to its time, this temporal art is never an anachronism. Art outlives its own time and continues to live in harmony with the movement of real life itself. In this sense, Greek art survived the death of a Greek society based on slavery. However, the impatient politician tends to see in art an anachronism, without realizing that in the dialectic of temporality and endurability, politics, not art, will be conquered by time. Art and politics have different rhythms, hence the necessity, as Gramsci pointed out, of not transforming a political criterion into an artistic one.[5]

Popular art transcends narrow affiliations to particular political ideologies and does not have a connection to one or another artistic school; its premise, according to Gramsci, is "historical, political, popular" and its roots "must penetrate the soil of popular culture."[6]

The artist who removes his roots from the popular soil ceases to identify with the sentiments, aspirations, and interests of the people, and does not feel the need to create a popular art. The cause of this break is sometimes found in the negative attitude of the artist toward a society which negates him as an artist and as a man, pushing him toward alienation; at other times it resides in the impossibility of discerning the location of the social forces—the people—with whom the artist could satisfy his need for communication. Finally, it may happen that the artist cannot find the audience which could encourage him to end his isolation. The artist and the people search for each other without finding each other; most often it is the people who search for the artist and do not find him; at other times, in this alienating industrial capitalist society, it is the artist who seeks the people without finding them. However, history offers us clear examples of solidarity between the artist and the people, examples which are so clear and recurrent that the current radical separation between art and the people appears in the light of the universal historico-artistic experience as a terrible and painful anomaly, in spite of attempts to regard it as a perfectly normal situation.

We again insist that what we have here is a schism between art and the people, because capitalism generously supplies the masses with the art which pleases them. The difference between the masses and the people is as radical as that between the quantitative and the qualitative, the dehumanized and the humanized, the inert and the alive, the passive and the active or creative. When we say people, we refer to the alive, fertile, and producing element of history, the motor and creative force of the historical process; in societies divided into classes, therefore, we cannot identify the people with the entire society or population, and even less with the emptiest and most inert sector of society, the reified and depersonalized masses. Nor is the people a general and abstract category; in each historical period it has a concrete content. The category of the people is constituted historically by the social classes and strata which create through their activity the principal material and spiritual values, and, by struggling against oppression and exploitation, ensure the continuity of the progressive unfolding of history. Throughout history, the fundamental strength of the people, their essence, resides in the working classes, to which must be added the intellectual strata and, during a particular period of history, the bourgeoisie, in its ascendant stage.

The people are the creative ferment of the historical process. Seen from that universal perspective, the people are definitively the force which ensures a continuous affirmation of what is human, throughout a difficult and complex series of struggles in which there are both victories and defeats, rises and falls.

When we speak of an art in which we discover an affirmation of what is universally human, a capacity to communicate with all men across boundaries of time, class, or nationality, we do not mean human in the abstract, either in the sense of man in general or the individual. Marx's criticism of the philosophers of the period immediately antecedent to his, Hegel, Feuerbach, Stirner, etc., is a spirited and constant effort to remove man as a concrete, real being from the abstractions in which those philosophers attempted to place him. Feuerbach's man in general was as abstract as Stirner's individual who believed he affirmed himself in his absolute uniqueness. Marx pointed out that man is a social being; the individual is a node of social relations. Individuals group together on the basis of common interests and aspirations, even without being conscious of it, and thus form human communities which we call classes, peoples, nations, or societies. From the earliest times, men have been able to affirm themselves as such by entering into relationships with each other. Thus in his relationship with others, and even in his relationship with himself, man never ceases to be a social being. Even solitude is a social state. Among the social forces which emerge as a result of man's "social quality," the people appear as a fundamental historical force, which does not exclude the possibility that at determinate moments, without losing sight of this universal perspective, the people might be passive, inert, and encumbered with a host of defects, prejudices, and limitations.

Inasmuch as art is an affirmation, expression, and objectification of man, understood in a concrete way as a social and historical being, art sinks its roots in that profound and authentic vein of humanity, the people. Because of this popular content, art bases itself on the here and now but does not become a prisoner of time; by virtue of its popular essence, art elevates itself to the level of the universally human.

In this sense we can talk of both the popularity and universality of Greek tragedy, the theater of Lope de Vega, the painting of Goya, Shakespeare's drama, the novels of Tolstoy, Picasso's *Guernica,* or the murals of Siqueiros and Orozco. Through their great artists, the people find both their most indigenous and their most universal expression; the creations of these artists are true bursts of the people's soul. As the poet Miguel Hernandez said: "Our destiny is to place ourselves in the hands of the people. We poets are the wind of the people: we are born to be blown through their pores and to direct their eyes and feelings toward the most beautiful summits."

All truly popular art opens and enriches a profound vein of humanity. To make art for the people is to make universal art, to plunge into the particular—national and popular— human essence and emerge charged with universality. Those who succeed in establishing this particular dialogue achieve an enduring dialogue which only the great creations of all times have succeeded in establishing. That is why the poet Antonio Machado, looking askance at those who crack an indulgent smile when a connection is made between art and the people, says:

> To write for the people—my teacher used to say—what more could I want! . . . To write for the people is to write for men who belong to our race, who speak our language, three inexhaustible things which we will never know completely. To write for the people is to call oneself Cervantes, in Spain; Shakespeare, in England; Tolstoy, in Russia. It is the miracle of the geniuses of the word.[7]

Gramsci and Machado thus agree, although their situations were different: Gramsci physically separated from his people in a dark cell which became his grave; Machado hand in hand with his people in the tense and burning land of Spain, where the people defended its destiny.

Thus disencumbered of the mystifications associated with it, popular art is, in sum, the universal art of all times, which is not content with a beautiful form, although forged in beauty, and which offers the rich and profound ideological content which corresponds to the aspirations and hopes of a particular people in a historical stage of its development. Popular art is therefore "the wind of the people," its living language. There is also the art which aspires to be "beauty," as Gramsci said; this beauty is not sufficient, although it is undeniable that such art can realize certain aesthetic values. But when a people wants to express itself and through its voice express the whole man, it must have an art imbued with the popular essence, and then it is artists such as a Lope de Vega, a Cervantes, a Goya, or a Tolstoy, who take that essence and return it to us as a universal human essence. That is the art which Marx, Engels, Lenin, Lunacharsky, and Gramsci appreciated, without ignoring its aesthetic merits, regardless of what time, society, or class interest it was connected to.

Whether considering Aeschylus, Goethe, or Balzac, Marx regarded their creations as sublime expressions of the universal humanity the proletariat is called on to realize, as well as characteristic expressions of a particular people. Fused in those works of art, in their popular essence, are the circumstantial and the enduring, the particular and the universal. Marx would have agreed with the previously quoted words of Machado and Gramsci on a truly popular art, without thereby closing his eyes to other fields, since he regarded art in all its manifestations as constant living proof of the creative existence of man. But wherever art is required to profoundly penetrate its time and authentically express a people or a nation, it cannot fail to be truly popular.

Notes

1. Antonio Gramsci, *Letteratura e vita nazionale,* pp. 100-1.
2. Ibid., p. 28.
3. Ibid.
4. Ibid.
5. Gramsci delimits the artistic and political levels and sees, in principle, a certain opposition between them:

"With regard to the relationship between literature and politics it is necessary to keep in mind that the literary man must necessarily have perspectives which are less precise and definite than those of the political man, he must be less 'sectarian,' so to speak, but in a 'contradictory' manner. For the political man, all images which are 'fixed' a priori are reactionary; the political man considers all movements from the perspective of their future. The artist, instead, must have images which are 'fixed' and solidified in a definitive form. The political man sees man as he is, and at the same time, as he should be in order to achieve a determinate goal; his work consists precisely in impelling men to move, to leave their current selves and to 'conform' to a specific goal.

"The artist necessarily presents, in a realistic way, 'what there is' in a determinate moment which is personal, non-conformist, etc. Therefore, the political man, from his point of view, is never satisfied with the artist, and never will be. He will always find the artist to be behind his times, an anachronism which is surpassed by the real movement." Ibid., p. 30.
6. Ibid., p. 31.
7. Antonio Machado, *Juan de Mairena* (Buenos Aires: Losada, 1943), vol. 2, pp. 67-68.

23. *Cultured, Individual, and Professional Art, and Popular and Collective Art*

Throughout its history, artistic creation has followed two distinct fundamental paths: cultured, professional creation by specific individuals in whom artistic talent is apparently exclusively concentrated, and the collective and anonymous creation of the people. There is thus the history made up of a succession of outstanding artists who constitute a radiant constellation of vigorous individualities who shine across the centuries with their own light, and there is a history of art without names. This is not the false and artificial anonymous history of which Wölfflin dreamt. It is a dark and silent history which starts with the primitive epics or even further back with the dances or songs which in prehistoric times accompanied man in his pain, fears, and hopes, and which endure across the centuries and into the present, in different forms, but without losing their collective and anonymous character, singing of new pains, fears, and hopes.

This collective and popular art pales by comparison to the art handed down to us by that constellation of individual creative geniuses. Taken as a whole, it seems to be losing in its struggle with time, for its vitality has been declining, especially in the last two or three centuries. Certainly, in some countries the popular artistic heritage is kept alive and even enriched; these countries are mostly those which, for whatever reason, have remained in the rear of modern capitalist development and therefore have not gone through the spiritual expropriation which mechanized production brought with it. Truly popular creation does not exist in highly industrialized capitalist countries; its manifestations often are only dim reminders of a creative impulse which no longer exists. How could the creative impulse exist when the very foundation of artistic creation, work, a universal expression of the creative nature of man, has been converted into an impersonal, dehumanized, and mechanical activity: alienated labor under the conditions of capitalist production?

We have seen that the destruction of the foundation of artistic creation has been most extensive and profound in capitalist society. In ancient society, characterized by the low level of development of the productive forces so that "the free and full development of the individual and of society was inconceivable" (Marx), production was at the service of man; hence ancient society nevertheless permitted a certain realization of man's creative capacity. In the Middle Ages it was possible for artisans to show in their work their free creative individuality. With the development of capitalist production, and particularly with the emergence of large industries, labor loses its vital, creative character and the creative capacity of the people is limited or annulled. The disappearance of creative labor dries the fountains of true popular creation, which results in a constantly greater impoverishment of folkloric traditions. We find then only consumers, the passive, impersonal, and dehumanized consumers who correspond to the artistic sub-products offered under capitalism by mass art.

Capitalism thus creates conditions which are hostile to the flowering of a popular art, both by exhausting the creative capacity of human labor, which is the foundation of popular art, and by distributing artistic substitutes on a large scale in order to keep the people separated from the great professional, cultured art of all times as well as from true popular creation. By virtue of the resulting alienation the people end by not recognizing themselves in their own products, in the anonymous or collective creations which express them.

Capitalist expropriation thus becomes expropriation of the creative capacity of the people, previously manifested, with varying degrees of richness, in labor and in art. The more extensive the sphere of influence of the law of capitalist material production, the more limited the sphere of popular artistic creation, of an art of and for the people. Thus, the capitalist expropriation of the English peasants in the seventeenth century, with all its concomitant pain and misery, meant not only a radical change in living conditions which put an end to the peasants' way of life, but also an expropriation of the individual, free, and creative characteristics of their labor, and thus the disappearance of the popular art which had flourished on the basis of that labor.

Capitalism tends in principle to limit the sphere of art as collective popular creation. Capitalism sees in popular art not an expression of the creative vitality of a people which does not resign itself to being expropriated, but rather a curious, local, and picturesque phenomenon. Popular art thus appears as a degraded artistic expression.

Marx and Engels showed the highest respect for art as cultured, individual, and professional creation, as demonstrated by their profound admiration for the outstanding exponents of such art (Aeschylus, Cervantes, Shakespeare, Goethe, Heine, Balzac, etc.). But without questioning the fundamental importance of those individual zeniths of artistic creation, they descended from the heights to observe and admire the fruits of the collective creation of the people. They were not attracted by their local color or picturesqueness; their interest did not lie in the fact that the people placed itself in those works as an object of representation; nor were they interested in them as monuments of the past from which they could glean the ideas, illusions, hopes, values, or prejudices of peoples of other times, or as testimonies of an extinct world. These factors had a certain value, and folkloric and ethnographic science had made important discoveries regarding them in Marx's and Engels' time. But popular creation interested Marx and Engels primarily as an expression of man's creative capacity, not as the subject of ethnographic research. They regarded popular art as a living phenomenon, as was all true art. Its vitality was manifest in its being an unexhausted fountain of aesthetic pleasure, in its capacity to resist time and the social and historical conditions which gave it birth. Because of its endurability, the artistic creation of the people shares the authentic destiny of great individual creations: it transcends human particularities to enrich what is universally human.

In showing that capitalism is by its essence hostile to art, Marx had in mind the radical opposition between capitalist production and man as a creative being. But Marx's thesis is applicable not only to art as individual creation, but also as popular creation. The destiny of art as popular collective creation is therefore connected to the destiny of man as a creative being. That is why one can observe today a rebirth of popular art in the socialist countries, that is, in those countries where human labor begins to reclaim its creative nature. The restoration of the aesthetic or creative principle of human labor in those countries creates favorable conditions for the development of the creative capacity of the people in art.

While they exalted popular art as an expression of the creative capacity of the people, Marx and Engels were careful not to idealize it or set it up against art as individual creation. When we examine the possibilities for popular creation under capitalism, we must not lose sight of the fact that the opposition between capitalism and popular creation can be radical and absolute, as demonstrated by the example of the popular art of English peasants during the seventeenth century. From this radical hostility, the romantics drew the conclusion that popular creation could only unfold in the conditions of the past, particularly those of the Middle Ages. Marx and Engels, who were the first to reveal the objective mechanism of that opposition, tried to show the relationship between popular creation and the conditions existing at their time. Under capitalist conditions popular creation can only survive for sure in rural areas, to which capitalist material and spiritual expropriation has not yet reached; but it can also exist in modern cities, according to Marx and Engels, in the form of revolutionary poetry and songs, as an expression of the class consciousness of workers. Thus the people manifest their creative capacity in art, in spite of hostile conditions faced by popular, nonprofessional creation in capitalist societies.

We noted before that Marx and Engels did not idealize popular art or oppose it to individual creation. In the hostile conditions of societies divided into classes, particularly in capitalist conditions, which destroy the foundation of artistic creation and castrate the creative impulse of the people, thereby limiting the possibilities for anonymous, popular art, it is inevitable that the creative means are concentrated almost exclusively in individuals who devote themselves professionally to art. These individuals do not have to sacrifice their creative energies to a type of human labor which is the very negation of their creative capacity. This cultured art is not only an expression of man's creative capacity (which has been negated or alienated in labor and diminished in collective or anonymous art), but it can also become a truly popular art, by virtue of its roots in the most profound aspirations and hopes of the people. Individual creation thus preserves the creative possibilities which popular collective creation cannot realize in the particular conditions of capitalist society.

24. The Social Division of Artistic Labor and the Development of the Personality

Marx perceived that true human wealth resides in the universal unfolding of the personality. "The *rich* human being is simultaneously the human being *in need of* a totality of human manifestations of life."[1] Man affirms himself as an essentially human being the more universally he unfolds his personality, the more rich and varied the realms in which he exercises his faculties. Human richness is one of needs and relations with oneself, with others, and with reality. In order to affirm himself as a free, conscious, and creative being, man must transcend the limitation implicit in the channeling of his energies into a unique and exclusive task, no matter how important it might be. His freedom is inseparable from the universality of his personality. Speaking of the new type of man who would realize his true human potential in a communist society, Marx stated: "Man appropriates his total essence in a total manner, that is to say, as a whole man."[2] This total unfolding of his personality is denied in capitalist society by the division of labor.

The division of labor under capitalism isolates man in the confines of a limited activity, and endows the development of his personality with a one-dimensional character, which at times assumes the form of monstrous specialization. Unable to develop universally in his limited sphere of action, he clings to his particularity and restricts and mutilates his being.

Concrete and real man is divided along with the division of labor. Marx, in his *Manuscripts of 1844,* called this division of labor "the estranged and alienated form of human activity as an activity of the species,"[3] thus relating it to the phenomenon of alienation. In all of his works, from *The Poverty of Philosophy* and *Wage-Labor and Capital* to the masterwork of his mature years, *Capital,* Marx emphasized the opposition of the division of labor to the development of the individual. While he recognized that the division of labor has permitted man to increase his productive forces and his power over nature, he insisted that in the conditions of capitalist society the division of labor divides the concrete, real man, degrading and debasing him and separating him from the community. In contrast to the bourgeois economists who saw only the positive and necessary aspects of the division of labor, Marx repeatedly pointed out its profoundly negative aspect, especially insofar as it mutilates the personality.

Artistic activity does not escape the consequences of this historical law of the division of labor. We noted that art is divided into a cultured, individual, professional art and a popular, anonymous, nonprofessional art. The task of creation is so concentrated in exceptional individuals as to exclude the people, especially under capitalism. As early as 1846, in a polemic against Stirner, Marx said: "The exclusive concentration of artistic talent in particular individuals, and its suppression in the broad mass which is bound up with this, is a consequence of division of labor."[4]

The division of artistic creation into individual and popular creation in capitalist society furthers the appearance of a minority art. But it also leads to the form of spiritual expropriation which we have called mass art, in whose production the people play no part, although they play a part in consumption insofar as they are degraded in that consumption to the condition of masses. As we pointed out, the historical tendency of capitalism is to remove the people from the sphere of artistic creation in order to reduce it to a consumer of artistic sub-products. The collective, popular art which is not only consumed but also produced by the people, finds conditions hostile to its development.

The division of artistic labor tends to concentrate the process of creation in exceptional individuals and eliminate from that process the simple, amateur artists, those not endowed with an exceptional creative talent, and of course the people. So despite the fact that art as the product of exceptional personalities can and indeed does yield extraordinary fruit, its concentration in particular individuals helps, under certain socio-historical conditions, to limit the creative capacity of man. If art represents one of the highest and most specifically human forms of appropriating reality, if man manifests himself in all his richness by realizing and objectifying his essential powers in a concrete-sensuous object, then the tendency to concentrate artistic talent in exceptional individuals limits that part of man which feels an inner need to create, as Marx put it, "according to the laws of beauty," to affirm his true human nature. Since art makes manifest the creative principle which exists in labor in a limited form, the universal development of the personality requires that every man, as a creative being, be a man-artist, that is, that he have a creative attitude toward the world and toward things. Despite the aesthetic and human values which art as an exceptional activity performed by a minority of specially gifted individuals may bequeath us, it perpetuates the mutilation of the personality, since it denies that personality access to a sphere which is vital to it. The concentration of artistic talent in a small number of individuals preserves the principle of the division of labor, with all its evils, in a sphere which must by its nature be universal—the sphere of creation. The affirmation of this principle also results in the division of men into creators and consumers, thus preventing the truly human development of the individual as a creative being.

By placing art in a historical perspective, Marx did not fail to see the ambivalence of art as individual creation. The division of artistic labor has social roots, and its evils, like those of the division of labor in general, will not disappear until the necessary social conditions are created in a society in which man can realize his total personality. In a society which tends to affirm each individual in his or her particularity and in which alienated labor is the expression of the negation of the creative capacity, man cannot develop as a creative being on a universal scale. Because of the general expropriation of man's creative essence, the concentration of human creative power in exceptional individuals is a necessity and, moreover, a guarantee of the survival of the creative principle in an economic and social world which is hostile to it. In the same way that the general division of labor signified an advance because human activity became autonomous and specialized, and thus immeasurably raised man's power over nature, art saved itself as a creative activity and was able to reach the highest peaks insofar as it became autonomous and artists limited themselves to the world of art. But this autonomy was achieved within the framework of society, by means of the division of labor, as Marx and Engels pointed out. The division of labor made possible not only the existence but the flourishing of artistic activity. Marx and Engels wrote:

> Sancho imagines that Raphael produced his pictures independently of the division of labor that existed in Rome at the time. If he were to compare Raphael with Leonardo da Vinci and Titian, he would know how greatly Raphael's works of art depended on the flourishing of Rome at that time, which occurred under Florentine influence. . . .[5]

The objective basis for the concentration of artistic creative power in exceptionally gifted individuals is also the basis for the expropriation of creative talent from large sectors of the working population by means of alienating and reifying their existence.

The hostility of capitalism to art, manifested on the level of creation as well as that of enjoyment or consumption, is expressed further in the division of artistic labor which leads to the concentration of creative talent in a few individuals and to the separation of the artist from society. Not until the individual sees in the community a necessary condition for his development, and not until the schism within real and concrete man disappears, will art cease to be an exclusive, privileged sphere. Marx believed this would come about with a radical change of society, with communism, when the division between professional and popular art would disappear and the human need to create and to enjoy the fruits of artistic activity would not be limited to a privileged sector of society, but would become common and universal.

Because man is by nature a creative being, and because communist society will reestablish man in his creative nature, artistic activity will become an increasingly more vital human need. Naturally, this creative capacity will manifest itself with different degrees of intensity, success, and quality in different individuals, but it will manifest itself to some degree in all individuals, since work itself, by ceasing to be totally alienated labor and becoming a creative human activity, will realize the aesthetic principle of "creation according to the laws of beauty," a principle which will be given its highest expression in art.

And, above all, communist society will give free rein to creative aptitudes; it will neither expropriate them nor suppress them on a large scale, which happens to popular art under capitalism. That is why Marx and Engels stated that the question is not, "as Sancho imagines, that each should do the work of Raphael, but anyone in whom there is a potential Raphael should be able to develop without hindrance."[6] And the individual will do this not by limiting himself to and stockading himself in that activity but by realizing himself in a totality of vital manifestations, of which art will be superior, but not unique and exclusive. However rich the activity of an individual may be, his human richness as a concrete, real man will not be exhausted in it. The universal realization of the personality prevents the reduction of art to a professional activity, an exclusive sphere within the division of labor.

With a communist organization of society, there disappears the subordination of the artist to local and national narrowness, which arises entirely from division of labor, and also the subordination of the artist to some definite art, thanks to which he is exclusively a painter, sculptor, etc., the very name of his activity adequately expressing the narrowness of his professional development and his dependence on division of labor. In a communist society there are no painters but at most people who engage in painting among other activities.[7]

Marx and Engels conceived of a society of men-artists, insofar as both art and labor are expressions of the creative nature of man. As a total manifestation of the essential powers of man, human labor has an aesthetic potential which art fully realizes. In communist society, therefore, every man will be a creator, an artist. In this society of artist-men the artist is not cut off from society and does not exhaust the totality of his being in artistic activity, no matter how developed it might be. The artist of communist society is above all a concrete, total man, whose need for a totality of vital manifestations is incompatible with limitation to an exclusive activity, even if it is the activity in which he manifests himself most universally and profoundly, art.

Notes

1. *Manuscripts,* p. 144.
2. Ibid., p. 138.
3. Ibid., p. 159.
4. Karl Marx and Frederick Engels, *The German Ideology* (New York: International Publishers, 1970), p. 109.
5. Ibid., p. 108.
6. Ibid.
7. Ibid., p. 109.

*
Concluding Remarks

We come to the end of our study. To clarify the meaning of Marx's thesis on the hostility of capitalism to art, to extract from it a series of fertile ideas, and to show its vital relevance to the present, we have dealt with the hostility of capitalist production to art on three levels: production or creation, consumption or enjoyment, and the social division of labor. In the course of our analysis we have shown that certain phenomena characteristic of our times which Marx did not know about—such as the existence of an inauthentic art or mass art—can be explained perfectly in the light of Marx's thesis. This analysis has been based on the idea that the opposition between art and capitalism is a radical, essential contradiction, rooted in the contradiction between capitalism and man, first proposed by Marx in 1844. Since art is an essential sphere of humanity, it suffers implacably from the hostility of capitalist production. That is the profound meaning of Marx's thesis, whose significance, validity, and relevance to the present we have tried to show.